Study Guide
to Accompany

DORNBUSCH AND FISCHER

MACROECONOMICS

*Study Guide
to Accompany*

DORNBUSCH AND FISCHER

MACROECONOMICS

sixth edition

RICHARD STARTZ

University of Washington

McGraw-Hill, Inc.

New York   St. Louis   San Francisco   Auckland
Bogotá   Caracas   Lisbon   London   Madrid
Mexico City   Milan   Montreal   New Delhi
San Juan   Singapore   Sydney   Tokyo   Toronto

STUDY GUIDE TO ACCOMPANY
DORNBUSCH AND FISCHER:
MACROECONOMICS

This book is printed on acid-free paper.

1 2 3 4 5 6 7 8 9 0 DOH DOH 9 0 9 8 7 6 5 4 3

ISBN 0-07-017846-1

This book was set in Times Roman by Ann Eisner.
The editors were Scott D. Stratford and Elaine Rosenberg;
the production supervisor was Kathryn Porzio.
The cover was designed by Joan Greenfield.
R. R. Donnelley & Sons Company was printer and binder.

CONTENTS

part four   INFLATION, UNEMPLOYMENT, BUDGET DEFICITS, AND
INTERNATIONAL ADJUSTMENT

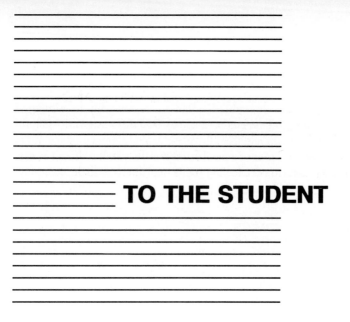

TO THE STUDENT

The study guide is designed for use with Dornbusch and Fischer's *Macroeconomics*, sixth edition. The only sensible reason for the existence of a study guide is to *make learning easier.*

FORMAT

Most of the twenty chapters have the following sections:

- **Focus of the Chapter:** A quick peek at the most important topics of the chapter.

- **Section Summaries:** A brief summary of each section of the text.

- **Key Terms:** A list of the most important technical terms used in the chapter.

- **Graph It:** Exercises that ask you to plot data, complete a graph, or fill in a chart. Most of these are quite simple. Think of the Graph It as being like warm-up exercises before a run or limbering-up scales for piano practice. Taking a pencil in hand gets your mind loosened up and focused on the subject at hand.

- **Review of Technique:** See below.

- **Fill-In Questions:** A test of the most important ideas and concepts of the chapter.

- **True-False Questions and Multiple-Choice Questions:** Tests of the detailed concepts of the chapter, sometimes requiring you to work out a few simple problems.

- **Problems:** At the end of each chapter. They require you to apply the concepts of the chapter to a specific problem.

- **Answers:** At the back of the book. They are given for every question in the study guide.

At the back of the study guide you will also find a glossary with definitions of many of the terms used in the text and the guide. You may find them especially helpful in working on the fill-in questions. In addition, there are some reference tables at the back of the book; these give various kinds of annual economic data for the United States. You may want to refer to those data to get a feeling for the real numbers in the economy.

HOW TO STUDY MACROECONOMICS

Do not! It wastes too much time. Instead—

Practice Macroeconomics

Practice; do not study. Having taught several hundred students with *Macroeconomics* from the first edition on, I have seen diligent students come in with the same problem over and over. They have read and reread the text several times, underlined all the important points, and spent hours and hours trying to memorize facts and theories. But they realize that somehow they have not quite caught on. As the authors of the text say, *active learning* is the only way to learn the material. Do not waste valuable hours trying to remember masses of material. Instead, spend a small amount of time trying to focus on the structure of the material. Since this is easier said than done, we have created this study guide to give you very specific questions to practice on. The questions in the study guide are not meant to serve just as lists of points to remember. Most questions have been picked to illustrate a basic principle. If you answer a question incorrectly, decide whether you have merely missed a minor point or whether you have overlooked a basic principle. The early questions in each chapter are quite easy, and later questions become progressively more difficult. Some of the problems are fairly advanced. While you may be able to answer all the fill-in questions in 2 minutes, the problems take time to work through. When it becomes necessary to choose between rereading the text for the third time and spending 20 minutes doing a hard problem, do the problem.

 Use this study guide *to learn more in less time.*

Review of Technique

A special feature of the study guide is the Review of Technique found in each chapter. Each one presents a quick review of some useful technical trick. Some of these are really very simple. Some are just a little bit advanced. You will probably find that you already know most of the material in each review, but a few years may have passed since you last had to use the information. The reviews allow you to brush up at your own leisure. They are not directly related to the material in the chapters in which they appear. When you have time, browse through all the reviews to find those most useful to use.

Computer Exercises

A set of computer-based exercises, *PC-Macroeconomics* Version 2.0, is now available to accompany the sixth edition of *Macroeconomics*. The computer modules are organized by chapter and operate on IBM-compatible personal computers under Lotus 1-2-3 or Quattro.[1] A guide to the operation of the modules is found in an appendix to the text.

ACKNOWLEDGMENTS

For the Original Edition

First, thanks must go to Rudiger Dornbusch and Stanley Fischer for, among other things, teaching me a great deal about macroeconomics. Susann Bizzari typed the original manuscript (and retyped it faster than I could edit). William Zahka, of Widener College, and Stephen Van der Ploeg, of Florida Atlantic University, provided very helpful reviews, as did several Wharton students.

Comments (and corrections!) on the study guide will be most appreciated.

For the Third Edition—Further Acknowledgments and Hints

Thanks continue to go to Professors Dornbusch and Fischer for continuing to teach me about macroeconomics. Thanks also go to the number of students who have sent corrections and suggestions. In response to several suggestions, this edition of the study guide is just a smidgen less technical than the earlier edition.

Here are two hints—the results of teaching several hundred students with the text and study guide.

1. Don't become overwhelmed by the details. Concentrate instead on the overall structure. The text has literally thousands of important details but only a dozen or so major themes. You can think of the themes as big branches and the details as leaves on a tree. It's much easier to trace down a specific detail by running out along the right branch than it is to build up an entire tree from a pile of leaves.

2. Study with a pencil in your hand and scribble in the margins or on scrap paper as you go. Pictures show structures better than words do. When the study guide describes how two curves interact, draw a rough graph right there in the guide. The picture you draw will stick with you much better than any words we can use.

---

[1] Lotus 1-2-3 is a registered trademark of Lotus Corporation. Quattro is a trademark of Borland Corporation.

For the Fourth Edition—Yet Another Acknowledgment and Hint

All the hard work in preparing this edition was done by Nick Pealy. Thanks to him, you'll find that this edition's coverage of the text material is even more thorough than in the past.

Hint: After the teaching of another thousand or so students, a bit more useful advice is available. The text has an enormous amount of detail but only a half dozen or so major themes. To test your understanding of the text, pretend to explain what you've learned to someone at a cocktail party.[2] Remember, you are supposed to explain how the entire economy works without using any technical terms.

For the Fifth Edition—More Acknowledgments and a High-Tech Hint

The world is getting to be more high-tech. (No doubt, this is not news to you.) At the request of a number of economists around the country, we've added some harder problems. So if you think a few of the problems are doozers—you're right. Of course, the idea is that if you chew on some hard problems in the study guide, everything you do later will seem easy.

The new material in this edition was prepared by Walt Fisher. Many thanks.

High-Tech Hint: Learning macroeconomics is akin to learning the piano in that it's better to practice than to read the book over and over. The newly available tutorial software is highly recommended. Give it a try!

Low-Tech Hint: Study with a friend. Two people will learn four times as much as each one studying alone.

For the Sixth Edition—Yet Another Further Acknowledgment and a Hint You Surely Already Knew If You Ever Thought about It

Morgan Lewis sat up many nights rearranging, rewriting, and revitalizing the material for this edition. My thanks for a super job.

The Hint You Knew: People learn in a variety of ways. In economics, some do best with a graphical approach, some like algebra, others find computer simulation provides the sudden "Aha!" The text, the available computer software, and this *Study Guide* provide a number of different paths to knowledge so you can pick your favorite. (Of course, nothing beats studying with a friend.)

RICHARD STARTZ

---

[2] Now you know how economists get their reputation for being boring. However, like most suggestions made by economists, this is a darn good one!

*Study Guide
to Accompany*

DORNBUSCH AND FISCHER

MACROECONOMICS

part one

INTRODUCING THE ECONOMY: FACTS AND FIRST MODELS

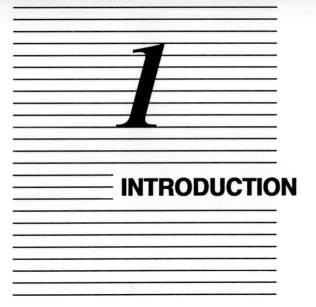

INTRODUCTION

FOCUS OF THE CHAPTER

- Our study of macroeconomics commences with an introduction to the principal concepts of macroeconomics and an overview of the textbook. We look at the questions of gross domestic product, unemployment, inflation, and economic growth.

SECTION SUMMARIES

1. Issues and Controversies

Contemporary macroeconomics is largely devoted to the study of the causes and consequences of three phenomena: unemployment, inflation, and economic growth. What government policy can do to promote economic growth or to lower the unemployment rate, for instance, has long been a matter of dispute among macroeconomists. Some macroeconomists, who can be identified as belonging to the monetarist or to the New Classical school, argue that since workers and firms adjust rapidly and efficiently to changing market conditions, there is little the government can do to assist the exchange of goods and services among private agents. These macroeconomists tend to believe, in fact, that the government's policy actions will impede the efficient adjustment of prices and quantities to changing market conditions.

    Another school of thought, which can be identified as New Keynesian, takes issue with such a view, and argues that since agents face significant costs of adjustment in responding to macroeconomic fluctuations, markets do not clear rapidly and thus undesirable phenomena, such as involuntary unemployment, will occur. The New Keynesians contend that proper government policies can overcome the effects of market failures.

2. Key Concepts

Gross domestic product (GDP) is the value of all goods and services produced in the economy in a year. *Real,* or *constant dollar,* GDP is the basic measure of economic activity. *Nominal,* or *current dollar,* GDP is the number of dollars needed to buy the entire gross domestic product. When prices go up, nominal GDP goes up even if real GDP doesn't change. In both the text and the *Study Guide,* "GDP" means "real GDP" unless we explicitly use the word "nominal." In order to measure the real value of goods and services—wiping away price changes—we often measure the value of goods in terms of 1987 dollars.

From 1960 through 1991, GDP grew at an average of 2.9 percent per year, although, of course, some years were good and some were bad. Trend growth in GDP is due to increased amounts of labor and of capital and to increased efficiency in using these factors of production. Year-to-year movements around trend depend on how much of the available resources are used. When unemployment is high, less is produced.

Macroeconomic performance is judged by the *inflation* rate, the *growth* rate of GDP, and the *unemployment* rate. Macroeconomics is largely the study of how these three economic variables behave, how they can best be controlled, and what limits we face in our attempts to control them.

Full-employment output, or *potential output,* is the level of GDP that the economy would produce if all resources were being used at just the right level. Actual output fluctuates around this level. The difference between *potential output* and actual output is called the *output,* or *GDP, gap.*

3. Relationships among Macroeconomic Variables

Output growth and unemployment are related by *Okun's law.* The trend growth of GDP is roughly 3 percent per year. If output grows faster than trend, unemployment falls. Okun's law suggests that GDP must grow about 2.25 percent per year above trend to lower unemployment by 1 percentage point.

Inflation is the rate of increase in prices. When prices are going up, the level of inflation is positive. When (on those rare occasions) prices are going down, the level of inflation is negative.

The *Phillips curve* describes a relation between inflation and unemployment: the higher the rate of unemployment, the lower the rate of inflation. This relation is fairly reliable in the short run (say, 2 years). In the long run, there is no tradeoff worth speaking about between inflation and unemployment.

4. Aggregate Demand and Supply

The overall concepts in studying unemployment, growth, and inflation are *aggregate demand* and *aggregate supply.* Basically, aggregate demand tells how much GDP consumers, business, and the government choose to buy given the overall level of prices.

Aggregate supply tells how much output is produced at a given price level. Figure 1-1 shows that the aggregate supply curve is flat at low levels of production and quite steep as production approaches potential GDP. In the flat region, changes in output occur with little price change. In the steep region, it is difficult to increase GDP; prices rise instead.

5. Outline and Review of the Text

Chapters 3 through 6 concentrate on aggregate demand. Later chapters consider aggregate supply as well as aggregate demand. You should think of the lessons of these early chapters as applying best at high levels of unemployment, that is, on the flat region of the aggregate supply curve.

Remember: In Chapters 3 through 6, *GDP really means aggregate demand for a given price level.*

6. Prerequisites and Recipes

The easiest way to study macroeconomics is to break the subject into smaller pieces. You may find it helpful to think of some chapters as "forest" (broad overview) chapters and others as "tree" (sophisticated detail) chapters. Chapter 2 describes national income accounting; it's a tree chapter in that it provides detail about national income accounting, but a forest chapter in that it provides an overview of how the economy is put together. Chapters 3, 4, and 5 (forest) give the "big picture" about aggregate demand. Chapter 6 (forest) introduces the international economy. Chapters 7 and 8 (forest) give a broad

FIGURE 1-1

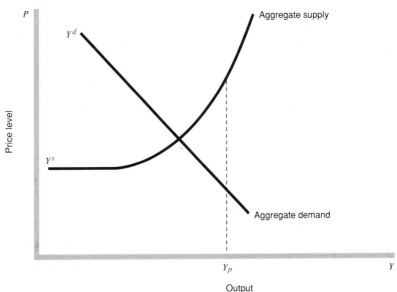

overview of how aggregate demand and supply combine. Chapter 9 (tree) presents a relatively new topic in macroeconomics: rational expectations. Long-term growth is the subject of Chapter 10 (forest). Chapters 11–14 (tree) take an in-depth look at the sectors contributing to aggregate demand. Chapter 15 is a tree chapter since it looks at the details of policy making. Chapters 16 and 17 look at inflation and unemployment in detail (trees). Chapters 18–19 examine policy issues regarding inflation, deficits, and debt (trees). Chapter 20 (tree) completes our examination of the international economy.

KEY TERMS

Monetarists	Phillips curve
Keynesians	Recovery or expansion
New Classical macroeconomist	Recession
GDP, nominal and real	Output gap
Trend, or potential, output	Okun's law
Peak	Rational expectations
Trough	Stabilization policy
Inflation	Activists
Growth	Aggregate demand and supply
Unemployment	New Keynesians
Business cycle	

GRAPH IT 1

The easiest way to see whether the economy is doing well is to chart real GDP. If GDP is going up by more than its usual trend, the economy is doing well—and vice versa. In Chart 1-1 you are asked to graph the annual rate of change in GDP from 1970 through 1991. Over this period, GDP grew about 3.11 percent each year *on average,* although some years had faster growth and some slower.

In order to fill out the chart, you must first calculate the rates of change of GDP and then plot them. For example, GDP was \$2,965.1 billion in 1971 and \$2,875.8 billion in 1970. So the 1971 annual growth rate was $100 \times [(2,965.1 - 2,875.8)/2,875.8]$ or 3.11 percent. We've filled in several years on the calculation table (Table 1-1) and the chart. You do the rest.

REVIEW OF TECHNIQUE 1

How to Review for This Course

Each person has a method of study that works best for her- or himself. In this review, we present some suggestions for breaking your studying up into manageable chunks. In each chapter, form a picture of the "forest" for that chapter before looking at the "trees." In

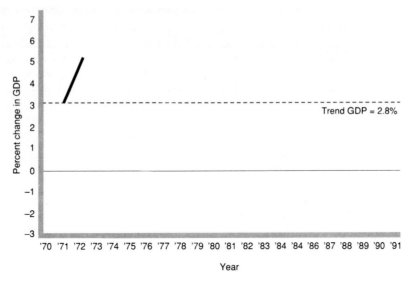

CHART 1-1
PERCENTAGE CHANGE IN GDP

this way, you have a framework on which to hang the details of the chapter. The text is far too rich for you to try to memorize a long list of unrelated facts and theories. Think of the difference in putting together a jigsaw puzzle when you know the general picture as compared with assembling it when you have no idea of the meaning of the big heap of pieces!

Figure 1-2 on page 9 presents one outline you can use for studying a chapter. You can start at the top with any of the suggestions for initial reading and work your way down to the RELAX box.

FILL-IN QUESTIONS

1. The value of production when all inputs are fully employed is called _____ _____.

2. The difference between production with fully employed inputs and actual production is the _____.

3. The bottom of the business cycle is called the _____.

TABLE 1-1

Year	GDP	Percent change from previous year
1970	2,875.8	
1971	2,965.1	3.11
1972	3,107.1	4.79
1973	——	——
1974	——	——
1975	——	——
1976	——	——
1977	——	——
1978	——	——
1979	——	——
1980	——	——
1981	——	——
1982	——	——
1983	——	——
1984	——	——
1985	——	——
1986	——	——
1987	——	——
1988	——	——
1989	——	——
1990	——	——
1991	——	——

SOURCE: See Table B of the Economic Data Tables.

4. Economic policymakers may try to improve economic performance by changing government spending and taxes, which are types of _____ policy.

5. Or they may try to do so by changing the money supply or interest rates, which are examples of _____ policy.

6. Both questions 4 and 5 are examples of _____.

7. GDP and unemployment are related through _____.

8. A time of high economic growth is called _____.

9. Times of economic weakness and contractions are termed _____ _____.

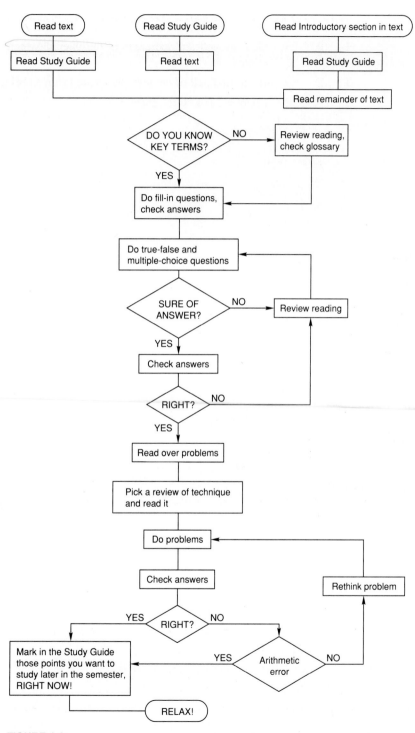

FIGURE 1-2

TRUE-FALSE QUESTIONS

T   F   1.   GDP growth and increases in the unemployment rate are positively
              related.

T   F   2.   In the first half of the text, prices are taken as being given.

T   F   3.   Chapter 1 is a "tree" chapter.

2

NATIONAL INCOME ACCOUNTING

FOCUS OF THE CHAPTER

- Under the heading "national accounting," we consider the several different ways in which the national economic pie can be sliced into its component parts.

- While we are taking apart GDP, we are also really learning how the different sources of aggregate demand can be added together to determine total national income.

SECTION SUMMARIES

1. Gross Domestic Product and Net Domestic Product

Gross domestic product (GDP) measures the value of all final output within the country. We measure only the value of final goods because counting both the value of a car and the value of the steel in the car would be double-counting. GDP includes the value of current production. It excludes the sales of existing goods from inventory. Goods are valued at their market price. To be precise, gross domestic product (GDP) measures the value of goods produced within a country, while gross national product (GNP) measures the value of goods produced by *domestically owned* factors of production. Net domestic product (NDP) is GDP minus depreciation; in other words, it is total current production minus an allowance for equipment that has worn out.

2.   Real and Nominal GDP

Because prices change from year to year, we distinguish real GDP from nominal GDP. Real GDP is a measure of physical production. Nominal GDP is the cost of that production at prevailing prices. The words "real" and "nominal" emphasize that real GDP is the useful measure of the economy's output.

Wherever the text or *Study Guide* uses the term "GDP," we mean real GDP, unless we specifically state that we are referring to nominal GDP.

GDP is measured only imperfectly, especially in regard to items such as government services and housework, which are difficult to value because they are not generally sold in the open market. The total incomes system of accounts (TISA) attempts to correct such deficiencies. GDP measurement is also made difficult by quality changes in goods and by the existence of the underground economy.

3.   Price Index

The three most important measures of the general price level are the GDP deflator, the consumer price index (CPI), and the producer price index (PPI). The GDP deflator equals the ratio of nominal GDP to real GDP. The CPI measures costs for a "typical" urban family. The PPI tracks prices of a range of goods used in production.

4.   Outlays and Components of Demand

GDP can also be divided up according to the various demands for purchasing output. The four sources of demand for purchasing output are personal consumption, private domestic investment, government purchases of goods and services, and net exports. Note that government transfers of income to individuals do not constitute part of demand for GDP. Nor are taxes directly part of GDP.

5.   GDP and Personal Disposable Income

For the nation as a whole, income must equal output. When one person buys an item, the money paid for it is part of another person's income. There are two qualifications to this. Replacement of worn machinery does not add to anyone's income even though it requires production. Therefore, income should be identified with NDP rather than GDP. Sales taxes and other indirect taxes also have to be deducted from the value of production since these payments are not directly part of anyone's income.

National income can be viewed as the sum of all payments to factors of production: wages, profits, and so on. National income can be further broken down into personal income and disposable personal income by subtracting those elements of income (principally taxes) that are not actually available for individuals to spend.

Disposable personal income must be either consumed or saved.

6.   Some Important Identities

Several important identities summarize the conventions of national income accounting. You should memorize the simple identities below. Be sure to learn the identities in terms of the economic concepts represented, not just as a set of abstract symbols.

$$Y \equiv C + I + G + NX$$ fundamental identity of aggregate demand

$$YD \equiv Y + TR - TA$$ sources of disposable income

$$YD \equiv C + S$$ uses of disposable income

$$BD \equiv (G + TR) - TA$$ budget deficit

$Y = $ GDP $\qquad$ $YD = $ disposable income

$C = $ consumption $\qquad$ $TR = $ transfers

$I = $ investment $\qquad$ $TA = $ taxes

$G = $ government purchases $\qquad$ $S = $ savings

$NX = $ net exports $\qquad$ $BD = $ government budget deficit

All these are summarized by the basic macroeconomic identity

$$C + G + I + NX \equiv Y \equiv YD + (TA - TR) \equiv C + S + (TA - TR)$$

which reduces to

$$S - I = (G + TR - TA) + NX$$

In the 1980s much attention was focused upon the "twin deficits"—the budget $(G + TR - TA)$ and trade deficits $(-NX)$.

KEY TERMS

Final goods

Value added

Market price

Factor cost

Gross domestic product (GDP)

Net domestic product (NDP)

Gross national product (GNP)

Depreciation

Measure of economic welfare (MEW)

Total incomes system of accounts (TISA)

The underground economy

Consumer price index (CPI)

Producer price index (PPI)

Assets

Liabilities

National income

Factor shares

Personal income

Transfers

Disposable personal income

Consumption

Government purchases

Government expenditures

Net exports

Final sales to domestic purchasers

Consumer durables

Government budget deficit

Twin deficits

Net national worth

GDP deflator

GRAPH IT 2

Economists spend a lot of time drawing straight lines on graph paper. This chapter's Graph It asks you to draw a line just for practice. We've taken two possible relations between consumption and income from Chapter 11. We've graphed the first in Chart 2-1. You are asked to draw the second in Chart 2-2. The two possible relations are

$$C = 6 + 0.90Y \quad \text{(ours)}$$
$$C = 47 + 0.73Y \quad \text{(yours)}$$

To draw a straight line, find two points on the line and then connect them. The easy point is found by taking $Y = 0$, and so $C = 6$. and we put a dot at 6 on the C axis. Since the slope of our relation is 0.90, consumption must go up 9 points for every 10 points of rise in income. From the first dot we counted off 10 positions to the right and then 9 positions up. We placed a second dot there and then drew the line connecting the two dots. Now you draw your relation on the blank graph.

REVIEW OF TECHNIQUE 2

Exogenous, Endogenous, and Policy Variables

Each subject in the text involves analyzing an economic model. A model is formed of one or more economic relationships that connect variables. Usually, these relationships are made specific by setting up one or more equations or graphs. At some philosophical level, everything studied in the book is all part of one large economic model. In practice, we break off small sectors of the economy to study in isolation.

Some variables are taken as inputs to a model. These are called *exogenous variables.* There are three general types of exogenous variables. Some economic variables are given by nature (the weather, for example), or at least are taken to be outside the scope of study of the model (investor psychology, for instance). Some economic variables can be set by policymakers. These are called *policy variables.* The rate of government spending and the level of the money stock are two important policy variables. Variables that may affect the reactions of the economy but that are not of any direct interest in and of themselves are called *parameters.* The marginal propensity to consume is an important economic parameter.

Endogenous variables are those that are determined internally by a given economic model. In supply-and-demand analysis, price and quantity are the endogenous variables. Whether a variable is endogenous or exogenous depends on context. When we study the simple multiplier model in Chapter 3, income and consumption are both endogenous. By contrast, in Chapter 11, in which we study advanced theories of consumption, income is taken to be exogenous and consumption is endogenous.

Two points are helpful in thinking about economic models. The first is of fundamental importance. The second is a useful trick.

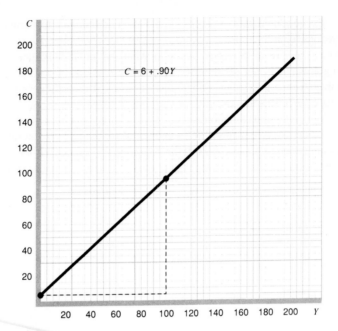

CHART 2-1
$C = 6 + 0.90Y$

CHART 2-2
$C = 47 + 0.73Y$

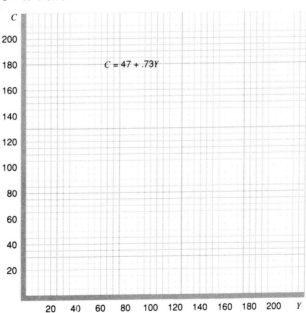

Exogenous variables determine the level of endogenous variables. The relation of exogenous to endogenous variables is one of cause to effect. A sensible question is: For a given change in an exogenous variable, what changes in the endogenous variable would be required? It is not sensible to ask about the effect of a change in an endogenous variable. A change in some endogenous variable is always the result of some more fundamental change in some exogenous variable.

When it comes time to find the solution of an economic model, try this procedure. Write down all the equations in the model. You should have the same number of equations and endogenous variables. If the numbers don't match, either some of the equations are just combinations of the other equations, or something fundamental has been omitted.

FILL-IN QUESTIONS

1. The value of all final goods and services produced within the country is _____ _____.

2. It is necessary to adjust GDP for _____ in order to calculate net domestic product.

3. The difference between net domestic product and national income is the difference between measuring the value of production at _____ and at _____.

4. A person's disposable income is (basically) either _____ or _____.

5. The principal difference between national income and disposable income is the addition of _____ and the subtraction of _____.

6. _____ attempts to account for economic "bads" as well as economic goods.

7. The ratio of nominal to real GDP is a useful price index called the _____ _____.

8. Net worth is the difference between _____ and _____ _____.

9. The excess of private savings over investment must equal _____ plus _____.

10. Net exports is the excess of _____ over _____ _____.

TRUE-FALSE QUESTIONS

T F   1. Investment equals private savings.

T F   2. Sale of a home adds to GDP.

T F   3. The real estate agent's commission on the sale of a home adds to GDP.

T F   4. Depreciation expenses are part of GDP.

T F   5. Depreciation expenses are part of disposable income.

T F   6. Purchase of common stock is part of investment.

T F   7. Purchase of a jeep by a camping enthusiast is part of consumption.

T (F) 8. Foreign corporate equities owned by domestic residents are not included in calculations of net national worth.

T F   9. The difference between gross investment and net investment is the same as the difference between GDP and NDP.

(T) F 10. Bonds issued by domestic corporations and owned by domestic residents are not included in calculations of net national worth.

MULTIPLE-CHOICE QUESTIONS

1. Which of the following is not part of aggregate demand?
   a. government spending
   b. taxes
   c. net exports
   d. investment

2. Which of the following is not a flow variable?
   a. net exports
   b. depreciation
   c. transfer payments
   d. national debt

3. Social Security payments are counted as part of
   a. government expenditure
   b. transfers
   c. taxes
   d. consumption

4. Benefits paid to government employees are counted as part of
   a. government expenditure
   b. transfers
   c. taxes
   d. consumption

5. Suppose investment and three of the following four items remain fixed. Which one of the four might have risen?
   a. government budget surplus
   b. saving
   c. net exports
   d. tax rates

$Y - G - TR = I - S + NX$

$Y = G + I + C + NX$ ①

$YD = Y + TR - TA$ ② $YD = S + C$ ③ $\Rightarrow C = YD - S$

From ② $Y = YD - TR + TA$ ③

put ③ into ① $YD - TR + TA = G + I + C + NX$

$YD - TR + TA = G + I + YD - S + NX$

6. Suppose GDP and NDP both rise by the same amount while three of the following four remain fixed. Which of the four could not have risen?
   a. gross investment
   b. net investment
   c. consumption
   d. net exports

7. An increase in the price of bicycles will show up in
   a. the GDP deflator
   b. the consumer price index
   c. the producer price index
   d. both a and b

8. If the price of apples goes up and the price of oranges goes down, this change would most likely be reflected in an increase in
   a. the GDP deflator
   b. the consumer price index
   c. the producer price index
   d. none of these

9. Which of the following is not part of national income?
   a. rental income
   b. welfare payments
   c. salaries
   d. net interest

10. The excess of savings over investment $(S - I)$ of the private sector is equal to
    a. net exports
    b. trade deficit
    c. budget deficit plus the trade surplus
    d. net investment

PROBLEMS

1. This is a problem of national income accounting. You are given the following facts about the economy: Consumption = $1,000, saving = $100, and government expenditure = $300. The government budget is balanced. What is the value of GDP? 1400

2. Suppose saving equals $200, the budget deficit is $50, and the trade deficit is $10. What is the level of investment?

3. If GDP = $1,000, government expenditure = $250, consumption = $500, net exports = $100, and the budget deficit = $40, what is the amount of disposable income?

4. If GDP = $500, consumption = $350, transfers less taxes = $20, investment = $150, and the budget deficit = $120, what is the amount of net exports? If this situation persists, what will happen to disposable income?

INCOME AND SPENDING

GDP or Y (income)

AD or Aggregate Demand

At Equilibrium AD = Y

or Aggregate Demand = Income
GDP

FOCUS OF THE CHAPTER

- The heart of Keynesian macroeconomic analysis is the idea that national income and the level of unemployment depend on *aggregate demand*.

- Aggregate demand is not exogenously fixed. As an accounting identity, however, GDP must be the sum of consumption, investment, and government spending. The classic example works through the response of consumption to income. Higher government spending increases GDP, since government purchases are a direct source of aggregate demand. This increase in GDP causes consumption to rise, and this rise causes yet a further increase in GDP.

- In order to find the equilibrium of the economy, it is necessary to combine the aggregate demand identity and the consumption function.

SECTION SUMMARIES

1. Aggregate Demand and Equilibrium Output

The fundamental identity of aggregate demand, $Y = C + I + G$, shows that the *actual* level of output must always equal the sum of all the different sources of aggregate demand. (Notice that we pretty much ignore the foreign sector until Chapter 6.) However, we can imagine a situation in which the *planned* levels of output are not equal to the *planned* levels of consumption, investment, and government spending. When the planned and actual levels are different, unintended inventory changes occur. When planned and actual levels are equal, the economy is in equilibrium. We use this fact to find the equilibrium of the economy by finding the level of GDP at which planned output equals the sum of planned consumption, investment, and government spending.

2. The Consumption Function and Aggregate Demand

Increased income causes increased consumption. When an individual receives an additional dollar of income, a fraction of that dollar is consumed and the remaining fraction is saved. The fraction of each additional dollar that is consumed is called the *marginal propensity to consume (MPC)*.

Since saving is just the difference between income and consumption ($S \equiv Y - C$), a given consumption function implies a specific saving function. Saving and consumption cannot be looked at independently.

In order to determine the equilibrium level of output, we set income equal to planned consumption, which is itself a function of income, plus planned investment. The equilibrium of the economy is found by solving for income as a function of the autonomous components of consumption and investment. We can write aggregate demand as $AD = \bar{C} + cY + \bar{I}$, or letting $\bar{A} = \bar{C} + \bar{I}$, as $AD = \bar{A} + cY$. For the economy to be in equilibrium, GDP must equal aggregate demand, or $AD = Y$.

The equilibrium level of GDP can be found by using the graphic technique illustrated in Figure 3-1. The 45° line represents $AD = Y$, and the second line is the graph of $AD = \bar{A} + cY$. The intersection of the two lines gives the value of GDP.

Alternatively, and equivalently, equilibrium may be found by equating investment and savings ($I = S$). (Both methods of finding equilibrium will require some minor modification when the public and foreign sectors are put back in the model.)

3. The Multiplier

A dollar increase in autonomous spending does not in general increase GDP by a dollar. The original increase adds directly to aggregate demand and also induces further spending. If the marginal propensity to consume is c, then a dollar increase in autonomous

FIGURE 3-1

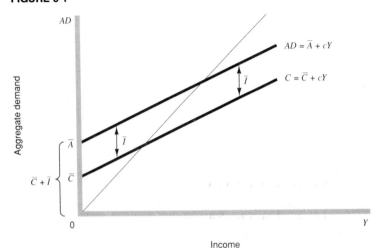

spending brings a further increase of c. But this further increase itself induces yet further increase—this increase causes yet another increase, and so forth. When all the increases are added up, the total addition to GDP is given by the *multiplier*. The value of the multiplier is $1/(1 - c)$. The change in GDP as a result of the original change in autonomous spending is

$$\Delta Y = \frac{1}{1 - c} \Delta \bar{A}$$

4. The Government Sector

Reintroducing the government sector requires two major modifications to our model. First, government spending belongs in the adding-up identity for GDP. Second, consumption truly depends on disposable income. If the government uses an income tax, the multiplier is reduced to

$$\Delta Y = \frac{1}{1 - c(1 - t)}$$

where the parameter t is the marginal income tax rate. As an example, if MPC is $\%$₁₀ and the tax rate is $\frac{1}{6}$, the multiplier will be 4. Because the multiplier is reduced, an income tax is called an *automatic stabilizer.* The multiplier for transfers is

$$\frac{c}{1 - c(1 - t)}$$

5. The Budget

The budget surplus is the difference between government income and government outgo. Symbolically, $BS = TA - G - TR$. The surplus responds to both exogenous changes in government expenditure and endogenous changes in tax collections due to changes in GDP.

For the special case where the change in government spending is exactly offset by a change in taxes, the multiplier is equal to 1 and output will rise by the amount of government spending. This result has been called the "balanced budget multiplier theorem."

6. The Full-Employment Budget Surplus

The *full-employment budget surplus* measures what the surplus would be if the economy were at full employment, with current expenditure policy and current tax rates. The full-employment budget surplus responds to changes in government expenditure and in tax rates but is immune to those changes in actual GDP that occur for other reasons, such as an increase in autonomous investment.

KEY TERMS

Aggregate demand
Equilibrium output
Unintended (undesired) inventory
  accumulation
Planned aggregate demand
Automatic stabilizer
Budget surplus
Budget deficit

Consumption function
Marginal propensity to consume (MPC)
Marginal propensity to save
Multiplier
Balanced budget multiplier
Full-employment (high-employment)
  budget surplus

GRAPH IT 3

For this Graph It, you are asked to use a graph to prove the following proposition: *For a given change in $\bar{A}$, a large marginal propensity to consume means a large change in GDP.* To prove this proposition requires a graph with five lines on it. We've provided the first three lines in Chart 3-1. You are asked to draw the last two.

The first line we drew was the 45° line for $AD = Y$. Then we drew the solid aggregate demand line for $AD = \bar{A}_0 + cY$ and the dashed aggregate demand line for

CHART 3-1

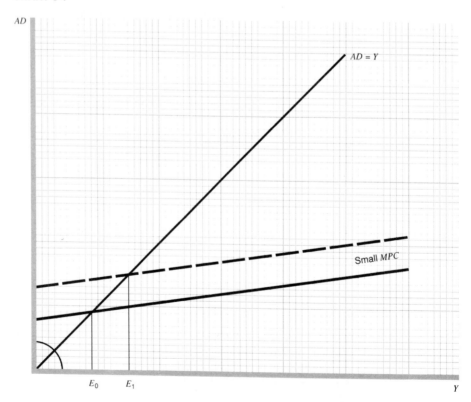

$AD = \bar{A}_1 + cY$, with $\bar{A}_1 > \bar{A}_0$. GDP is shown increasing from level E_0 to level E_1. Notice that both our aggregate demand lines were fairly flat, indicating that the marginal propensity to consume is small.

Now you draw a solid aggregate demand line that goes through point E_0 with a steep slope, indicating a large *MPC*. Then draw a dashed line parallel to your solid line, but higher by the same vertical distance as appears between the two lines we drew. Mark the point at which your dashed line hits the 45° line as E_2. You should be able to see that the distance from E_0 to E_2 is greater than the distance from E_0 to E_1.

REVIEW OF TECHNIQUE 3

Solving Problems Backward

Most of the theories we develop tell us how a given change in an exogenous variable, such as government spending, will affect some endogenous variable, such as GDP. Sometimes it is necessary to reverse the question and ask what change in an exogenous variable would either cause or account for a given change in an endogenous variable.

Suppose you are asked to lower the government budget deficit by $100 by lowering government spending. Assume that the income tax rate is 33⅓ percent and that the marginal propensity to consume is 0.9. Begin with the definition of the budget deficit.

Note: The symbol Δ (the Greek capital letter delta) is read "the change in."

$$BD = G - TA$$

$$\Delta BD = \Delta G - \Delta TA$$

ΔBD is -100, and ΔG is our final goal. We need to work backward to relate ΔTA to our final goal, ΔG. We know that $TA = tY$. Since the tax rate, t, is constant, we can write $\Delta TA = \Delta tY = t\Delta Y$. Hence,

$$\Delta BD = \Delta G - t\Delta Y$$

Now we need to work backward from ΔY to ΔG. We can use the multiplier formula derived in the book for this purpose:

$$\Delta Y = \frac{1}{1 - c(1 - t)} \Delta G = \frac{1}{1 - 0.9(1 - \frac{1}{3})} \Delta G = 2.5\Delta G$$

Now substitute this into the formula for the change in the budget deficit:

$$\Delta BD = \Delta G - t \cdot 2.5\Delta G = (1 - \frac{2.5}{3})\Delta G = \frac{1}{6}\Delta G$$

Thus, in this example, government spending must be decreased by $600.

In the questions that follow, we include a government sector but continue to omit the foreign sector.

FILL-IN QUESTIONS

1. When planned and actual spending are equal, the economy is in ___Equilibrium___ .

2. The relation between consumption and income is called ___Consumption Fn.___ .

3. A $10 increase in GDP induces an increase in consumption of $10 times the ___marginal propensity to consume___ (in the absence of an income tax).

4. The complement of the marginal propensity to consume is the ___marginal propensity to save___ .

5. An initial increase in autonomous spending has an effect on GDP that is magnified by the ___multiplier___ .

6. The difference between government expenditure and taxes is the ___Budget deficit___ .

7. A(n) ___Automatic Stabilizer___ is a program, such as the income tax, that reduces the impact of shocks to the economy without any direct government action.

8. The ___Full Employment Budget Surplus___ is the difference between tax receipts at full employment and government expenditure.

9. The balanced budget multiplier equals ___one___ .

10. In equilibrium, planned investment equals ___planned Saving___ and ___actual investment___ .

TRUE-FALSE QUESTIONS

T̶ F 1. Increasing transfers increases GDP.

T F̶ 2. Increasing the income tax rate increases GDP.

T̶ F 3. Increasing government purchases increases savings.

T̶ F 4. Increasing government purchases in the presence of a proportional income tax increases the budget deficit.

T (F) 5. Increased autonomous consumption, in the presence of an income tax, increases the full-employment budget surplus.

T F̶ 6. Increasing autonomous consumption increases savings.

T F̶ 7. An increase in the marginal propensity to consume reduces income.

(T) F̶ 8. In the absence of an income tax, an increase in government purchases together with an equal decrease in transfers will increase GDP by the amount of the increase in government purchases.

Full employment Budget doesn't depend on Ā

Tax and G.

NOT · Balanced Budget multiplier

T F̶ 9. In the presence of an income tax, an increase in government purchases together with an equal decrease in transfers will increase GDP by the amount of the increase in government purchases.

T F̶ 10. The greater the marginal propensity to save, the greater the impact on GDP of a change in government purchases.

MULTIPLE-CHOICE QUESTIONS

$$\frac{1}{1-c'} = \frac{1}{0.2} = 5$$

1. If the marginal propensity to consume is 0.8, then, in the absence of an income tax, the multiplier is
   a. 1
   b. 2
   c. 5
   d. 10

⑧ $Y = G + C$

$Y = \bar{G} + \bar{C} + c Y_D$

2. If the *MPC* is 0.8, then, in the absence of an income tax, the multiplier relating changes in transfer payments to changes in national income is
   a. 4
   b. 5
   c. 6
   d. 8

$Y = \bar{G} + \bar{C} + c(Y + TR)$

$Y = G + \bar{C} + cY + cTR$

3. In the presence of an *MPC* equal to 0.9 and a tax rate of 33⅓ percent, the multiplier is
   a. ½
   b. 2½
   c. 5
   d. 10

$\frac{1}{1 - c(1-t)}$

$\therefore \Delta Y = 2.5 \Delta G$

$\delta Y = \Delta G + c \Delta Y + c \Delta TR$

$\therefore \Delta G = -\Delta TR$

4. Using the same parameters as in question 3, a $30 increase in government spending leads to a change in the budget surplus of
   a. −$30
   b. −$5
   c. $5
   d. $30

$BS = TA - G$
$\Delta BS = t\Delta Y - \Delta G$
$\Delta BS = t \cdot 2.5 \Delta G - \Delta G$

$(1-c)\delta Y = \Delta G - c\Delta G$

$(1-c)\delta Y = (1-c)\Delta G$?

$\delta Y = \Delta G$.

5. Using the same information as in question 4, the increase in the full-employment budget surplus is
   a. −$30
   b. −$25
   c. $25
   d. $30

$\Delta BS = (t \times 2.5 - 1)\Delta G$
$= (\frac{1}{3} \times \frac{5}{2} - 1)30$
$= -\frac{1}{6} \cdot 30$

6. If *MPC* is 0.75, a $10 tax increase (marginal tax rate = 0) leads to a change in savings of
   a. −$30
   b. −$10
   c. $10
   d. $30

7. In equilibrium, investment equals
   a. private savings
   b. the budget surplus
   c. the sum of a and b
   d. neither a nor b

8. An increase in the income tax rate causes the full-employment budget surplus to
   a. increase
   b. decrease
   c. the answer depends on *t*
   d. the answer depends on *c*

9. In the presence of an income tax, the effect on GDP of equal and opposite changes in government purchases and transfers
   a. equals the change in government purchases
   b. depends on t
   c. depends on c
   d. depends on both t and c

10. Comparing the effect of government purchases on GDP in an economy with an income tax to the effect in an economy without an income tax, the effect in the former

   a. is greater   c. depends on the MPC
   b. is less   d. cannot be determined

PROBLEMS

1. Government purchases and taxes are $500 and $400, respectively. Investment equals $200. The autonomous part of consumption is $100. The marginal propensity to consume is 0.9. What is the level of GDP?   4400

2. The marginal propensity to consume is 0.9. The income tax is one-third of income. The government decides to increase spending in order to increase GDP by $750. How much should government spending increase? What happens to the budget deficit?
   $\Delta G = 300$ $\circ BD= 50$

3. The MPC and the marginal income tax rate are 0.9 and ⅓, respectively. The budget deficit is observed to increase by $15.
   a. What amount of change in investment would account for this? $\Delta I = -18$
   b. What amount of change in government purchases would account for this? $\Delta G = 90$

4. Let us introduce a foreign sector into the national economy. Recall that the national income identity for an open economy is $Y = C + I + G + NX$, where NX represents net exports, that is, the excess of exports over imports. The following equations describe the economy.

$$NX = \text{exports} - \text{imports} = 20 - 0.1Y$$
$$C = 20 + 0.75(1 - t)Y$$
$$\bar{I} = 25$$
$$\bar{G} = 15$$

$t = \frac{1}{15}$

6.7%

If the government seeks to maintain a zero trade balance on its current account ($NX = 0$), what proportional income tax rate should it set? Ignoring transfer payments to individuals, will there be a government budget surplus or deficit as a result of this trade policy?

$200 \times \frac{1}{15} = 13.33$

$G > TA$.

MONEY, INTEREST, AND INCOME

FOCUS OF THE CHAPTER

- *IS-LM* analysis is the core of modern macroeconomics.

- The simple model of Chapter 3 is extended to include the interaction of the money market with the goods market.

- The interest rate is now taken to be an endogenous model.

- Our previous analysis of the goods market will lead to formation of the *IS* curve. We posit a simple *LM* curve, a relation expanded on in Chapters 13 and 14.

SECTION SUMMARIES

1. The Goods Market and the *IS* Curve

The *IS* curve represents equilibrium in the goods market. The *IS* curve shows all those combinations of income and interest such that the goods market is in balance. The formula for the *IS* curve is found by combining the consumption function and the investment function with the aggregate demand identity. We know from Chapter 3 that consumption depends on income. Chapter 12 shows that investment depends negatively on the interest rate. The simplest version of the *IS* curve is derived below.

$$Y \equiv C + I + G$$
$$C = \bar{C} + cY$$
$$I = \bar{I} - bi \text{ (} i \text{ is the interest rate)}$$

$$Y = \bar{C} + cY + I - bi + G$$

$$Y = \frac{1}{1-c}(\bar{C} + \bar{I} + G) - \frac{b}{1-c}i = IS \text{ curve}$$

2.   The Assets Market and the *LM* Curve

The *LM* curve represents equilibrium in the assets market. It shows all those combinations of income and interest such that the asset markets are in balance. The *LM* curve is the schedule that equates money supply and money demand. Money demand, which is studied in detail in Chapter 13, depends positively on income and negatively on the interest rate. Money supply is taken to be exogenous. In this chapter we also assume that prices are fixed. The *LM* curve is given by

$$\bar{M}/\bar{P} = kY - hi \quad (LM \text{ curve})$$

$\bar{M}/\bar{P}$ is the exogenously given real money supply.

3.   Equilibrium in the Goods and Assets Markets

The *IS* and *LM* curves give us two independent relations between two endogenous variables, income and the interest rate. By solving the two equations simultaneously, we can find the equilibrium levels of income and interest. Figure 4-1 illustrates an *IS-LM* equilibrium. Figure 4-2 uses the *IS-LM* apparatus to show the effects of an increase in

FIGURE 4-1

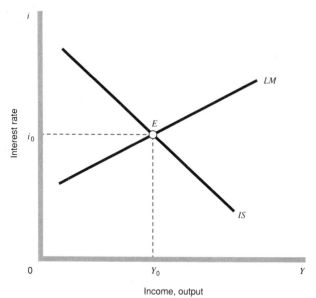

Income, output

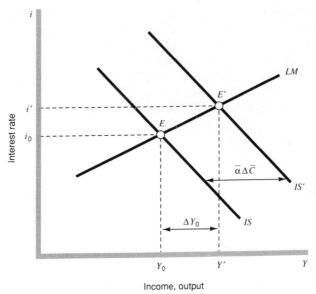

FIGURE 4-2

autonomous spending. Note that an expansion in autonomous demand, such as an increase in government purchases, increases both income and interest rates.

4. Adjustment toward Equilibrium

At any point other than the intersection of the *IS* and *LM* curves, the economy is out of equilibrium. The economy moves toward equilibrium according to whether there is an excess supply or demand for money and an excess supply or demand for goods. It is often reasonable to assume adjustment in the money market is very fast, so that the adjustment path to equilibrium moves along the *LM* curve.

5. A Formal Treatment of the *IS-LM* Model

Since our *IS* and *LM* curves are both represented by linear equations, we can solve them together algebraically to find equilibrium income. The final equation for income in terms of all exogenous variables is

$$Y = \frac{h\bar{\alpha}}{h + kb\bar{\alpha}} A + \frac{b\bar{\alpha}}{h + kb\bar{\alpha}} \frac{\bar{M}}{\bar{P}}$$

For obvious reasons, the first fraction is called the *fiscal policy multiplier* and the second is called the *monetary policy multiplier*. $\bar{\alpha}$ is the multiplier from Chapter 3 and equals $1/(1 - c)$ in the simplest model.

It is instructive to calculate the fiscal and monetary policy multipliers in the special cases of the liquidity trap and the classical case. The parameter h equals zero in the classical case, and so the fiscal policy multiplier equals zero and the monetary policy multiplier reaches its maximum value, $1/k$. In a liquidity trap, the parameter h approaches infinity, and so the fiscal policy multiplier approaches the simple multiplier α and the monetary policy multiplier goes to zero.

The final equation for the interest rate in terms of all the exogenous variables is

$$i = \frac{k\bar{\alpha}}{h + kb\bar{\alpha}} A - \frac{1}{h + kb\bar{\alpha}} \frac{\bar{M}}{\bar{P}}$$

KEY TERMS

IS curve	*IS-LM* model
LM curve	Wealth budget constraint (wealth constraint)
Bond	Liquidity trap
Money	Classical case
Portfolio decisions	Monetary policy multiplier
Real balances (real money balances)	Fiscal policy multiplier

GRAPH IT 4

Does tight monetary policy put people out of work? You might think that we could decide such a question just by graphing the unemployment rate against the real money stock. This would be a dangerous way to settle a scientific question because it ignores the influence of fiscal policy on unemployment. However, in recent years monetary policy seems to have been dominant, and so in this Graph It we are going to cast caution to the winds and graph the unemployment rate against the real money supply anyway.

As a first step, you should collect data on the unemployment rate, $M1$, and the consumer price index (CPI) for the years 1980 through 1991. Then calculate the real money supply by dividing $M1$ by the price level. Finally, plot unemployment against the real money supply on the graph provided. We've collected and calculated the first two data points to get you started (Table 4-1, p. 31, and Chart 4-1). What do you think? Will a big money supply reduce unemployment?

REVIEW OF TECHNIQUE 4

Graphing Equations

This review gives you a chance to apply your talent at freehand sketching to drawing economic graphs. Solving economic questions by drawing graphs is often easier than finding an algebraic solution. This is especially true in three different cases: first, when

TABLE 4-1

Year	Unemployment	M1	CPI	M1/P
1980	7.1	408.8	82.4	4.96
1981	7.6	436.4	90.9	4.80
1982	—	—	—	—
1983	—	—	—	—
1984	—	—	—	—
1985	—	—	—	—
1986	—	—	—	—
1987	—	—	—	—
1988	—	—	—	—
1989	—	—	—	—
1990	—	—	—	—
1991	—	—	—	—

SOURCE: *Economic Report of the President,* 1991.

CHART 4-1

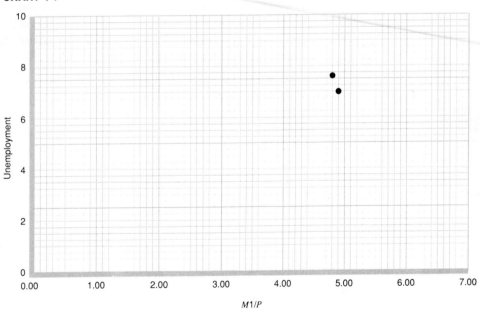

a qualitative solution is sufficient, as opposed to a specific numerical answer; second, when we know the general relation of economic variables in an equation but don't have a specific formula; third, when nonlinear equations are involved. In this Review of Technique, we go over some useful "tricks" for graphing an equation. In Review of Technique 5, we use graphs to solve two simultaneous equations.

Suppose we have an equation such as

$$X = aY + bZ$$

X, Y, and Z are three economic variables. Both coefficients, a and b, are greater than zero. We graph the relation between two of the variables while treating the third as exogenous. In Figure 4-3, we show X as a function of Y. Since a is positive, X goes up when Y goes up; therefore, the line slopes upward from left to right.

The important fact we used was that X goes up with Y. Even if we have only a general functional form, we can draw a representative graph so long as we know the direction of the relation between X and Y. Figure 4-4 gives a representative graph for $X = f(Y, Z)$ using only the fact that X and Y are positively related.

Sometimes it is convenient to be able to draw the relation between two right-hand variables while treating the left-hand variable as exogenous. (We do this when we draw the LM curve, for example.) Figures 4-5a, 4-5b, 4-5c, and 4-5d illustrate four steps we use to decide whether the line should slope upward or downward.

1. Pick any point that satisfies the equation.
2. Draw an arrow representing an increase in the horizontal variable.
3. Consider the point at the end of the arrow. The equation is out of balance at this point. Since b is positive, and since Z is higher than at the original point, the right-hand side must be too large. We ask the question, How must Y move in order to

FIGURE 4-3

$X = aY + bZ$ DRAWN FOR A FIXED VALUE OF Z

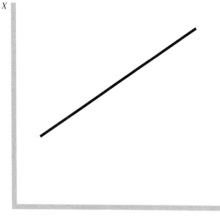

FIGURE 4-4
$X = f(Y, Z)$ DRAWN FOR A FIXED VALUE OF Z

FIGURE 4-5
GRAPHING THE RELATION BETWEEN THE RIGHT-HAND
SIDE VARIABLES WHILE HOLDING THE LEFT-HAND SIDE FIXED

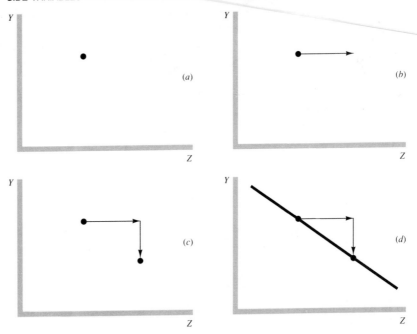

bring the right-hand side back into balance? Since a is positive, Y must decrease to bring the right-hand side back down to balance. Draw an arrow pointing down to show the decrease in Y.

4. Connect the original point to the end of the second arrow. In this case, the line slopes downward from left to right.

Frequently, we need to show how the graph shifts if the third variable changes. Suppose, in our example, that X increases. In which direction does the graph move? Figures 4-6a and 4-6b illustrate two different ways of figuring this out.

1. Pick any point on the original line. Since X is higher than before, we need to increase the right-hand side to return the equation to balance. This can be done by increasing Y. Draw a line above and parallel to the original line.
2. Alternatively, the right-hand side can be increased by increasing Z. Draw a line to the right and parallel to the original line.

Generally, the two methods are equivalent.

FIGURE 4-6
GRAPHING THE SHIFT OF A LINE

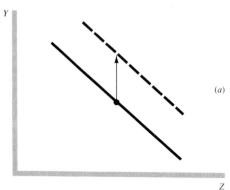

(a)

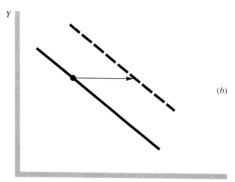

(b)

FILL-IN QUESTIONS

1. Both the *IS* curve and the *LM* curve represent combinations of _____ and the _____ .
2. The *IS* curve represents equilibrium in the _____ market.
3. The *LM* curve represents equilibrium in the _____ market.
4. A(n) _____ produces an increase in the money supply and an equal decrease in outstanding bonds.
5. The interest rate rises when there exists an excess _____ money.
6. The key sector of aggregate demand linking the money market and the goods market is _____ .
7. The ratio of nominal money to the price level is called _____ .
8. The interest rate and level of output are jointly determined by simultaneous _____ _____ in the goods and money markets.
9. Holding the real money supply constant, the _____ shows how much an increase in government spending changes the equilibrium level of income.
10. The size of the increase in equilibrium level of income from an increase in the money supply is determined by the _____ .

TRUE-FALSE QUESTIONS

T F 1. Increased government spending moves the *IS* curve upward to the right.

T F 2. Increased money supply moves the *LM* curve downward to the right.

T F 3. For a given money supply, there is a positive relation between interest and income along the *LM* curve.

T F 4. For a given level of autonomous spending, there is a positive relation between interest and income along the *IS* curve.

T F 5. Decreasing the money supply increases investment.

T F 6. Increasing government spending increases investment.

T F 7. Equal increases in government purchases or transfers have the same effect on the *IS* curve.

T F 8. Tax rates don't matter in the *IS-LM* model.

T F 9. For a given level of output there can be more than one equilibrium interest rate.

T F 10. An increase in government spending changes equilibrium income levels by an amount proportional to the monetary policy multiplier.

MULTIPLE-CHOICE QUESTIONS

1. Lower exogenous taxes lead to
   a. higher income
   b. higher interest rate

   c. both
   d. an increase in neither one

2. A lower money supply leads to
   a. higher income
   b. higher interest rate

   c. both
   d. an increase in neither one

3. An increase in the money supply increases
   a. interest rates
   b. investment

   c. both
   d. neither

4. An increase in government purchases increases
   a. interest rates
   b. investment

   c. both
   d. neither

5. The less sensitive money demand is to changes in the interest rate, the more an increase in the money stock
   a. increases GDP
   b. lowers interest rates

   c. both
   d. neither

6. Rapid adjustment in the money market means the economy is always on
   a. the *IS* curve
   b. the *LM* curve

   c. both
   d. neither

7. Expansionary fiscal policy tends to
   a. raise consumption
   b. lower investment

   c. both
   d. neither

8. A high *MPC* means a relatively
   a. steep *IS* curve
   b. flat *IS* curve

   c. steep *LM* curve
   d. flat *LM* curve

9. A high interest sensitivity of investment means a relatively
   a. steep *IS* curve
   b. flat *IS* curve

   c. steep *LM* curve
   d. flat *LM* curve

10. A high income tax rate means a relatively
    a. steep *IS* curve
    b. flat *IS* curve

    c. steep *LM* curve
    d. flat *LM* curve

A small negative slope is steep

PROBLEMS

1. The following equations describe the economy.

$$C = 100 + 0.8YD \quad \text{(consumption)}$$
$$I = 200 - 1{,}000i \quad \text{(investment)}$$
$$L = YD - 10{,}000i \quad \text{(money demand)}$$

Initially, government purchases are $550 and taxes are $500. The real money supply equals $900.
   a. Derive the formulas for the IS curve and LM curve.
   b. What are the initial levels of GDP, the interest rate, consumption, and investment?

Owing to a drop in investor confidence, the autonomous component of investment drops by $90.
   c. By how much do income, the interest rate, and investment drop?
   d. By how much should the money supply be changed in order to return GDP to its original level? What will the new interest rate be?
   e. Draw three graphs to illustrate the equilibria in b, c, and d.

2. The following equations describe the economy.

$$C = 90 + 0.9YD \quad \text{(consumption)}$$
$$I = 200 - 1{,}000i \quad \text{(investment)}$$
$$L = YD - 10{,}000i \quad \text{(money demand)}$$

There is a 33 percent proportional income tax. Government purchases equal $710. The real money supply is $500.
   a. What are the initial values of investment and the budget deficit?
   b. How large a change in the money supply would give the government a balanced budget?

3. Some economists maintain that it is inappropriate to use national income as an argument in the money demand function, because the government does not employ money balances to make purchases of goods and services. They maintain that consumption spending is a more appropriate argument to use, since money balances are held primarily by households. Let us compare two economies in which one has the traditional specification of money demand, while the other has the specification suggested here.

$$C = \bar{C} + C(1-t)Y$$
$$I = \bar{I} - bi$$
$$G = \bar{G}$$
$$M/P = \bar{M}/\bar{P}$$

Margin handwritten notes

$L = kY - hi$

$\bar{I}_{GM}$

$h\bar{\alpha}$, $b\bar{z}$

$\dfrac{h\bar{\alpha}}{h + \alpha b\, k}$ $\dfrac{b\bar{z}}{h + \alpha b\, k}$

$\dfrac{h\bar{\alpha}}{h + \alpha b\, k}$ $\dfrac{b\bar{\alpha}}{h + \alpha b\, k}$

$\alpha_{G} = \overline{1 - c(1-t)}$

$Y = \alpha_{G}(\bar{A} - bi)$ IS

α_{g} is small

h is small

$$\text{Traditional: } L = kY - ki$$
$$\text{Special:} \quad L = kC - ki$$

Solve for the reduced form fiscal and monetary policy multipliers. Are the policies more or less powerful under the special specification of money demand than under the traditional specification? Provide an intuitive as well as an algebraic explanation.

4. Provide a rationale for the following specification of the consumption function.

$$C = \bar{C} + C(1 - t)Y - di \qquad \text{(assume } d > 0)$$

How is such a specification likely to affect the slope of the *IS* curve? How will the government's ability to conduct fiscal and monetary policy be influenced thereby? For your answer, use spending functions specified in the previous problem along with the traditional formulation of the money demand.

MONETARY AND FISCAL POLICY

FOCUS OF THE CHAPTER

- The effectiveness of fiscal policy depends on the slopes of the *IS* and *LM* curves.

- The fiscal policy–monetary policy mix determines the composition of output as well as the overall size of aggregate demand.

- In the final section, we algebraically combine the *IS* and *LM* schedules to determine the equation for aggregate demand in terns of autonomous spending and the real money supply.

SECTION SUMMARIES

1. Monetary Policy

When the Federal Reserve makes an *open market purchase,* the money supply is increased while the outstanding supply of bonds is reduced. Notice that this operation reduces the interest rate but does not initially change private wealth. The lower interest rate induces increased investment, which means that GDP rises. The flatter the slope of the *IS* curve, the greater the impact of an increase in the money supply on GDP.

Figure 5-1 uses the *IS-LM* to show the effects of an increase in the money stock. Note that an expansion in the money stock increases income and decreases interest rates.

With a horizontal *LM* curve, called the *liquidity trap,* an increase in the money supply does not move the *LM* curve, and so income is unaffected. A vertical *LM* curve, called the *classical case,* or quantity theory case, gives the maximum effect of an increase in the money supply.

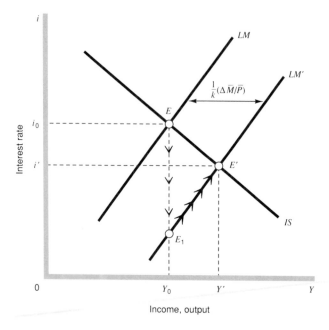

FIGURE 5-1

2. Fiscal Policy and Crowding Out

An increase in government spending increases GDP and the interest rate. The increased interest rate lowers investment. Thus, part of the increase in government spending is offset by a decrease in investment. This is called *crowding out*. In the quantity theory case, there is 100 percent crowding out; the increase in government spending is totally offset by a drop-off in investment, and so GDP does not increase at all. The flatter the *LM* schedule, the greater the increase in GDP. Thus, fiscal policy has maximum power in the case of the liquidity trap and zero power in the quantity theory case.

Three rules summarize the effect of a fiscal expansion:

a. Income increases more, and interest rates increase less, the flatter the *LM* schedule.
b. Income increases more, and interest rates increase less, the flatter the *IS* schedule.
c. Income and interest rates increase more the larger the multiplier and thus the larger the horizontal shift of the *IS* schedule.

Did the large government budget deficits during the 1980s crowd out investment? Not necessarily, since high budget deficits may be associated with higher income, and thus higher saving, rather than lower investment. In the real world the extent of crowding out depends on both the slope of the *LM* curve and the extent to which the Federal Reserve accommodates fiscal policy. The Federal Reserve *accommodates* fiscal policy when it increases the money supply (moves the *LM* curve right) to prevent interest rates from rising as the *IS* curve moves right.

3. The Composition of Output and the Policy Mix

Either fiscal or monetary policy can be used to expand aggregate demand. However, expansionary fiscal policy discourages investment, while expansionary monetary policy encourages investment. The choice of a policy mix, particularly between spending policy and tax policy, also depends on whether you favor a large government sector or a small one.

4. The Policy Mix in Action

The 1964 tax cut combined expansionary fiscal policy with accommodating monetary policy. In 1968 and 1969, tight fiscal and monetary policy were used to contract the economy, but these steps failed to slow inflation. From 1979 to 1982, the Reagan administration used expansionary fiscal policy together with an extremely tight monetary policy. The tight monetary policy predominated, and the economy underwent the greatest contraction since the Great Depression of the 1930s. The inflation rate was reduced drastically.

The *real interest rate* is the nominal interest rate minus the inflation rate.

KEY TERMS

Crowding out
Monetary-fiscal policy mix
Monetary accommodation
Monetizing budget deficits
Composition of output
Investment subsidy

Real interest rate
Nominal interest rate
Open market operations
Classical case
Liquidity trap

GRAPH IT 5

For this chapter's Graph It, we ask you to use graphs to demonstrate that an increase in the money stock generates a large increase in income if the *LM* curve is vertical (the *classical case*), a moderate increase in income if the *LM* curve has a moderate positive slope, and no change in income at all if the *LM* curve is horizontal (the *liquidity trap*). In Chart 5-1, we've provided three graphs, one under the other, with initial *IS* and *LM* curves filled in. On the middle graph, we've also drawn a dashed line showing the *LM* curve moved to a distance, Δ, to the right. Note that the equilibrium moved from E_0 to E_2. Now you draw new *LM* curves on the upper and lower graphs and show the new equilibria, E_1 and E_3. You should find that the horizontal distance from E_0 to E_2 is less than the distance from E_0 to E_1 and greater than the distance from E_0 to E_3.

If you are out of practice in moving lines around on a graph, you might want to try the Review of Technique in this chapter.

CHART 5-1

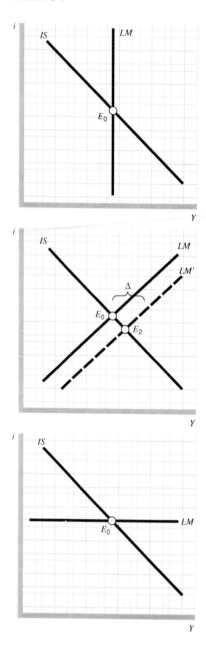

REVIEW OF TECHNIQUE 5

Graphic Solution of a Two-Equation Model

Many economic models can be reduced to a problem of two unknown variables described by two equations. *IS-LM* analysis and supply-and-demand analysis are the best-known examples of such systems. In this Review of Technique, we use graphs to solve a two-equation model and then to show how the equilibrium of the system shifts when exogenous parameters shift.

Equations (5-1) and (5-2) are a pair of simultaneous equations. The unknown variables are X and Y. Q and Z are exogenous variables. The coefficients are all positive.

$$Y = a_1X + a_2Z \tag{5-1}$$

$$Y = -b_1X - b_2Z + b_3Q \tag{5-2}$$

Notice that these are totally made-up equations. (We want you to work on technical tools for the moment and not use your economic intuition.) If you find algebraic coefficients such as *a* distracting, you can cross them out and replace a_1 with 7, a_2 with 3, or whatever you like.

The two equations are graphed in Figure 5-2. The intersection of the two lines, the point (Y^*, X^*), is the one combination of X and Y that satisfies both equations.

We are frequently concerned with discovering how the solution to a system of equations is changed by a shift in one of the exogenous variables. Discovering the changes in income and the interest rate induced by an increase in government spending, which are predicted by the *IS-LM* model, is a typical example. We illustrate effects of increasing the exogenous variable Q in Figure 5-3. Equation (5-2) shifts upward and to the right to

FIGURE 5-2

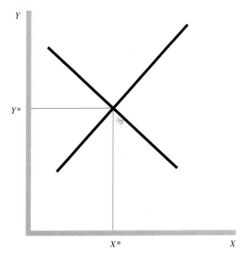

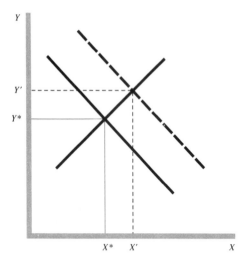

FIGURE 5-3
FINDING THE NEW INTERSECTION WHEN ONE
RELATION SHIFTS

the dashed line. At the new equilibrium (Y', X'), both X and Y are higher than at the original equilibrium. Notice that we are able to make very strong qualitative statements about the direction of change of the unknown variables even though we have very limited information about the two equations. In principle, we could find exact numerical solutions by drawing the graph with sufficient care. Practically speaking, we rarely do this. Graphs are used mainly for qualitative analysis.

If Z increases, both equations shift. As illustrated in Figure 5-4, equation (5-1) shifts upward to the left and equation (5-2) shifts downward to the left. (Go back to Review of Technique 4 if you are unsure why the motion is in the direction indicated.) Since both equations shift to the left, the equilibrium surely shifts to the left; in other words, X will be lower. On the other hand, since one equation shifts up and the other shifts down, the new intersection might be either above or below the original point. The change in Y might be either positive or negative. In order to know the change unambiguously, we would need to know the relative values of a_2 and b_2.

The slope of equation (5-1) determines how a shift in equation (5-2) changes X and Y. A practical example of this is the question of how the slope of the IS curve determines the effectiveness of monetary policy. Figure 5-5 illustrates two different hypothetical versions of equation (5-1). The narrow line represents a line with a higher value for a_1, and therefore a greater slope, than the original equation (5-1); the distance from (Y^*, X^*) to (Y', X') is the change that would occur with the original value of a_1. The distance from (Y^*, X^*) to (Y'', X'') illustrates the change caused by the hypothetically higher value of a_1. The higher slope of the narrow line results in a larger shift in Y and a smaller shift in X.

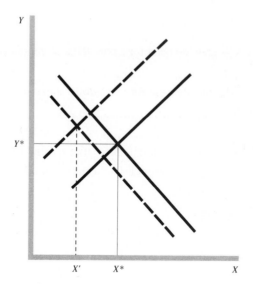

FIGURE 5-4
FINDING THE NEW INTERSECTION WHEN BOTH
RELATIONS SHIFT

FIGURE 5-5
IMPACT OF A SHIFT IN ONE RELATION DEPENDS
ON THE SLOPE OF THE OTHER RELATION

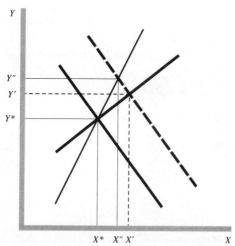

FILL-IN QUESTIONS

1. The increase in aggregate demand for a one-dollar increase in the money stock is given by the _____.

2. The increase in aggregate demand for a one-dollar increase in autonomous spending is given by the _____.

3. Because of _____, an increase in government purchases increases GDP by less than one might think after reading Chapter 3.

4. _____ provides a "good set of wheels" on which expansionary fiscal policy can roll.

5. The choice of the proper _____ affects the division of aggregate demand between consumption and investment; that is, it affects the

   _____.

6. A flat region of the *LM* curve is known as the _____.

7. A vertical *LM* curve is called the _____.

TRUE-FALSE QUESTIONS

T F   1. The effectiveness of monetary policy depends on the *LM* curve, not the *IS* curve.

T F   2. The effectiveness of fiscal policy depends on the *IS* curve, not the *LM* curve.

T F   3. In the liquidity trap, the demand for money responds a great deal to the interest rate.

T F   4. In the classical case, the demand for money does not respond at all to the interest rate.

T F   5. Expansionary monetary policy increases the budget deficit.

MULTIPLE-CHOICE QUESTIONS

1. Which of the following administrations employed restrictive fiscal policy:
   a. Kennedy-Johnson
   b. Nixon
   c. Reagan
   d. all of the above

2. The major postwar recession occurred in
   a. 1962–1963
   b. 1968–1969
   c. 1973–1974
   d. 1981–1982

$L = kr - hi$ $I = I_p - bi$

$\dfrac{h\bar{\alpha}}{h+\bar{\alpha}bk}$ $\dfrac{b\bar{\alpha}}{h+\bar{\alpha}bk}$.

3. A higher *MPC* increases
   a. the fiscal policy multiplier   c. both
   b. the monetary policy multiplier   d. neither

4. A higher interest sensitivity of investment increases
   a. the fiscal policy multiplier   c. both
   b. the monetary policy multiplier   d. neither

$\alpha = \dfrac{1}{1 - C(1-t)}$

5. A high interest sensitivity of money demand increases
   a. the fiscal policy multiplier   c. both
   b. the monetary policy multiplier   d. neither

$S - I = (G + TR - TA) + NX$ 6. A high income sensitivity of money demand increases
   a. the fiscal policy multiplier   c. both
   b. the monetary policy multiplier   d. neither

7. A high income tax rate decreases
   a. the fiscal policy multiplier   c. both
   b. the monetary policy multiplier   d. neither

8. According to the model in this chapter, a balanced budget increase in taxes and spending generally increases GDP
   a. not at all
   b. by less than the amount of the increase
   c. by exactly the amount of the increase
   d. by more than the amount of the increase

9. Increased transfer payments increase
   a. the interest rate   c. both
   b. the budget surplus   d. neither one

10. Expansionary fiscal policy together with tight monetary policy produces
    a. high GDP—interest rates might go up or down
    b. low GDP—interest rates might go up or down
    c. high interest rates—GDP might go up or down
    d. low interest rates—GDP might go up or down

PROBLEMS

1. Find the transfer policy multiplier in terms of *h, b,* etc., assuming that
   a. transfers are not taxed.
   b. transfers are taxed, like all other incomes, at the rate *i.*

2. Suppose that government purchases rise by $1 billion while transfers fall by $1 billion. (Assume that transfers are not taxed directly, but that there is an income tax at rate t on all income.)
   a. What happens to GDP?
   b. What happens to the budget surplus?

3. In 1985, the interest rate on Treasury bills was 7.48 percent. The consumer price index rose from 315.5 in December 1984 to 327.4 in December 1985.
   a. What was the inflation rate over 1985?
   b. What was the real interest rate?

4. Consider the following *IS-LM* model, which omits government spending and taxes but takes into account the distinction between nominal and real interest rates.

$$C = \bar{C} + cY$$
$$I = \bar{I} - br$$
$$L = kY - hi$$
$$M = \bar{M}$$
$$P = \bar{P}$$
$$i = r + \pi^e$$

Investment demand depends on the real return on alternative assets. By contrast, real money demand depends on both the real return on bonds and the expected return on goods (expected inflation), that is, the nominal rate. How are output and the real and nominal rate affected by an increase in expected inflation? Expected inflation is an exogenous variable in this model.

5. Consider an economy in which government spending is not simply exogenous, but responds negatively to deviations of GDP from its potential, full-employment level. $G = \bar{G} + d(YP - Y)$, where YP = potential, or full-employment, GDP, and $d > 0$. How is the *IS* curve affected by this change, and what is the implication of this for the effectiveness of monetary policy? Show your result analytically, using the standard equations and explain.

6

INTERNATIONAL LINKAGES

FOCUS OF THE CHAPTER

- All countries engage in international trade, exporting some goods to foreign countries and importing other goods from abroad. Most countries also engage in international finance, borrowing from or lending to other nations. A country that engages in international trade or finance is said to have an open economy.

- The U.S. economy is linked to other nations by the exchange rate, that is, the value of other currencies relative to the U.S. dollar. When the value of other currencies is relatively high, the United States exports more and imports less. The U.S. economy is also linked to other nations by the relative level of domestic and foreign interest rates. When U.S. interest rates are relatively high, foreigners invest capital in the United States.

- We extend the *IS-LM* framework to include the effects of international trade. We also add a new consideration, the position of the balance of payments surplus or deficit.

- Exchange rates may be either fixed (set by central bank intervention) or floating (determined in the marketplace). Capital may be mobile (easily moved to the country with the highest interest rate) or relatively immobile. The effect of fiscal and monetary policy in an open economy varies considerably according to these two factors.

SECTION SUMMARIES

1. The Balance of Payments and Exchange Rates

The *balance of payments* measures the difference between total payments leaving the country and total payments entering the country. The two principal parts of the balance are the *current account* and the *capital account.* The current account is made up of the *trade balance,* the difference between exported goods and imported goods, plus net exports of services and net transfers abroad. The *capital account* is the difference between U.S. investment abroad and foreign investment in the United States, including both real and financial investment. Throughout most of the 1960s, our current account was in surplus, although the account reversed itself dramatically by the early 1980s. The U.S. capital account ran a large deficit until the 1980s when it moved into a surplus condition.

Foreigners usually want to be paid in their own currency, not dollars. When our balance of payments is in deficit, more dollars leave the country than return, and so the Fed and foreign central banks must turn these excess dollars into foreign currency. These *official reserve transactions* must just match the overall balance of payments deficit.

The exchange rate is the price of one currency in terms of another. If there are two deutsche marks (DM) per dollar, we say the German exchange rate is 0.50, or that each deutsche mark is worth 50 cents. Under a *fixed exchange rate* regime, the central banks *intervene* in the market in order to peg the prices of different currencies. The German central bank can buy or sell any amount of deutsche marks at 50 cents each. If a country is in persistent deficit, it may run out of the reserves needed to keep buying up its own currency. In that case, the bank must either borrow reserves from the central banks or lower the value of its currency.

Under *flexible exchange rates,* the prices of different currencies are decided by the laws of supply and demand. The price of deutsche marks changes continually in the same manner as the price of stocks on the stock exchange. Under fixed exchange rates, countries usually keep the value of their currency constant for a number of years. In a *clean floating* system, the central banks allow supply and demand to operate without interference. In practice, the world operated on a system of *managed,* or dirty floating, in which central banks intervene in a limited way.

The exchange rate can be defined either as the value of foreign currency in terms of U.S. dollars or as the value of U.S. dollars in foreign currency. The text, as a matter of convention, always uses the former, and so the German-U.S. exchange rate rises, for example, from $0.60 to $0.70. An *appreciation* of the dollar means that the exchange rate falls. *Devaluation (revaluation)* refers to a depreciation (appreciation) deliberately brought about by the government under a fixed exchange rate system.

2. Exchange Rate Measures and the U.S. Dollar

A bilateral exchange rate measures the price of a foreign country's currency in terms of the dollar. The effective or multilateral exchange rate measures the price of a representative basket of foreign currencies, the price being stated in units of foreign currency per dollar. Each currency receives a weight that reflects the importance of the currency to the United States in international trade.

The real exchange rate measures the prices of goods produced in a foreign country relative to the prices of those same goods produced at home. The real exchange rate is given by the expression

$$R = \frac{e \cdot P_f}{P}$$

where R is the real exchange rate, e is the currency exchange rate, and P_f and P are the foreign and domestic price levels.

3. Trade in Goods, Market Equilibrium, and the Balance of Trade

We return now to our *IS-LM* model and *add back in* net exports, *NX*. We differentiate between spending by domestic residents and total spending on domestic goods.

$$\text{Spending by domestic residents} \equiv A \equiv C + I + G$$
$$\text{Spending on domestic goods} \quad \equiv Y \equiv A + NX$$
$$\equiv (C + I + G) + NX$$

At first glance, it may appear that purchases of imported goods are omitted from spending by domestic residents. Remember that all purchases are already counted in consumption and the other sectors of aggregate demand.

We use X and Q to represent exports and imports, respectively. Exports depend positively on foreign income, Y_f, and on the real exchange rate, R. Imports depend positively on domestic income, Y, and negatively on the real exchange rate. The text defines functions $A( )$, $Q( )$, $X( )$, and $NX( )$.

$$A \ = A(Y, i)$$
$$NX = X(Y_f, R) - R \cdot Q(Y, R)$$
$$NX = NX(Y, Y_f, R)$$

We can combine these to find the goods market equilibrium, or *IS* curve.

$$Y = A(Y, i) + NX(Y, Y_f, R)$$

This *IS* curve can be combined with the *LM* curve of Chapter 4 to find overall equilibrium. Once we know equilibrium GDP, we can compare exports and imports to find the overall trade surplus. Figure 6-1 shows the equilibrium of the economy at point E and also the level of GDP at which $NX = 0$. Since point E is shown to the left of the $NX = 0$ line, the economy has a trade surplus.

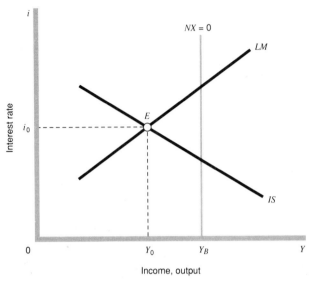

FIGURE 6-1
GOODS AND MONEY MARKET EQUILIBRIUM

We can use this extended *IS-LM* diagram to explore the impact of several economic changes on GDP and the trade balance. Consider an increase in autonomous spending on domestic goods, for example, the use of expansionary fiscal policy. This moves the *IS* curve as shown in Figure 6-2, increasing GDP and reducing the trade surplus.

FIGURE 6-2
EFFECTS OF AN INCREASE IN DOMESTIC SPENDING

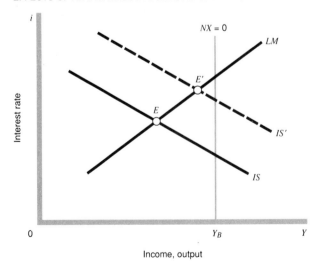

Consider now an increase in exports. As shown in Figure 6-3, this moves the *IS* curve to *IS'* and also moves the *NX* = 0 line rightward, since imports (and therefore higher income) are now required in order to have balanced trade. GDP increases. The trade surplus also improves as shown.

Just as our model of the U.S. economy depends on our exports to Germany, so too the state of the German economy depends on our imports from Germany. Thus, all nations are interdependent. If U.S. income rises, we import more from Germany. This leads to an expansion of German GDP, leading to more purchases of U.S. goods by Germany and a further increase in U.S. GDP. This is called the *repercussion effect.*

4. Capital Mobility

Policymakers need to watch both internal balance, keeping the economy close to full employment, and external balance, keeping the balance of payments close to even.

Interest rates adjusted for exchange rate risk tend to be equalized across countries with well-developed capital markets. Investors move money out of low-interest-rate countries into high-interest-rate countries until rates are brought into line. Changes in the interest rate induce capital flows so that a policy that creates a current account balance may be associated with a capital account imbalance. Capital flows into the United States when the U.S. interest rate rises above comparable world rates.

In the short run, by using both fiscal and monetary policy, we can choose both a level of GDP and a rate of interest. By choosing the appropriate rate of interest, we can have a capital account surplus that just offsets a current account deficit. Under fixed exchange rates, we should expand income through fiscal policy whenever there is

FIGURE 6-3
EFFECTS OF AN INCREASE IN EXPORTS

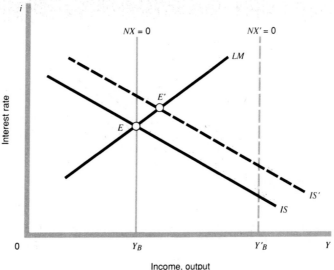

Income, output

unemployment and should use tight monetary policy whenever there is a balance of payments deficit. In addition to the problems of fiscal and monetary policy discussed in Chapter 15, a country is not indifferent to the makeup of the balance of payments. After all, if you run a large, permanent capital account surplus, eventually someone else will own your country.

5. The Mundell-Fleming Model: Perfect Capital Mobility under Fixed Exchange Rates

When capital is perfectly mobile, domestic and foreign assets are perfect substitutes. Consequently, interest rate differentials between domestic and foreign assets cannot persist. Were yields on similar assets different from one another, investors would shift all of their investments to the asset with the highest yield.

When exchange rates are fixed, a country cannot pursue an independent monetary policy. If the domestic interest rate were above the world interest rate, investors would move their investment into domestic assets. In order to buy domestic assets, foreigners must exchange their own currencies for dollars. Central banks, including the Federal Reserve, are required to supply the dollars to meet the demands of these investors at the established exchange rates. The final result is that the influx of dollars into the domestic economy increases the domestic money supply and shifts the *LM* curve outward.

An understanding of the interaction between perfect capital mobility and a worldwide regime of fixed exchange rates leads us to conclude that fiscal policy can be used to increase domestic GDP, but that monetary policy is completely ineffective.

6. Perfect Capital Mobility and Flexible Exchange Rates

The Mundell-Fleming model is a tool for evaluating the relative effectiveness of domestic fiscal and monetary policy when capital is perfectly mobile and exchange rates are flexible.

Flexible exchange rates imply that the balance of payments must be zero. Perfect capital mobility implies that the domestic interest rate must equal the world interest rate.

A disturbance in the goods market, such as an increase in foreign demand for domestic goods, shifts the *IS* curve outward, as in Figure 6-4. Consideration of the domestic goods market alone would suggest that E' is the equilibrium. But at E', i exceeds i_f, so that investors will wish to increase their holdings of domestic assets. The increased demand for dollars raises the exchange rate (the price of dollars), and the relative price of domestic goods rises. The *IS* curve shifts leftward as foreign demand for domestic goods falls and domestic demand for imports rises.

An increase in the domestic money stock (Figure 6-5), on the other hand, will have powerful effects on domestic income. As the *LM* curve shifts to the right, the domestic interest rate falls below the world interest rate, capital flows out, and the dollar depreciates. Domestic goods become cheaper to foreigners and imports become more expensive at home. Net exports rise, which shifts the *IS* curve rightward. The economy ends up at E'.

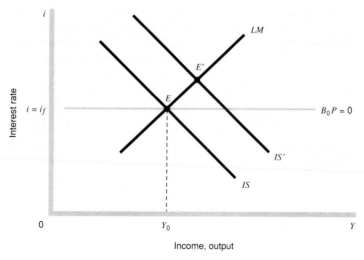

FIGURE 6-4
EFFECTS OF AN INCREASE IN THE FOREIGN DEMAND FOR DOMESTIC GOODS
WHEN THE EXCHANGE RATE IS FLEXIBLE AND CAPITAL IS PERFECTLY MOBILE

On occasion, an individual country will engage in a beggar-thy-neighbor policy of depreciating its currency. The domestic balance of payments will improve at the expense of the country's trading partners. Trading partners may counter the home country's depreciation with a competitive depreciation of their own.

FIGURE 6-5
EFFECTS OF AN INCREASE IN THE MONEY STOCK WHEN EXCHANGE RATES
ARE FLEXIBLE AND CAPITAL IS PERFECTLY MOBILE

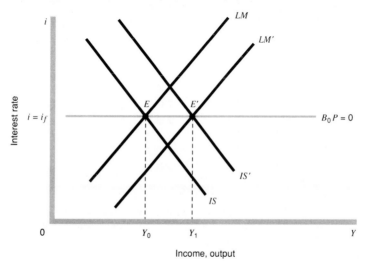

KEY TERMS

Exchange rate	Real exchange rate
Current account	Depreciation
Capital account	Appreciation
Balance of payments	Repercussion effects
Fixed exchange rate	Capital mobility
Floating exchange rate	Internal and external balance
Intervention	Mundell-Fleming model
Dirty floating	Beggar-thy-neighbor policy
Clean floating	Trade balance
Nominal exchange rate	

GRAPH IT 6

Does an increase in the exchange rate really cut exports? *By how much?* In this Graph It, we ask you to prepare a graph (Chart 6-1) with exports on the vertical axis and the value of the U.S. dollar (1/*e* in the textbook's terms) on the horizontal axis, using the data in Table 6-1.

TABLE 6-1

Year	Real exports	Value of the dollar
1967	130.0	120.0
1968	140.2	122.1
1969	147.8	122.4
1970	161.3	121.1
1971	161.9	117.8
1972	173.7	109.1
1973	210.3	99.1
1974	234.4	101.4
1975	232.9	98.5
1976	243.4	105.6
1977	246.9	103.3
1978	270.2	92.4
1979	293.5	88.1

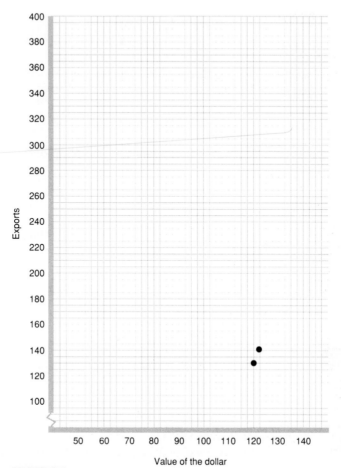

CHART 6-1

REVIEW OF TECHNIQUE 6

Solving Two Equations Algebraically

Some students find that a little algebra adds precision to economic arguments . . . and then some students find that it doesn't help at all. The text uses very little algebra, although there are spots such as the end of Chapter 5 where algebra comes in handy. This review provides some algebra practice for those who want it.

   In Review of Technique 5, we solved a system of two equations in two unknowns by using a graph. Now we will solve the same system algebraically. The equations are

$$Y = a_1 X + a_2 Z$$
$$Y = -b_1 X - b_2 Z + b_3 Q$$

Since the equations come in a form with the same variable on the left-hand side, the simplest method is to set one equation equal to the other.

$$a_1 X + a_2 Z = -b_1 X - b_2 Z + b_3 Q$$

Equation (6-1) gives the final formula for X in terms of the exogenous variables.

$$X = -\frac{a_2 + b_2}{a_1 + b_1} Z + \frac{b_3}{a_1 + b_1} Q \qquad (6\text{-}1)$$

We find the final equation for Y by substituting the value of X, above, into either of the original equations and collecting common terms.

$$Y = -b_1 \left(-\frac{a_2 + b_2}{a_1 + b_1} Z + \frac{b_3}{a_1 + b_1} Q \right) - b_2 Z + b_3 Q$$

$$= \left(\frac{b_1(a_2 + b_2)}{a_1 + b_1} - b_2 \right) Z + \left(\frac{-b_1 b_3}{a_1 + b_1} + b_3 \right) Q$$

$$= \frac{b_1 a_2 - a_1 b_2}{a_1 + b_1} Z + \frac{a_1 b_3}{a_1 + b_1} Q \qquad (6\text{-}2)$$

We can use equations (6-1) and (6-2) to answer the same questions about changes in Q or Z as we did in Review of Technique 5. If Q increases, then both X and Y increase, since the coefficient on each is positive. If Z increases, X definitely falls, since the coefficient in equation (6-1) is negative. On the other hand, Y might either rise or fall, as $(b_1 a_1 - a_2 b_1)$ might be either positive or negative. These answers are the same as those obtained from the graphical analysis. Of course, if we had exact values for each coefficient, we could make precise calculations for X and Y.

FILL-IN QUESTIONS

1. The value of foreign currency in terms of the U.S. dollar is called the _____ _____.

2. The _____ measures the net flow of goods and services out of the country.

3. Net investment by foreigners in the United States is measured by the _____ _____.

4. The net flow of dollars into the country from abroad is the _____.

5. Governments can peg the value of their currency in a(n) _____ or let the market determine the value in a(n) _____.

6. In practice, governments often intervene occasionally in foreign exchange markets in what is called a(n) _____.

7. _____ of the dollar makes foreign currency relatively more valuable.

8. When the government reduces the value of its currency under fixed exchange rates, the action is called a(n) _____.

9. When exchange rates are fixed and capital is perfectly mobile, the money supply is _____.

10. When capital is perfectly mobile and exchange rates are fully flexible, the _____ _____ always balances.

TRUE-FALSE QUESTIONS

T F 1. Expansionary fiscal policy increases the trade surplus.

T F 2. Expansionary monetary policy increases the capital account surplus.

T F 3. Devaluation improves the trade balance.

T F 4. Devaluation increases GDP.

T F 5. Devaluation increases the domestic cost of living.

T F 6. An increase in U.S. GDP generates a drop in German GDP.

T F 7. An increase in U.S. interest rates leads to an increase in German interest rates.

T F 8. The central bank can meet a temporary balance of payments deficit by using up reserves of foreign currency and gold.

T F 9. The central bank can meet a permanent balance of payments deficit by using up reserves of foreign currency and gold.

MULTIPLE-CHOICE QUESTIONS

1. High U.S. GDP leads to
   a. high U.S. exports
   b. high U.S. imports
   c. both high exports and imports
   d. neither

2. High German GDP leads to
   a. high U.S. exports
   b. high U.S. imports
   c. both
   d. neither

3. Contractionary fiscal policy increases
   a. the current account surplus
   b. the capital account surplus
   c. both types of surplus
   d. neither type of surplus

4. Contractionary monetary policy increases
   a. the current account surplus
   b. the capital account surplus
   c. both types of surplus
   d. neither type of surplus

5. Beginning with an increase in autonomous U.S. spending, the repercussion effect through the German economy
   a. leads to a further increase in U.S. GDP
   b. leads to a further decrease in U.S. GDP
   c. produces no further changes in U.S. GDP
   d. completely offsets the initial change in U.S. GDP

6. If the deutsche mark is initially worth 25 cents and Germany revalues its currency by 50 percent, the German exchange rate
   a. rises
   b. falls
   c. remains unchanged
   d. cannot be determined from the information given

7. In an open economy, the simple multiplier is _____ in a closed economy.
   a. larger than that
   b. smaller than that
   c. no different from that
   d. any of a, b, or c

8. Combined expansionary fiscal and monetary policy, used so as to keep the interest rate constant, causes the capital account surplus to
   a. increase
   b. remain unchanged
   c. decrease
   d. do any of a, b, or c

9. An increase in foreign income when capital is perfectly mobile and exchange rates are fixed causes
   a. domestic output to rise
   b. foreign income to rise again
   c. neither a nor b
   d. both a and b

PROBLEMS

1. Initially, the deutsche mark is worth 25 cents. Suppose the dollar is devaluated by 50 percent and then by an additional 20 percent. What is the new exchange rate?

2. The domestic import schedule is given by $Q = R \cdot (a \cdot R + B \cdot Y)$, where a and b are constants. If an increase in R is to reduce Q in a fixed-exchange-rates world, what is the sign of a?

3. The marginal propensity to consume is 0.9, investment and exports are autonomous, and imports are as described below. What is the multiplier on government spending?

$$Q = \bar{Q} + 0.1Y \text{ (U.S. imports)}$$

4. Suppose that the U.S. economy is as described in question 2 and that the German economy has an *MPC* of 0.8, investment is purely autonomous, and German imports are as given below. Further assume that all trade between Germany and the United States is bilateral. What is the multiplier of U.S. government spending on German GDP?

$$Q_G = \bar{Q}_G + 0.2Y_G \text{ (German imports)}$$

5. With perfect capital mobility and fixed exchange rates, how will the domestic economy be affected by an increase in government spending and an increase in the money stock which, in combination, maintain interest rates constant?

6. When capital is perfectly mobile and exchange rates are perfectly flexible, by what mechanism does an increase in the money stock raise GDP?

7. The OPEC cartel caused increases in the price of oil in 1973–1974 and again in 1979–1980 that brought about a large redistribution of world income to the countries of the oil cartel. The OPEC countries have a larger marginal propensity to save than that of the rest of the world. What effect will such a redistribution have on *world* income and the world *real* interest rate if the world *nominal* money supply is constant? Discuss and provide a graphical explanation using a world *IS-LM* diagram with the real rather than nominal interest rate represented on the vertical axis. What might be appropriate world monetary and fiscal responses to such OPEC actions?

part two

AGGREGATE DEMAND, SUPPLY, AND GROWTH

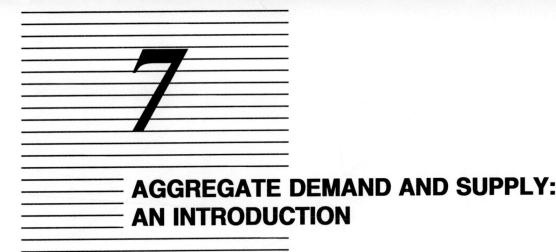

AGGREGATE DEMAND AND SUPPLY: AN INTRODUCTION

FOCUS OF THE CHAPTER

- *Aggregate supply* and *aggregate demand* each give a relationship between the overall price level and output. Together, the aggregate supply and demand schedules determine GDP and the price level.

- The aggregate supply schedule describes how much output firms are willing to supply at a given price level.

- The aggregate demand schedule summarizes the *IS-LM* equilibrium of Chapters 4 and 5, with the *LM* curve repositioned for changing price levels.

- Aggregate supply and demand schedules are not related to the ordinary supply and demand schedules of microeconomics, although they look alike.

SECTION SUMMARIES

1. Introducing Aggregate Demand and Supply

The slope of the aggregate supply schedule splits movements of the aggregate demand schedule into changes in prices and changes in output. If the aggregate supply schedule is steep, as in Figure 7-1a, then an increase in aggregate demand mostly increases prices and leaves GDP relatively unchanged. If the aggregate supply schedule is relatively flat, as in Figure 7-1b, then an increase in aggregate demand mostly increases GDP and leaves prices relatively unchanged.

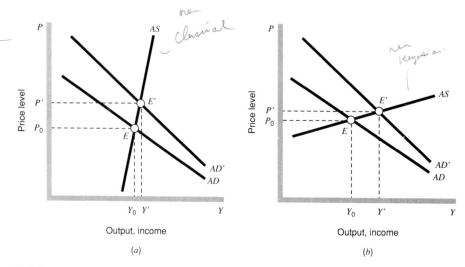

FIGURE 7-1

2. The Aggregate Demand Curve

The aggregate demand curve summarizes the *IS-LM* model for given fiscal and monetary policy, but changing price levels. At a high price level, the real money supply is low, and so aggregate demand is low. Thus the aggregate demand curve slopes downward. The slope of the aggregate demand curve is determined by the *monetary policy multiplier* of Chapter 5. If the monetary policy multiplier is large, then the aggregate demand curve is relatively flat, and vice versa. Expansionary fiscal or monetary policy shifts the *IS-LM* equilibrium out at a given price level and thus shifts the aggregate demand curve to the right.

3. Aggregate Demand Policies

A fiscal expansion shifts the aggregate demand curve outward to the right by an amount indicated by the fiscal policy multiplier. An increase in the nominal money stock also shifts the aggregate demand curve to the right. The shift is more easily measured as a shift up by the same proportion as the money stock increases.

4. The Aggregate Supply Curve

The aggregate supply curve describes the quantity of output firms are willing to supply at a given price level. The aggregate supply curve reflects conditions in the factor markets. Two special cases of aggregate supply are the Keynesian case, a perfectly horizontal aggregate supply curve, and the classical case, a perfectly vertical aggregate supply curve.

5. Fiscal and Monetary Policy under Alternative Supply Assumptions

With a Keynesian-case aggregate supply curve, prices are constant, and the conclusions of the first five chapters of the text hold without modification. With a classical aggregate supply curve, prices rise when aggregate demand increases. In the case of expansionary fiscal policy, there is full crowding out and interest rates rise so much that investment falls by an amount equal to the increase in government spending. With expansionary monetary policy, the price level rises in proportion to the increase in the money supply, and so the real money supply and GDP are unchanged.

6. The Quantity Theory and the Neutrality of Money

The *quantity theory* emphasizes the idea that changes in the money supply are responsible for most changes in the price level. Money is said to be *neutral* if an increase in money increases prices but leaves all real variables—GDP, unemployment, and the interest rate —unchanged. The pure quantity theory is equivalent to the notions that the velocity of money is constant and that real GDP is unaffected by changes in money—neither of which is true. Modern quantity theorists believe that the aggregate supply curve is vertical in the long run, but sloped in the short run. Thus the money supply will affect GDP in the short run but not in the long run.

KEY TERMS

Aggregate supply curve	Full crowding out
Aggregate demand curve	Quantity theory of money
Keynesian aggregate supply curve	Neutrality of money
Classical aggregate supply curve	Monetarism

GRAPH IT 7

The aggregate demand schedule represents the solutions of the *IS-LM* system at different price levels. Chart 7-1 shows an *IS-LM* diagram drawn above an aggregate demand diagram. We've drawn an *IS* curve and an *LM* curve based on a price level P_0. The equilibrium income is E_0. We've marked off this same income level on the aggregate demand diagram at price P_0. This gives us one point on the aggregate demand schedule. Now you draw in two new *LM* curves, one based on $P_1 < P_0$ and another based on $P_2 > P_0$. Mark the points E_1 and E_2 and drop vertical lines to mark the points on the aggregate demand diagram. Connect the three points on the aggregate demand diagram and mark the line *AD*.

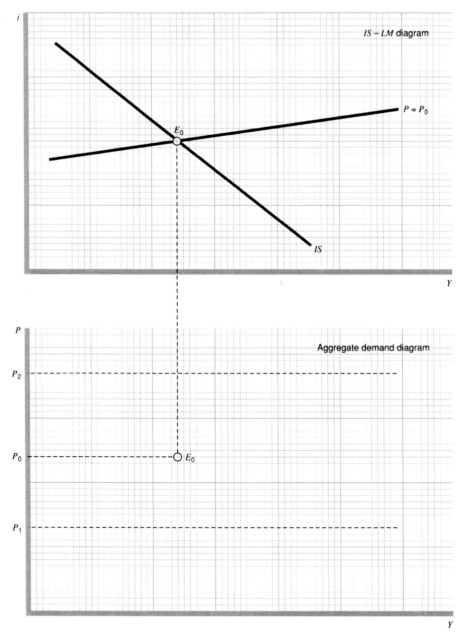

CHART 7-1

REVIEW OF TECHNIQUE 7

Logarithms

Logarithms turn out to be extremely useful for "back-of-the-envelope" economic calculations. Logarithms are intimately related to the calculation of percentage changes. The formal, and not very important, definition of logarithm is that

$$X = \ln Y$$

if and only if

$$Y = e^x$$

where e is an irrational number (pi is another irrational number) approximately equal to 2.71828. (Technically, this stands for a natural logarithm, as distinguished from logarithms based on numbers other than e.) Before the days of calculators, tables of logarithms were used to speed calculations.

If you look up the logarithms of 100, 101, and 110 in a table or if you press the appropriate buttons on your calculator, you will find that $\ln 100 = 4.605$, $\ln 101 = 4.615$, and $\ln 110 = 4.700$. Notice that $\ln 101$ minus $\ln 100$ is approximately 1 percent (more precisely, 0.00995). The natural log of 110 minus $\ln 100$ is about 10 percent (more precisely, 0.0953). As you can see, *the change in the logarithm of a variable approximately equals the percentage change in the variable itself.* Several useful points to remember about logarithms are:

$$\ln (X \cdot Y) = \ln X + \ln Y$$
$$\ln (X/Y) = \ln X - \ln Y$$
$$\ln (X^Y) = Y \cdot X$$
$$\ln (1 + x) \cong x \text{ for very small } x \ (\cong \text{ means "approximately equal to")}$$

Today, logarithms are no longer needed to speed calculation. However, knowing the facts above allows us to solve many problems by inspection, never actually calculating a logarithm. See Review of Technique 8 for a very useful example of this.

FILL-IN QUESTIONS

1. The aggregate demand function depends on _____.
2. It also depends on _____.
3. The aggregate demand function represents those combinations of income and price level found through _____ analysis.
4. The displacement of investment by government spending is called _____

   _____.

5. The proposition that proportional changes in the nominal money supply and the price level have no real effect is referred to as _____.

6. The relation between output and prices that summarizes the economy's ability to produce goods and services is the _____ schedule.

7. The relation between output and prices that summarizes the various possible *IS-LM* equilibria is the _____ schedule.

8. In the Keynesian model, the aggregate supply curve is _____.

9. In the classical model, the aggregate supply curve is _____.

TRUE-FALSE QUESTIONS

T (F) 1. Movements up and left along the aggregate demand schedule correspond to decreasing interest rates in the *IS-LM* equilibrium.

T (F) 2. A flat aggregate demand schedule results from a low *MPC*.

(T) F 3. A flat aggregate demand schedule results from a low interest sensitivity of money demand.

(T) (F) 4. A flat aggregate demand schedule results from a low interest sensitivity of investment.

(T) F 5. Aggregate demand (*AD*) is increased by increased government spending.

(T) F 6. Combinations of *IS* and *LM* curves can be used to trace out the aggregate supply curve.

T (F) 7. Increased government spending increases interest rates if the aggregate supply curve is Keynesian.   *Not tru ; P is not chgd.*

(T) F 8. Increased government spending increases interest rates if the aggregate supply curve is classical.

(T) F 9. Increased nominal money supply decreases interest rates if the aggregate supply curve is Keynesian.

T (F) 10. Increased nominal money supply decreases interest rates if the aggregate supply curve is classical.

MULTIPLE-CHOICE QUESTIONS

Note: The price level is held constant in Questions 1 and 2.

1. Increasing the money supply
   a. increases aggregate supply
   b. decreases aggregate supply
   c. increases aggregate demand
   d. decreases aggregate demand

2. Increasing government spending
   a. increases aggregate supply
   b. decreases aggregate supply
   c. increases aggregate demand
   d. decreases aggregate demand

3. There is a positive relation between GDP and the price level along
   a. the aggregate demand curve
   b. the aggregate supply curve
   c. both these curves
   d. neither of these curves

4. There is a negative relation between GDP and the price level along
   a. the aggregate demand curve
   b. the aggregate supply curve
   c. both these curves
   d. neither of these curves

5. There is a negative relation between GDP and the interest rate along
   a. the aggregate demand curve
   b. the aggregate supply curve
   c. both these curves
   d. neither of these curves

6. A high marginal propensity to save implies
   a. that the aggregate supply curve is relatively flat
   b. that it is relatively steep
   c. that it is relatively flat only if *MPS* is greater than 0.5
   d. nothing about aggregate supply

7. If the nominal money supply doubles, eventually the price level will
   a. remain unchanged
   b. double
   c. increase by a factor of less than 2
   d. increase by a factor of more than 2

8. If autonomous spending doubles, eventually the price level
   a. will remain unchanged
   b. will double
   c. will more than double
   d. cannot be determined without more information

9. An increase in the nominal money supply will cause investment to increase in
   a. the long run
   b. the short run
   c. both the short and the long run
   d. neither the short nor the long run

10. An increase in government spending will cause investment to decrease in
    a. the long run
    b. the short run
    c. both the short and the long run
    d. neither the short nor the long run

PROBLEMS

Use the following equations for questions 1, 2, and 3:

$$Y = 2A + 4(M_{-1}/P_{-1}) \qquad \text{(aggregate demand)}$$
$$P = P_{-1}\{1 - 0.8[1 - (Y/Y_p)]\} \qquad \text{(aggregate supply)}$$
$$I = 1,000 - 2,000i \qquad \text{(investment)}$$

In the long run, assume the supply curve is classical and $P = P_{-1}$. Also note that we assume there is a one-period lag before monetary policy works.

Potential GDP is 4,000. Initial levels are $A = 1,000$, $M = 50,000$, and $P = 100$. Consumption is a function of current income only.

1. Suppose government spending increases by 500. What are the levels of GDP and the price index in the year of the increase? In the two following years?

2. What is the price level in the long run? By how much does investment change? The interest rate?

3. Suppose that, instead of increasing government spending, the money supply had been doubled. In the long run, what would be the level of the price index, the change in investment, and the change in the interest rate?

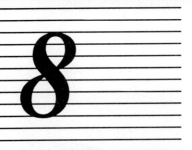

AGGREGATE SUPPLY: WAGES, PRICES, AND EMPLOYMENT

FOCUS OF THE CHAPTER

- The frictionless neoclassical model is a benchmark for the amount of production possible—potential GDP—when all prices are fully flexible.

- Money wages adjust slowly. When the wage differs from its long-run value, GDP differs from potential GDP.

- The Phillips curve describes the relation between wage change and unemployment. The aggregate supply curve is derived from the Phillips curve by looking at the relation of prices to wages and of output to employment.

- The aggregate supply curve is inherently dynamic. In the long run it will move to bring the economy to full employment.

- Expectations of inflation are implicitly held constant in this chapter. This important assumption is reexamined in Chapter 16.

SECTION SUMMARIES

1. Wages, Prices, and Output: The Facts

Unemployment fluctuates much more than the frictionless neoclassical model implies should be the case. Furthermore, money wage rates respond slowly to shifts in aggregate demand, which, again, is inconsistent with the neoclassical model. Shifts in aggregate demand appear to affect output and employment well before they affect prices and money wages.

The Phillips curve

$$\frac{W - W_{-1}}{W_{-1}} = -\varepsilon(u - u^*)$$

makes precise the notion that wages respond slowly to shifts in aggregate demand (unemployment). As u rises above u^* (natural rate of unemployment), money wages fall. As u falls below u^*, money wage rates rise. The rate at which money wages change from last period's level depends upon ε as well as $u - u^*$. The larger ε is, the more rapidly wages change.

At one time it was argued that policy makers could choose any combination of inflation and unemployment along the Phillips curve. Friedman and Phelps argued that the Phillips curve was not stable over time and that in the long run the economy would return to the natural rate of unemployment. Econometric evidence supports Friedman and Phelps's argument.

2. The Wage–Unemployment Relationship: Why Are Wages Sticky?

Using the definition of the unemployment rate

$$u = \frac{LF - N}{LF}$$

where LF is the size of the labor force and N is the actual level of employment, we can rewrite the Phillips curve in terms of the level of employment:

$$u = W_{-1} \left[1 + \varepsilon \left(\frac{N - N^*}{LF} \right) \right]$$

Wages rise ($W > W_{-1}$) whenever employment is above full employment ($N > N^*$).

Wage employment contracts are renegotiated only periodically, since negotiation is costly. Renegotiation dates are usually staggered, so that at any point in time, only a faction of all workers' wages are rising or falling in response to current changes in the cost of living or productivity. Wages in economies with low inflation rates are usually set in nominal terms, so that real wages do not adjust to changes in goods prices immediately. Therefore, nominal wages may remain fixed for long periods. Fluctuations in the real wage cause the terms on which employers can hire workers to change over time and, thus, produce fluctuations in employment.

3. The Aggregate Supply Curve

The aggregate supply curve relates prices and output. Prices depend on costs, which we can think of as unit labor costs, $1/a$, times the money wage, w, plus a percentage markup, z, to cover the costs of materials, capital, and profits.

$$P = \frac{w}{a}(1 + z)$$

In the wage adjustment equation, we now substitute prices for wages and GDP for labor to get aggregate supply.

$$P = P_{-1}\left[1 + \varepsilon\left(\frac{Y - YF}{YF}\right)\right]$$

Note the three properties of aggregate supply.

a. If wage adjustment is slow, the aggregate supply curve is relatively flat.
b. The position of the aggregate supply curve depends on the past history of prices.
c. The aggregate supply curve shifts over time because today's price becomes yesterday's price tomorrow. (Reread the last sentence if necessary. It actually does make sense. A different P_{-1} tomorrow means that the aggregate supply curve has a new position tomorrow.)

4. The Effects of a Monetary Expansion

Figures 8-1, 8-2, and 8-3 show the short-, medium-, and long-run responses of the economy to an increase in the money stock. The aggregate demand curve shifts to the right. At first, prices rise very little and output goes up almost as much as the horizontal shift in aggregate demand. Since we are now above full employment, prices rise and the aggregate supply curve gradually shifts up. The aggregate supply curve keeps shifting up until output returns to potential GDP, at a higher price than when we started, as in Figure 8-3 (see page 77).

5. Supply Shocks

An aggregate supply shock, an increase in the price of raw materials, for example, shifts the supply curve up. This increases prices and reduces output. If potential GDP has not fallen (and it may have), the aggregate supply curve will eventually return to its initial position. Aggregate demand policy can be used to accommodate supply shocks, stabilizing output but raising prices.

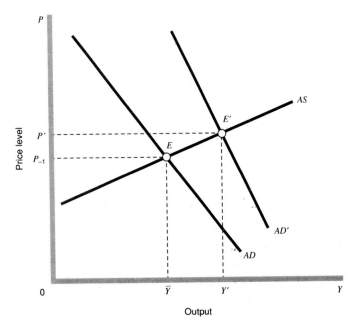

FIGURE 8-1

FIGURE 8-2

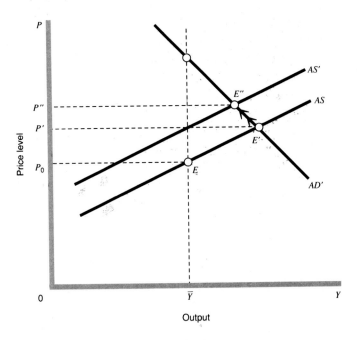

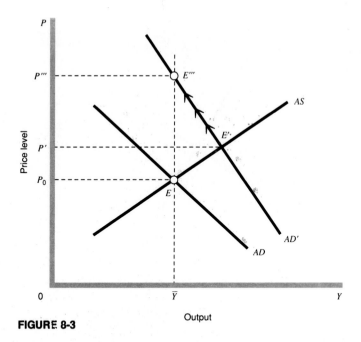

FIGURE 8-3

Output

KEY TERMS

Frictionless neoclassical model
Frictional unemployment
Natural rate of unemployment
Phillips curve
Labor productivity
Supply shock

Unit labor costs
Markup
Sticky wages
Adverse supply shock
Accommodation of supply shocks
Coordination problem

GRAPH IT 8

Graph It 8 asks you to implement fiscal policy (or at least to figure out how far to move the *IS* curve). Chart 8-1 shows *IS* and *LM* curves in the top diagram and aggregate supply and demand curves in the bottom diagram. Initially, equilibrium is at point E_0. Then a supply shock moves the aggregate supply curve up. The new equilibrium, with lower output and higher prices, is at point E_1. Draw in a new *IS'* curve that will move the economy to point E_2, and mark off the horizontal distance by which you moved the *IS* curve.

Hold it! Not so fast! Prices are higher at E_1 than at E_0. This means that real balances are lower and that the *LM* curve has already shifted left. Draw in the *LM'* curve corresponding to this movement along the aggregate demand curve. Then draw in *IS'* and measure the distance.

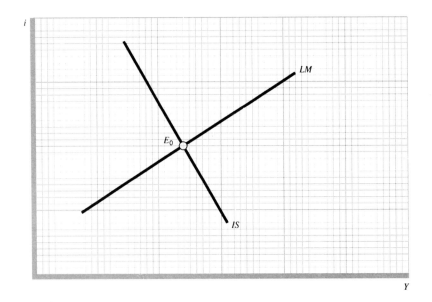

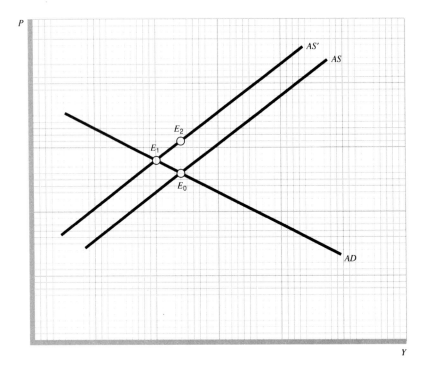

CHART 8-1

REVIEW OF TECHNIQUE 8

Constant Elasticity Formulas

Certain formulas show that one variable has a constant elasticity with respect to another. These formulas are extremely convenient because the variables involved always have the same relation in terms of percentage changes. The formula

$$X = AY^a Z^b$$

can be rewritten by taking logarithms of both sides.

$$\ln X = \ln A + a \ln Y + b \ln Z$$

Since the change in a natural log is the percentage change in the underlying variable, we can find directly the effect of a percentage change in Y or Z. Letting $\%\Delta$ mean percentage change,

$$\Delta \ln X = a \, \Delta \ln Y + b \, \Delta \ln Z$$

or

$$\%\Delta X = a\%\Delta Y + b\%\Delta Z$$

In other words, if Y goes up by 1 percent, X goes up by a times 1 percent. By definition, then, the elasticity of X with respect to Y equals a, and the elasticity of X with respect to Z equals b.

In future chapters we will see several examples of this type of formula. For example, the Baumol-Tobin money demand formula can be written

$$\frac{M}{P} = (bY)^{\frac{1}{2}}(2i)^{-\frac{1}{2}}$$

The claim in Chapter 13 that the elasticity of money demand with respect to income equals ½ is thus seen to be true.

FILL-IN QUESTIONS

1. The fact that wages change slowly is due to _____ .

2. The rate of _____ is the percentage change in the general price level per annum.

3. The _____ is the relation between inflation and unemployment derived from the aggregate supply curve.

4. The ratio of output to labor input is called _____.

5. The theory that prices are set by a constant percentage over variable costs is the _____ theory.

6. Events that change costs or shift the supply or demand for labor are called _____ _____.

$Y = aN$

TRUE-FALSE QUESTIONS

T F 1. Average output per worker generally rises during a boom.

T F 2. The concept of diminishing returns indicates that additional labor leads to lower output.

T F 3. Aggregate supply (AS) is increased by increased potential GDP.

T F 4. AS is increased by an increased labor force.

T F 5. An increase in materials prices pushes the aggregate supply curve up.

T F 6. Unit labor cost is the inverse of labor productivity.

T F 7. The government should always accommodate an adverse supply shock.

MULTIPLE-CHOICE QUESTIONS

1. Adverse supply shocks
   a. increase prices and increase output
   b. decrease prices and increase output
   c. increase prices and decrease output
   d. decrease prices and decrease output

2. Movement of the aggregate supply curve moves the economy to potential GDP
   a. instantly   c. slowly
   b. quite quickly   d. never

3. An increase in the money stock increases GDP in
   a. the short run   c. both
   b. the long run   d. neither

4. A drop in autonomous spending decreases GDP in
   a. the short run   c. both
   b. the long run   d. neither

5. The position of the aggregate supply curve depends on
   a. potential GDP   c. both
   b. past prices   d. neither

PROBLEMS

1. Suppose that the fraction of the labor force that becomes unemployed for each one percentage point deviation of GDP from potential GDP is 0.4 percent. Further assume that nominal wages drop 2 percent for each 1 percent increase in unemployment. Initially, the economy is in full employment and the consumer price index (CPI) is 100. If the government increases GDP by 10 percent and maintains it at its new level, what will the CPI be after 1 year? After 2 years?

2. According to the aggregate supply curve theory developed in this chapter, what is the inflation rate when the economy is at full employment?

3. (Refer to the Review of Technique in this chapter for help with this question.) The Federal Reserve would like to know the demand for real money balances in order to estimate the response of inflation to the Fed's nominal monetary policy. Assume that the money demand equation is

$$\ln \frac{M}{P} = a_0 + 0.555 \ln Y - 0.185 \ln i$$

   a. If $\%\Delta M = 3$, $\%\Delta Y = 2$, and the level of i is at 5 percent and unchanging, what is the rate of inflation?
   b. If monetary growth increases to 6 percent, what is the long-run response of money demand and inflation, allowing the nominal interest rate to change?

THE RATIONAL EXPECTATIONS EQUILIBRIUM APPROACH

FOCUS OF THE CHAPTER

- The rational expectations approach is a recent development in economic theory.

- The rational expectations approach argues that markets clear themselves and monetary policy cannot systematically affect output or employment.

- As the name suggests, economic agents form their expectations in a rational manner, using all available information as well as possible.

- The model insists upon equilibrium—that is, all markets must clear.

SECTION SUMMARIES

1. The Frictionless Neoclassical Model of the Labor Market

In the *frictionless neoclassical model of the labor market,* all firms are competitive and produce with a fixed amount of capital. Each firm's demand curve for labor slopes downward, a result of the fact that the marginal product of labor falls as additional workers are used in production. Firms hire labor up to the point at which the marginal cost of labor—the real wage—is equal to the marginal product of labor.

The supply curve of labor to the economy is an upward-sloping function of the real wage rate. As the real wage rises, more workers enter the labor force. The economywide real wage rate is determined by the intersection of the aggregate demand curve for labor and the supply curve of labor to the economy.

Employment is always at its *full-employment level* in the frictionless neoclassical model. Any disturbance that causes the price level to rise or fall produces immediate pressure in the labor market for the money wage rate to rise by the same proportion. Output and employment immediately return to their full-employment levels. The aggregate supply curve is vertical.

Even at full employment there will be frictional unemployment. Frictional unemployment is associated with normal turnover in the labor market. The unemployment rate at full employment is called the *natural rate of unemployment.*

2. The Market-Clearing Approach: The Lucas Supply Curve

A theory of business cycles that does not rely, as the Keynesian theory does, on sticky wages and prices is the Lucas hypothesis. The Lucas hypothesis suggests that the source of fluctuations in employment and output lies in the fact that different agents in the economy have different information about the aggregate price level. Lucas takes the case in which firms have better information than workers about those factors that affect movements in the aggregate price level. He then asks what would happen if an expansion in the nominal money supply by the Federal Reserve is anticipated by firms but not by workers. Firms anticipate that the monetary expansion will lead to an equiproportional rise in the aggregate price level. This will represent a fall in the real wage from the point of view of firms because workers do not anticipate the rise in the price level and thus do not bid up the *nominal* wage to a level that keeps their *real* wage constant. The response of firms to the fall in the actual real wage can be represented as an increase in the demand curve for labor along a constant labor supply curve. Employment and output rise as a result. Workers, who have not revised upward their expectation of the price level, believe they have the incentive to supply more labor, since they view the rise in the nominal wage that results from an increase in labor demand as an increase in the real wage. However, once workers realize that the actual price level exceeds their expectations and that, as a consequence, their real wage has fallen, they will reduce their labor supply until the real wage as well as employment and output have returned to their original levels. The interactions between workers and firms concerning expectations of the price level can be summarized in the *Lucas supply curve*. The Lucas supply curve describes output as a positive function of the ratio of the actual to the expected price level.

3. A New Keynesian Alternative

New Keynesian macroeconomics presents a rigorous alternative to the equilibrium model. The key distinction between the models is that new Keynesian theory assumes that wages in the labor market can be fixed by contract at the beginning of a period while prices of goods may change within the period. Firms and businesses agree upon wages that they expect will produce equilibrium in the labor market based upon their expectations about the price level.

4. Real Business Cycles

Members of the rational expectations equilibrium school have attempted to explain business cycles while adhering to the notion that all markets clear. Real business cycle theory takes the view that business cycles are mainly a consequence of real shocks, such as shifts in labor productivity (supply shocks), and government spending. Equilibrium business cycle theorists believe that business cycles are propagated by large swings in the supply of labor over time, a phenomenon that is known as the *intertemporal substitution of leisure.*

Appendix

The production function is a technological relation telling us how much output can be produced for a given combination of factor inputs. In the short run, when cooperating factors of production are in fixed supply, the marginal product of labor will be falling as more labor is added to the production process. The marginal product of labor measures the contribution to total output of an additional unit of labor (another worker). Firms will hire a worker as long as the contribution to total output is greater than the cost of hiring, which is the real wage.

KEY TERMS

Classical labor market	Real business cycle approach
Market-clearing approach	Economic disturbances
Production function	Propagation mechanism
Marginal product of labor	Rational expectations
Lucas model	Intertemporal substitution of leisure
Unanticipated money	Frictionless neoclassical model

GRAPH IT 9

Graph It 9 asks you to consider the special case where the aggregate supply curve is vertical. Using Chart 9-1, show the shift in the aggregate demand schedule when there is an increase in the money stock.

REVIEW OF TECHNIQUE 9

The Expectations Mechanism

In many chapters we have modeled expectations of some economic variable as depending on past levels of the variable. To see how this works, suppose we have some variable X

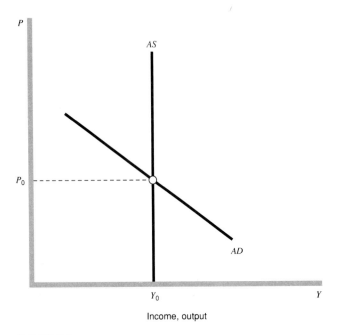

CHART 9-1

and that the expectation of X, X^e is based on the last 3 years' value of X according to the following formula

$$X^e = 0.75_{-1} + 0.2X_{-2} + 0.05X_{-3}$$

Suppose X rises by one unit for a year and then returns to its original level. What happens to X^e over the next several years?

Nothing happens in the year that X changes, since X^e does not depend on this year's X. Next year, X^e is up by 0.75 unit. The year after that, X_{-1} has returned to its original level and X_{-2} is up by one unit, so X^e is up by 0.2 unit from its original level and thus is 0.55 unit lower than it was in the first period following the change in X. In the next period, X^e is only 0.05 unit higher than its original level, and thereafter X^e is back to its original level.

Suppose, instead, that X went up one unit permanently. In the first period following the change, X^e is up by 0.75 unit, just as in the case of a temporary change. In the next period, X_{-1} and X_{-2} are both up by one unit, and so X^e climbs another 0.2 unit to reach 0.95 unit above its original level. In the third and following periods, X^e is up by one unit. Notice that we force the long-run change in X^e to be the same as a permanent change in X by making sure that the weights in the expectations equation add to 1.

Figures 9-1 and 9-2 illustrate the changes in X and X^e worked through above.

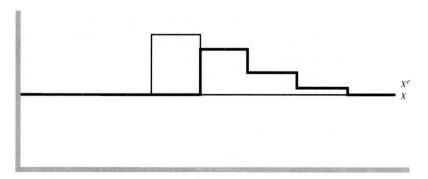

FIGURE 9-1
CHANGE IN EXPECTATIONS (HEAVY LINE) FOLLOWING A TEMPORARY
INCREASE IN X (LIGHT LINE)

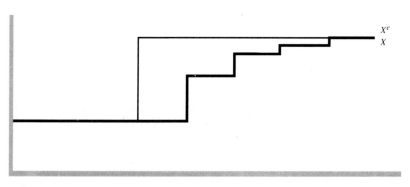

FIGURE 9-2
CHANGE IN EXPECTATIONS (HEAVY LINE) FOLLOWING A PERMANENT
INCREASE IN X (LIGHT LINE)

FILL-IN QUESTIONS

1. The relatively new school of economic thought that holds the belief that only unanticipated changes in monetary policy have any real effect is the _____ _____ school.

2. _____ theory suggests that economic fluctuations have nothing to do with money, but rather arise from shocks to productivity and aggregate supply changes.

3. The amount by which temporary wage fluctuations affect how much people work depends on the _____.

4. Assuming that the labor market is always in equilibrium, the aggregate supply curve is _____ at the full-employment level of output.

5. According to the _____, prices are flexible and prices and output are determined by perfect competition.

TRUE-FALSE QUESTIONS

T (F) 1. Rational expectations theorists believe that anticipated changes in the money supply are a major determinant of economic activity. *unanticipated.*

T F 2. Rational expectations equilibrium does not allow for imperfect information. *It allows for imperfect info but NOT system at.*

T F 3. Equilibrium wages rise in proportion to prices under the assumptions of the frictionless neoclassical model.

T F 4. Unanticipated changes in the money supply can affect the level of output.

T F 5. The New Keynesian approach argues that unanticipated money supply changes can increase output since many wages are fixed by contracts.

T F 6. The frictionless neoclassical model is a reasonably good short-run description of the economy.

T F 7. The frictionless neoclassical model is a reasonably good long-run description of the economy.

MULTIPLE-CHOICE QUESTIONS

1. In the frictionless neoclassical model, the real wage
   a. is unchanging over time
   b. equals the marginal product of labor
   c. equals the nominal wage
   d. is higher than in the Keynesian model

2. Rational expectations theory suggests that
   a. only unexpected changes in the stock of money affect the price level
   b. only unexpected changes in the stock of money affect the level of output
   c. only expected changes in the stock of money affect the price level
   d. only expected changes in the stock of money affect the level of output

3. The idea that surprise increases in the money supply increase GDP is associated with
   a. Keynesians   c. rational expectations theory
   b. monetarists   d. all of the above

4. The fundamental assumption of the rational expectations theory is that
   a. some people will always be unemployed
   b. there is no uncertainty regarding prices and wages
   c. the labor market is always in equilibrium
   d. individuals do not make systematic forecast errors

5. New Keynesian economic theory differs from rational expectations theory by suggesting that
   a. wages can be fixed in the short run by contracts
   b. unanticipated changes on the money stock have real effects on output
   c. there is increasing marginal productivity of labor
   d. workers do make systematic forecast errors

LONG-TERM GROWTH AND PRODUCTIVITY

FOCUS OF THE CHAPTER

We study two related topics here:

- *Potential output*

  1. Potential output is determined by factor inputs and the state of *technology*.
  2. Technology is described by a *production function*.

- *Long-term growth:* By studying how factor inputs change over time, in particular how saving leads to the accumulation of capital, we can predict how potential output will change in the future.

- *In this chapter we always assume that GDP equals potential GDP.* We allow no role for aggregate demand or for incorrect expectations.

SECTION SUMMARIES

1. Sources of Growth in Real Income

Output depends on factor input and on the technology applied to that input. The *production function* relates output to input. Using Y to represent output and K and N to represent capital input and labor input, respectively, we can write a production function as

$$Y = AF(K, N)$$

The rate of growth of output can be written as

$$\frac{\Delta Y}{Y} = (1 - \theta) \frac{\Delta N}{N} + \theta \frac{\Delta K}{K} + \frac{\Delta A}{A}$$

where θ is capital's share in income (about 0.25 in the U.S. economy) and A represents the level of technology. Thus the three sources of growth are more labor, more capital, and improved technology. A 1 percent increase in labor increases output by about three-fourths of 1 percent, while a 1 percent increase in capital increases output by about one-fourth of 1 percent.

2.   Empirical Estimates of the Sources of Growth

Since 1929, economic growth has averaged about 2.9 percent per year. Of this, about 1.9 percent has been due to increased input and the remainder to increased output per unit of input. The most important sources of growth have been population growth and increases in knowledge.

3.   Growth Theory

Growth theory is the study of the growth of factor inputs and the resultant growth in output. We assume that population grows at a constant percentage rate, $\Delta N/N \equiv n$. We also assume no technological change.

It is sometimes convenient to think about output *per capita* (Latin for "by head," that is, per person). We write output per capita as $x \equiv Y/N$ and capital per worker, also called the capital-labor ratio, as $k \equiv K/N$ (see Figure 10-1). We assume that the production function has *constant returns to scale* (see Review of Technique 17).

The *steady state* of the economy is the position in which capital per worker is constant. Just enough is saved to replace machinery that has worn out and to provide machines for new workers. Output per head is constant whenever capital grows as fast as population.

$$\frac{\Delta K}{K} = n$$

The change in capital is the difference between saving and depreciation. We assume that people save a constant fraction, s, of their income and that depreciation is a constant percentage, d, of the existing capital stock.

$$\Delta K = \text{saving} - \text{depreciation}$$
$$= sY - dK$$

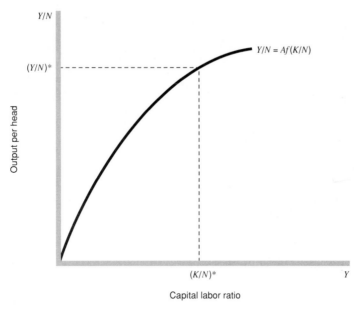

FIGURE 10-1
THE PRODUCTION FUNCTION

Dividing both sides by K and subtracting n from both sides,

$$\frac{\Delta K}{K} - n = \frac{\Delta Y}{K} - n - d$$

Recognizing that the rate of growth of capital minus the rate of growth of labor is the rate of growth of capital per head and that the ratio of output to capital is the same as the ratio of per capita output to per capita machinery, we can write

$$\frac{\Delta k}{k} = \frac{sx}{k} - (n + d)$$

$$\Delta k = sx - (n + d)k$$

This final formula looks formidable. All it says is that the amount of capital each worker has available rises when saving goes up and falls when depreciation rises or when capital must be spread out among more workers.

The growth process can be studied in terms of Figure 10-2. The x curve gives the level of output per head as a function of the capital-labor ratio. This is a graph of the production function. This sx curve shows the amount saved. The $(n + d)k$ line is the investment requirement, the amount needed to prevent capital per worker from falling.

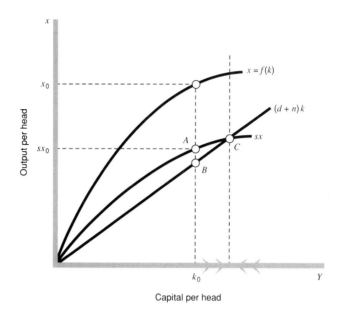

FIGURE 10-2
SAVINGS, INVESTMENT, AND CAPITAL ACCUMULATION

   To the left of point C, saving is above the investment requirement, and so capital per worker is growing. To the right of point C, saving is less than required investment, and so capital is falling. Point C is the steady state of the economy, the point at which the capital-labor ratio is neither rising nor falling. Steady-state per capita output is found by reading x off the production function directly above point C. Note that while C shows the long-run equilibrium of the economy, nothing prevents the economy from being away from steady-state equilibrium most of the time.
   An increase in the saving rate increases steady-state per capita GDP. It does not change the growth rate of per capita GDP permanently. In the steady state, population growth reduces per capita GDP. Even though GDP grows faster with higher population growth, it does not grow rapidly enough to keep up with the increasing population. Thus, faster population growth means a lower steady-state per capita GDP.

4. Endogenous Growth Theory

Endogenous growth theory attempts to make economic growth rates determined within the theory instead of exogenously. There are two basic ways of endogenizing the steady-state growth rate:

   a. The rate of technical progress can be made endogenous.
   b. Assuming constant returns to factors of production, the steady-state growth rate will be affected by the rate at which those factors are accumulated.

Persistent growth differences between countries can exist when the countries have different savings and investment levels. Neoclassical growth theory predicts these differences can exist for only a finite period. Robert Barro describes a result known as *conditional convergence,* which explains the link between endogenous growth theory and neoclassical theory.

5. Supply-Side Economics

Supply-side economists argue that potential GDP can be increased by improving incentives to supply labor or to invest in new capital. While such effects clearly exist, they are fairly small and unlikely to have much short-run significance. They may be of greater importance in terms of very long-run economic well-being.

6. Growth and Development

Economic development is the process by which the accumulation of factors of production, including human capital, contributes to the economic well-being of an economy. Successful economic development is generally characterized by an increase in the productivity of the agricultural sector of the economy. This permits the population to be fed by only a small fraction of the total labor force, thus enabling industrialization to take place. The most successful development strategies have been those that stress the growth of the exporting sector and that, after a period of protection, expose domestic producers to foreign competition. Such competition maintains an efficient scale of production in domestic import-competing industries.

KEY TERMS

Potential output	Limits of growth
Production function	Import substitution
Growth accounting	Newly industrializing economies (NIEs)
Sources of growth	Neoclassical growth theory
Technical progress	Endogenous growth theory
Growth of total factor productivity	Infrastructure investment
Supply-side economics	Human capital
Steady state	Convergence
Labor productivity	Development economics
Economic development	Exogenous
Outward-oriented strategy	Endogenous
Catching-up hypothesis	

GRAPH IT 10

We know that an increase in investment increases both aggregate demand and aggregate supply. Aggregate demand rises because of the increase in I in the $C + I + G$ expression, and aggregate supply rises because of the increase in the capital stock. How do the two effects compare? We'll use 1979 as a base year because 1979 was a year in which the economy was approximately at full employment. Assume that we could increase investment spending by 20 percent and that the aggregate demand multiplier on investment is 2.0.

Fill out Table 10-1. Notice that the table title refers to the short run and the long run. If we permanently increase investment, we permanently increase aggregate demand. In other words, aggregate demand goes to a new, higher level and stays there, but it doesn't keep increasing.

In Table 10-2 we try to figure out the increase in aggregate supply. Aggregate supply goes up because increased investment increases the capital stock. We know from studies of the production function that a 1 percent increase in the capital stock increases output by about one-fourth of 1 percent. It turns out that the capital stock is roughly 3 times GDP. Using these facts, fill in Table 10-2 to calculate the supply side of the impact of a 1-year and a 5-year increase in investment. (Use the same annual investment increase as in Table 10-1.)

REVIEW OF TECHNIQUE 10

Levels versus Rates of Change

Economic variables change over time. The difference between the *level* of a given variable and the *rate* at which it *changes* over time is critical. Sometimes the rate of change of an economic variable is itself an important economic variable. For example, the *rate of inflation* is the percentage *rate of change of the price level*. It is quite possible for the rate of change to be falling while the level of the variable is rising. For example,

TABLE 10-1
SHORT- AND LONG-RUN INCREASE IN AGGREGATE DEMAND

BILLIONS OF DOLLARS

(1) 1979 investment	‾‾‾‾‾‾
(2) 20% increase	‾‾‾‾‾‾
(3) Increase in GDP [2 × (2)]	‾‾‾‾‾‾
(4) Actual 1979 GDP	2,488.6

TABLE 10-2
SHORT- AND LONG-RUN DECREASES IN AGGREGATE SUPPLY

BILLIONS OF DOLLARS

	1 Year	5 Years
(1) Increase in annual investment	$_____	$_____
(2) Cumulative increase in capital	_____	_____
(3) Total capital (roughly 3 × GDP)	_____	_____
(4) Line (2) as percent of total capital	_____ %	_____ %
(5) Relative increase in production [¼ × (4)]	_____ %	_____ %
(6) Increase in *AS* [GDP × (5)]	$_____	$_____
(7) As fraction of increase in *AD* [100 × (6)/[(3) from Table 10-1]]	_____ %	_____ %

suppose inflation falls from 13 percent a year to 8 percent a year. The *price level,* of course, keeps rising so long as the inflation rate is above zero.

It is sometimes useful to distinguish between a smooth change in the level of a variable and a sudden jump in its level. If the price level changed from 100 to 110 over a year, the inflation rate over the year would be 10 percent per year. If the same change took place over a month, the inflation rate on the basis of that month would be 120 percent per year. If the change took only a day, the inflation rate would be 3,650 percent per year. The smaller the time period, the greater the *rate* of change. If an economic variable actually jumps, then the rate of change when the variable jumps is infinite or, perhaps more correctly, undefined.

Figure 10-3 shows the level and rate of change of an arbitrary economic variable. Be sure you see how the figure in panel (*b*) is derived from the one in panel (*a*).

FILL-IN QUESTIONS

1. When all factors of production are fully employed, we say that the economy is producing _____ GDP.

2. Total output divided by the number of people is _____ GDP.

3. Output per worker is a measure of labor _____ .

4. The technological relation between output and inputs is described by the _____ _____ .

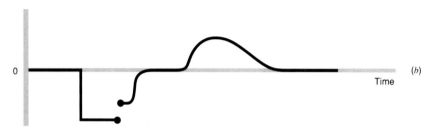

FIGURE 10-3
LEVEL AND RATE OF CHANGE OF A VARIABLE

5. The addition of one unit of capital, with other inputs fixed, increases output by the

   _____ .

6. Payment to capital as a fraction of GDP is called _____ .

7. Technology is said to have _____ when a proportional increase in all inputs results in a proportional increase in output.

8. GDP per person is constant in the _____ .

9. Continuing growth of GDP per person is due to _____ .

TRUE-FALSE QUESTIONS

T   F   1. An exogenous addition to the capital stock leads to an immediate in-
            crease in per capita GDP.

T   F   2. An exogenous addition to the capital stock leads to an increase in
            steady-state per capita GDP.

T   F   3. An increase in the saving rate leads to an immediate increase in per
            capita GDP.

T   F   4. An increase in the saving rate leads to an increase in steady-state GDP.

T   F   5. An increase in the saving rate leads to an increase in the steady-state
            rate of growth of GDP.

T F 6. An increase in the rate of population growth leads to an immediate drop in per capita GDP.

T F 7. An increase in the rate of population growth leads to a drop in steady-state per capita GDP.

T F 8. An increase in the rate of population growth leads to a drop in steady-state GDP.

T F 9. A higher depreciation rate leads to lower steady-state capital.

T F 10. A higher depreciation rate leads to lower steady-state GDP.

MULTIPLE-CHOICE QUESTIONS

1. The most important factor responsible for growth in GDP in the United States has been
   a. population growth
   b. technological change
   c. capital accumulation
   d. stimulative government spending

2. The most important factor responsible for per capita growth of GDP in the United States has been
   a. population growth
   b. technological change
   c. capital accumulation
   d. stimulative government spending

3. Over the last 97 years, per capita GDP has grown about
   a. 0.5 percent per year
   b. 2 percent per year
   c. 6 percent per year
   d. 8 percent per year

4. Productivity growth has fallen in recent years because
   a. more inexperienced workers have entered the labor force
   b. spending on research and development has slowed
   c. more of GDP is in the service industries
   d. all of the above

5. Assuming everyone is in the labor force, an increase in population causes
   a. an immediate increase in GDP
   b. an immediate increase in GDP per capita
   c. immediate increases in both
   d. no increases in either

6. A 15 percent increase in the capital stock leads to an increase in GDP of
   a. 0 percent
   b. between 0 and 15 percent
   c. 15 percent
   d. more than 15 percent

7. Labor's share of GDP in the United States is approximately
   a. 2 percent
   b. 25 percent
   c. 75 percent
   d. 98 percent

8. If the capital stock increases 15 percent while the labor force increases 7 percent, the capital-labor ratio increases approximately
   a. 2 percent
   b. 4 percent
   c. 8 percent
   d. 15 percent

9. If half the capital in the economy were to be destroyed, per capita GDP would drop
   a. not at all
   b. by less than half
   c. to one-half its original level
   d. by more than one-half

10. If population were suddenly to double, per capita GDP would
    a. remain unchanged
    b. double
    c. drop by less than one-half
    d. drop by more than one-half

PROBLEMS

The Cobb-Douglas production function is

$$Y = AK^a N^{1-a}$$

1. Find the function that gives per capita GDP based on capital per person, using the Cobb-Douglas production function above.

2. Prove that if $a = 0.25$, labor's share of GDP will be 75 percent.

3. Assume that labor's share of GDP is 75 percent and capital's share is 25 percent. If the labor supply increases by 10 percent and the supply of capital increases by 20 percent, by how much does GDP increase? GDP per capita?

4. Assume that at a point along a transitional path to steady state, the growth rate of the capital-labor ratio is 10 percent. What is the capital-labor ratio at this point if the savings rate is 30 percent, the rate of depreciation is 5 percent, and the rate of population growth is 10 percent? Use the production function given above and set $A = 1$. What will be the steady-state capital-labor ratio?

5. Assume the economy is initially in long-run equilibrium. Suppose half the capital of society is destroyed. Show the time path of per capita GDP.

6. Assume the economy is initially in long-run equilibrium. Suppose that the savings rate increases. Show the time path of per capita GDP.

part three

BEHAVIORAL FOUNDATIONS

CONSUMPTION AND SAVING

FOCUS OF THE CHAPTER

- Consumption is the largest sector of aggregate demand.
- Consumption this year depends not only on disposable income this year, but also on income in the past and expectations of future income.
- People try to spread their available lifetime resources over their entire lifetime. A transitory change in income makes little difference to lifetime resources and thus does not much affect consumption. A permanent change in income makes a great difference to lifetime resources and thus greatly affects consumption.

SECTION SUMMARIES

1. The Life-Cycle Theory of Consumption and Saving

The *life-cycle* theory is based on the notion that individuals plan in order to spread their available income over their entire lifetime. In particular, people save during their working lives in order to provide for retirement. Consumption is a function of wealth and of life-time disposable income. Instead of simply stating a marginal propensity to consume, we can calculate the *MPC* based on the number of years a person has remaining until retirement and on life expectancy.

2. Permanent-Income Theory of Consumption

The *permanent-income* theory argues that people gear consumption to their long-term consumption opportunities. This is the same basic theme as the life-cycle theory, but is made operational by assuming that, as a practical matter, people estimate their long-run opportunities by making a projection based on current and past income. This assumption suggests that a transitory change in income will have little lasting effect on consumption, but that a permanent change will have a large effect on consumption.

3.   Excess Sensitivity, Liquidity Constraints, and Uncertainty

Researchers have found that household consumption systematically responds too much to changes in current household income, forcing macroeconomists to qualify the claim that consumers behave precisely according to the life-cycle–permanent-income hypothesis. This *excess sensitivity* may be the result of liquidity constraints on households, whereby households are unable to borrow or lend freely so as to smooth consumption over time. Uncertainty about future income prospects also may help explain household consumption patterns.

4.   Further Aspects of Consumption Behavior

The household savings rate in the United States is the lowest among the group of countries that also includes the United Kingdom, Japan, Canada, Italy, and France. The U.S. national savings rate, which includes corporate and government saving as well as household saving, is the lowest in this group.

Arguments have been made that policy measures to increase interest rates on savings will increase household saving, but empirical evidence suggests that changes in interest rates have little effect on saving in the United States.

The Barro-Ricardo hypothesis is the claim that a tax cut matched by an increase in government borrowing to hold government expenditures constant will have no effect on the interest rate. According to the Barro-Ricardo hypothesis, consumers view the increase in government debt as an increase in future taxes and, therefore, save their current tax cut for payment of future taxes.

5.   Consumption and the *IS-LM* Framework

The more sophisticated consumption function of this chapter can be put back in the *IS-LM* framework. The slope of the *IS* curve and the values of the fiscal policy and monetary policy multipliers now depend on the time frame of a policy action. Because the short-run *MPC* is less than the long-run *MPC,* the short-run multipliers are less than the long-run multipliers.

We can also see that a rise in the value of the stock market increases wealth and thus consumption, although the magnitude of this effect is fairly small.

KEY TERMS

Life-cycle hypothesis

Dissaving

Permanent income

Rational expectations

Liquidity constraints

Myopia

Relative-income hypothesis

Dynamic multiplier

Excess sensitivity of consumption

Barro-Ricardo hypothesis

Net national saving

Buffer-stock saving

GRAPH IT 11

Graph It 11 asks you to replicate one of the most important scientific investigations of postwar macroeconomics, the discovery of the life-cycle–permanent-income theory of consumption. As you know from Chapter 11, the marginal propensity to consume seems fairly low when we look at consumption over 2 or 3 years, but the *MPC* is quite high when looked at over decades. In this Graph It you will replicate that result.

Table 11-1 presents invented consumption and income data for three groups of 3 years. Ignore for the moment all but the first group. Plot the three points on the blank graph (Chart 11-1). Draw a straight line that fits the three points as well as you can. What's the slope (*MPC*) of the line?

Now do the same for each of the two other groups. Do you get the same slope for each line? (You should.) Think of these as short-run consumption functions measured in three different decades.

TABLE 11-1
CONSUMPTION AND SAVING

	GDP	Consumption
Group 1	50	49
	60	54
	70	59
Group 2	10	13
	20	18
	30	23
Group 3	80	76
	90	82
	100	86

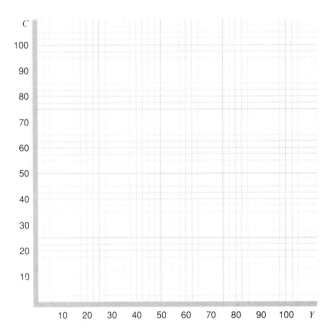

CHART 11-1

Now draw a single consumption function line for all nine points. (It won't fit exactly, of course.) This represents a long-run consumption function. What's your estimate of the long-run *MPC?*

REVIEW OF TECHNIQUE 11

Dynamic Simulation

As soon as lags are introduced into an economic model, the model becomes *dynamic* instead of *static*. This shift makes it necessary to keep track of all the variables as they change over time. In this review, we present a simple table that makes this easy. Suppose we have the following economic model:

$$Y = C + I + G$$
$$C = 0.6Y + 0.3Y_{-1}$$
$$I = 100$$

Initially, *G* equals 20 and *Y* has been 1,200 for several years. Suppose *G* now increases to 40 for 1 period and then returns to 20. We can use Table 11-2 to trace out the impact on GDP for the next several periods. Note first of all that

TABLE 11-2a

Period	Y	Y_{-1}	I	G
0	1,200	1,200	100	20
1			100	40
2			100	20
3			100	20

TABLE 11-2b

Period	Y	Y_{-1}	I	G
0	1,200	1,200	100	20
1	1,250	1,200	100	40
2	1,237.5	1,250	100	20
3	1,228.125	1,237.5	100	20

$$Y = 0.6Y + 0.3Y_{-1} + I + G$$
$$Y(1 - 0.6) = 0.3Y_{-1} + I + G$$
$$Y = 0.75Y_{-1} + 2.5I + 2.5G \qquad (11\text{-}1)$$

In Table 11-2a, we have provided all the information we have before beginning the problem. The entire trick is to recognize that Y_{-1} in period 1 is the same as Y was in period 0. (That, after all, is what the subscript "−1" tells us.) In Table 11-2b we have indicated this relation by the diagonal line connecting the two numbers. Using this fact, we can employ equation (11-1) to find Y in period 1.

$$Y = 0.75(1{,}200) + 250 + 2.5(40) = 1{,}250$$

We can repeat the same "trick," noting that Y_{-1} in period 2 is the same as Y in period 1.

$$Y = 0.75(1{,}250) + 250 + 2.5(20) = 1{,}237.5$$

Table 11-2b runs the simulation up through period 3.

Now we repeat the same problem, except that G is increased from 20 to 40 permanently. Table 11-3a sets up the problem for you. Using equation (11-1), fill in the rest of the table *before* you look at the answer in Table 11-3b.

TABLE 11-3a

Period	Y	Y$_{-1}$	I	G
0	1,200	1,200	100	20
1	_____	_____	100	40
2	_____	_____	100	40
3	_____	_____	100	40

TABLE 11-3b

Period	Y	Y$_{-1}$	I	G
0	1,200	1,200	100	20
1	1,250	1,200	100	40
2	1,287.5	1,250	100	40
3	1,315.625	1,287.5	100	40

FILL-IN QUESTIONS

1. The hypothesis that people plan consumption on the basis of their wealth and all future income is called the _____ theory.

2. Estimates of long-term consumption opportunities based on previous and current income are called _____ income.

3. Using up wealth to provide for consumption is called _____.

4. The long-run average propensity to consume is about _____.

5. The long-run marginal propensity to consume is about _____.

6. The immediate response of GDP to a change in autonomous aggregate demand depends on the _____ multiplier.

7. The eventual response of GDP to a change in autonomous aggregate demand depends on the _____ multiplier.

8. The marginal propensity to consume depends on the number of _____ years compared with the number of _____ years.

9. The gradual adjustment of output to a shock illustrates a(n) _____ lag.

TRUE-FALSE QUESTIONS

T F 1. The permanent-income theory suggests that the long-run marginal propensity to consume is less than the short-run marginal propensity to consume.

T F 2. Modern consumption theory suggests that consumption is proportional to long-run income.

T F 3. A worker aged 20 who expects to retire at 65 and who has a life expectancy of 50 years should have a marginal propensity to consume out of income of 0.9.

T F 4. A worker aged 20 who expects to retire at age 65 and who has a life expectancy of 50 years should have a marginal propensity to consume out of wealth of 0.02.

T F 5. The long-run *MPC* and *APC* are approximately equal.

T F 6. If a simple linear consumption function has a positive intercept, then the average propensity to consume falls as income rises.

T F 7. Temporary changes in income produce relatively small changes in consumption.

T F 8. The decision to leave an inheritance increases current consumption.

T F 9. A growing population will have higher per capita savings than a static population.

T F 10. The permanent-income theory and the life-cycle theory are fundamentally the same.

MULTIPLE-CHOICE QUESTIONS

1. According to the life-cycle theory, an individual's marginal propensity to consume out of permanent labor income
   a. rises over time
   b. falls over time
   c. remains constant
   d. may be a, b, or c, depending on circumstances

2. According to the life-cycle theory, an individual's marginal propensity to consume out of transitory labor income
   a. rises over time
   b. falls over time
   c. remains constant
   d. may be a, b, or c, depending on circumstances

3. The weights used on income and all the lagged income to estimate permanent income should probably add up to
   a. 0
   b. between 0 and 1
   c. 1
   d. more than 1

4. If the marginal propensity to consume out of permanent income is 0.9 and the weight on current income in estimating permanent income is two-thirds, the short-run simple Keynesian multiplier is
   a. 1
   b. 2.5
   c. 3
   d. 10

5. The life-cycle and permanent-income theories are associated with the
   a. Keynesian school
   b. monetarist school
   c. both
   d. neither

6. According to the life-cycle theory, wealth during the working years
   a. rises over time
   b. remains constant
   c. falls over time
   d. may either rise or fall, depending on the *MPC*

7. During a temporary recession, the average propensity to consume
   a. falls
   b. remains constant
   c. rises
   d. is neither a nor b nor c

8. During a temporary boom, the average propensity to save
   a. falls
   b. remains constant
   c. rises
   d. is neither a nor b nor c

9. The role of the stock market in determining consumption is shown most directly through the
   a. simple linear consumption function
   b. permanent-income theory
   c. life-cycle theory
   d. both b and c

10. When the expansionary effects of a permanent tax cut are compared with those of a temporary tax cut, the former tax cut
    a. is more expansionary
    b. has the same effect
    c. is less expansionary
    d. is a, b, or c, depending on the *MPC*

PROBLEMS

1. Assume the typical consumer expects to work for 40 years and to live for 10 years beyond retirement. Assume consumers have perfect foresight. Disregarding any multiplier effects, how does consumption change this year as a result of a $100 annual tax cut on workers' income that
   a. is permanent, and will begin immediately?
   b. will last only for the current year?
   c. is permanent, but will not go into effect until next year?

2. Assume that the typical consumer has a marginal propensity to consume of 0.8. Consumers must use historical information to estimate permanent income. Research has shown that they estimate permanent income by using a weight of 0.75 on current disposable income and 0.25 on lagged disposable income. Disregarding any multiplier effects, how much does consumption change in the first year and in the second year as a result of a $100 tax cut that
   a. is permanent.
   b. is effective for 1 year only.

3. The following equations describe an economy:

C	$= c(1 - t)Y^P$	Consumption
Y^P	$= \theta Y + (1 - \theta)Y_{-1} \quad 0 < \theta < 1$	Permanent income
I	$= \bar{I} - br$	Investment
Y	$= C + I + \bar{G}$	National income identity
$\bar{M}/P = kY - hr$		Money demand

   Calculate the fiscal and monetary policy multipliers for this economy. Compare these multipliers to the multipliers that would be calculated if consumption depended solely on current disposable income, that is, $\theta = 1$.

4. Let the following set of equations describe the economy.

   $$C = c(1 - t)Y^P$$
   $$I = 0.1(Y - Y_{-1}) - 1{,}000r$$
   $$Y^P = 0.6Y + 0.4Y_{-1}$$
   $$Y = C + I + G$$
   $$\bar{M}/\bar{P} = 0.8Y - 2{,}000i$$

Y^P is the estimate of permanent income out of which consumers spend. Investment demand is given by a modified accelerator model. The real rate is r, and the nominal rate is i. The *MPC* is $c = 0.8$, and the tax rate is $t = 0.5$.

Let the price level be fixed. What is the *initial* impact on GDP and the budget deficit of a one-unit increase in government spending? Assume that the increase in government spending is permanent. What will be the *long-run* impact on output and the budget deficit?

INVESTMENT SPENDING

FOCUS OF THE CHAPTER

- The second key sector of aggregate demand is investment spending.

- Investment is less than 20 percent of GDP, but investment is very volatile and, thus, changes in investment account for much of the change in GDP.

- Investment demand is especially important because it contains the main link through which monetary policy affects aggregate demand.

- Increased interest lowers investment because capital becomes more expensive.

- Decreases in expected sales lead manufacturers to reduce investment, thereby reducing aggregate demand.

- The three investment subsectors are *business fixed investment, residential investment,* and *inventory investment.*

SECTION SUMMARIES

1. Business Fixed Investment: The Neoclassical Approach

Businesses use machinery, equipment, and structures in the course of producing final output. These make up the stock of *business fixed capital.* We develop a theory of the *desired capital stock. Investment* is a *flow* that is the addition of new machinery to the existing capital stock. Investment closes the gap between the desired capital stock and the existing capital stock.

Manufacturers decide on how much capital they want by considering three factors: how much output they expect to sell; what the *marginal product of capital* is; and how much capital cost to incur, or the *rental* or *user cost of capital.* The more output that must be produced, the more the required amount of capital. The higher the rental cost, the less capital will be used, since capital is more expensive. The most important component of the rental cost is the interest rate. Several other components are discussed below.

More capital always means that greater output can be produced, but each additional unit of capital adds less and less additional production. However, each additional unit of capital costs as much to add as the previous unit. Thus, there is declining marginal product but constant marginal cost. The intelligent business manager adds just enough capital so that the last unit produces just as much as it costs.

Firms base their expectations of future sales on a period comparable to the life of the machinery. Current sales affect capital demand to the extent that they change expectations of sales over the life of the machinery.

The rental cost of capital is basically the market interest rate, since this is the opportunity cost of using funds to buy capital instead of "investing" in bonds. However, capital wears out over time. This depreciation cost must be covered to keep machines working well. If depreciation is d percent per year, then the cost of capital is

$$rc = i + d$$

In the presence of inflation, we distinguish the *real interest* rate from the *nominal interest* rate. The difference is the expected rate of inflation, denoted π^e. Since, on average, the price of goods produced will go up at the rate of inflation, the rental cost of capital properly depends on the real rate of interest. This leads to the following formula for the rental cost of capital:

$$rc \equiv r + d \equiv i - \pi^e + d$$

The rental cost of capital must be adjusted to account properly for taxes. Under the *investment tax credit,* the government pays some portion, τ, of the cost of new equipment to the firm in the form of a tax rebate. This rebate lowers the effective cost of equipment and therefore increases the demand for capital. The *corporate income tax* is essentially a proportional tax on corporate profits. Because of the complexities of the tax code, theory alone leaves the effects of the corporate income tax ambiguous.

The rate of investment depends on the difference between the desired and actual capital stock. An important element of the way firms plan to adjust their capital stock is the gradual adjustment hypothesis. Each period firms close some portion of the gap between desired capital, K^*, and the capital available at the beginning of the period, K_{-1}. If the fraction of the gap closed each period is λ, then the investment function is

$$I = K - K_{-1} = \lambda(K^* - K_{-1})$$

The timing of investment with respect to changes in the investment tax credit is especially important. A temporary investment tax credit means that a firm gets a tax break on any investment done now, but none on any done in the future. It pays the firm to invest right away not only because capital is cheaper, but also because any investment planned for the future should be made immediately instead. This means that a temporary tax credit has a much larger effect on current investment than a permanent tax credit.

2. Business Fixed Investment: Alternative Approaches

In practice, firms rarely think of calculating a desired capital stock as such. Rather, they use a *discounted cash flow analysis* to compare the cost of adding a machine with the present value of the flow of profits the machine will provide. High interest rates mean future profits have a lower value today, thus making adding an additional machine less desirable. Discounted cash flow analysis and computation of a desired capital stock are really just two different ways of looking at the same problem.

The *accelerator* model states that the desired capital stock is proportional to income and that investment is proportional to the change in income. The accelerator model is a special case of investment theory with instantaneous adjustment to the desired capital stock and a constant ratio of desired capital to income.

3. Residential Investment

The price and quantity of housing depend on the supply and demand for homes. Investment in housing occurs when the demand for homes rises above the available stock. The demand for housing falls when interest rates, especially mortgage rates, rise. The ability of people to buy new homes depends on the availability of mortgage money. Most home mortgages are made available through thrift institutions. These institutions raise money through savings accounts. When interest rates rise above the rate allowed by law on savings accounts, consumers pull their money out of savings, cutting off the flow of mortgages. This is called *disintermediation.* New types of savings instruments appear to have made disintermediation a less serious problem than in the past.

4. Inventory Investment

Unintended inventory accumulation occurs when sales fall unexpectedly. On the other hand, when sales are expected to fall, firms intentionally reduce inventories. This intentional reduction feeds back very quickly to accelerate movements in aggregate demand. This is the *inventory cycle.*

Appendix

The chapter appendix explains the relation between coupon rates, yields, and the prices of bonds. On a *Consol,* or perpetual bond, the yield is the coupon payment divided by the price of the bond. More generally, the price of a bond is the present discounted value (*PDV*) of all the payments on the bond. The *PDV* is found by reducing the value of future payments according to the interest rate and the time when the payment is due.

KEY TERMS

Business fixed investment

Residential investment

Inventory investment

Desired capital stock

Marginal product of capital

Rental (user) cost of capital

Cobb-Douglas production function

q-theory

Real interest rate

Gradual adjustment hypothesis

Discounted cash flow analysis

Flexible accelerator model

Disintermediation

Inventory cycle

Present discounted value

Credit rationing

GRAPH IT 12

Chapter 12 explains that investment forms a relatively small part of aggregate demand, but the changes in investment are responsible for much of the change in aggregate demand. Another way to say this is that investment is a small but volatile sector. In this Graph It, you are asked to demonstrate both parts of the relationship. In Chart 12-1, you are asked to plot 12 years of GDP and investment data. You will see from this graph that GDP and investment are related, but only moderately. In Chart 12-2, you are asked to plot the annual change in GDP and the annual change in investment. This second graph shows that the relation between investment volatility and aggregate demand volatility is very strong.

Table 12-1 provides data on GDP and gross investment. We've also left space for you to fill in the annual change data you will need for plotting the second chart.

By the way, if you are also taking a statistics course, you might compare the correlation coefficient of GDP and investment versus the change in GDP and investment.

TABLE 12-1

Year	GDP	I	$Y_t - Y_{t-1}$	$I_t - I_{t-1}$
1980	3,776.3	594.4		
1981	3,843.1	631.1	66.8	36.7
1982	3,760.3	540.5	_____	_____
1983	3,906.6	599.5	_____	_____
1984	4,148.5	757.5	_____	_____
1985	4,279.8	745.9	_____	_____
1986	4,405.5	735.1	_____	_____
1987	4,540.0	749.3	_____	_____
1988	4,718.6	773.4	_____	_____
1989	4,836.9	789.2	_____	_____
1990	4,884.9	744.5	_____	_____
1991	4,848.4	672.6	_____	_____

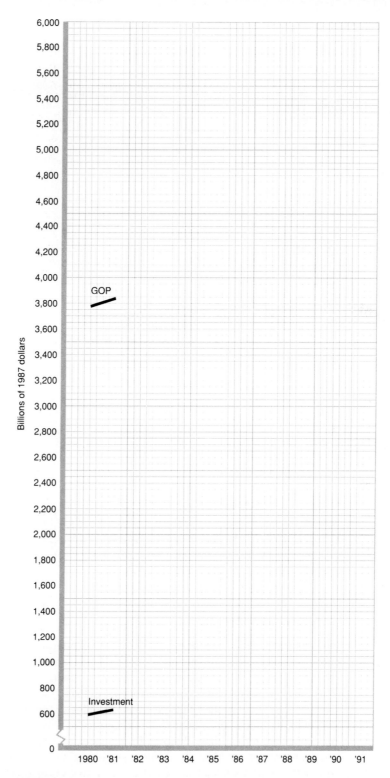

CHART 12-1

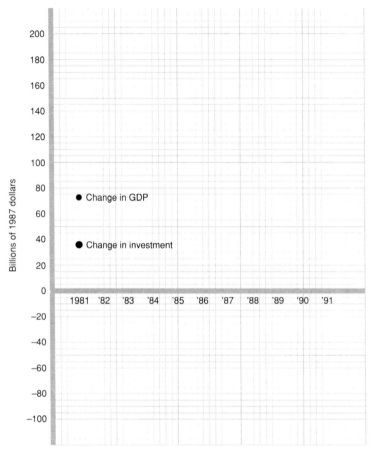

CHART 12-2

REVIEW OF TECHNIQUE 12

Units of Measurement

We generally write our equations and variables without specific reference to the units by which we measure economic quantities. However, care must be taken to see that units of measurement are consistent throughout an equation.

We typically measure most quantities in dollars. However, behind this convenience we have carefully matched units. Speaking loosely, we say that investment is the change in the capital stock. To be precise, it is necessary to remember that investment is a rate of change per unit of time. It we go from a stock of 25 machines to 75 machines in 1 year, investment would be 50 machines per year. If the same change takes place over a 6-month period, we would say that the rate of investment is 100 machines per year.

The variable whose units of measurements are most frequently confused is the interest rate. Interest rates are typically quoted at an annual percentage rate. We can write an interest rate as "5 percent" or "0.05" or even as "500 basis points" (a basis point is 1/100 of a percentage point). It is understood, though, that the rate is 5 percent *per year*. Obviously, which manner we choose doesn't matter so long as we are consistent.

A frequent source of confusion is the statement that the "interest rate rose 20 percent." If the original rate was 5 percent, what is the new rate? The careless answer is 25 percent, 5 plus 20. The correct answer is 6 percent. Obviously, 20 percent of 5 is 1. So a 20 percent increase of a 5 percent interest rate is one percentage point, raising the interest rate from 5 to 6.

FILL-IN QUESTIONS

1. The three principal investment sectors are _____, _____, and _____.

2. Investment is a _____ devoted to maintaining the _____ _____ of capital.

3. The contribution of an extra unit of capital to a firm's profit is the _____ _____.

4. The cost of using capital for a year is the _____.

5. In planning how much capital to have, firms must estimate _____ sales.

6. When the government gives firms a rebate for new capital investment it is called an _____.

7. The difference between gross and net investment is _____.

8. The flight of money from savings institutions during periods of high interest rates is called _____.

9. The cycle of aggregate demand fluctuation that causes inventory fluctuation, causing more aggregate demand fluctuation, is called the _____.

TRUE-FALSE QUESTIONS

T   F   1. Increased interest rates cause increased investment.

T   F   2. Rising GDP causes increased investment.

T   F   3. A permanent increase in the investment tax credit decreases current investment.

T   F   4. High mortgage rates lead to increased investment.

T	F	5.	In the short run, the supply of housing is more or less fixed.
T	F	6.	A surprise sales boom leads to a drop in inventories.
T	F	7.	An expected sales boom leads to a drop in inventories.
T	F	8.	Changes in investment are directly proportional to income, according to the accelerator model.
T	F	9.	The actual capital stock adjusts gradually to the desired capital stock.
T	F	10.	Restrictive monetary policy decreases investment.

MULTIPLE-CHOICE QUESTIONS

1. The effect of an increase in the corporate income tax on investment
   a. is an increase
   b. is a decrease
   c. is nonexistent
   d. theoretically is any of a, b, or c

2. Comparing the impact on current investment of a permanent versus a temporary increase in the investment tax credit, we find that a permanent increase is
   a. more effective
   b. less effective
   c. the same
   d. theoretically a, b, or c

3. Empirically it has been found that an increase in the desired capital stock causes investment to
   a. rise instantly, then gradually drop off
   b. respond in an upside-down-U pattern
   c. rise, then return immediately to zero
   d. fall gradually

4. An increase in the depreciation rate causes net investment to
   a. rise
   b. remain the same
   c. fall
   d. theoretically do any of a, b, or c

5. An increase in the depreciation rate causes gross investment to
   a. rise
   b. remain the same
   c. fall
   d. theoretically do any of a, b, or c

6. If the nominal interest rate is 12 percent and the inflation rate is 6 percent, the real interest rate is
   a. 18 percent
   b. 2 percent
   c. 6 percent
   d. 8.4 percent

7. According to the simple accelerator model, the response of investment to a permanent increase in GDP is to
   a. rise, then return to zero
   b. rise gradually, then fall gradually
   c. rise to a new permanent level
   d. remain unchanged

8. Net investment is the change in the capital stock
   a. according to the flexible accelerator
   b. according to the simple accelerator
   c. always
   d. never

9. The response of the housing stock to economic conditions is
   a. very rapid
   b. quite slow
   c. slow during a boom, quick during a downturn
   d. quick during a boom, slow during a downturn

10. The response of the stock of inventories to economic conditions is
    a. very rapid
    b. quite slow
    c. slow during a boom, quick during a downturn
    d. quick during a boom, slow during a downturn

11. The price of a bond increases
    a. with the market interest rate
    b. with the coupon payment
    c. both
    d. neither

PROBLEMS

1. Assume that the demand for capital is determined by the equation $K^* = 0.25Y/rc$. The nominal interest rate is 12 percent (that is, $i = 0.12$), the inflation rate is 6 percent, and capital depreciates at 10 percent per year.
   a. Initially, income is $16,000. What is the desired capital stock?
   b. Now income doubles. What is the new desired capital stock?
   c. Given the simple accelerator model of investment, what is the rate of net investment? Of gross investment?

2. Suppose the desired capital stock jumps from $2,000 to $3,600. If companies close half the gap between existing and actual capital each year and if depreciation is 10 percent, what are the values of gross and net investment for each of the 3 years following the change?

3. A friend offers to lend you $1,000. You agree to pay him $220 in 1 year and to make a final payment in 2 years. The prevailing interest rate is 10 percent. You and your friend wish to agree on a fair final payment. How large should the final payment be?

4. A temporary cut in the personal income tax has very little effect on current consumption. By contrast, a temporary increase in the investment tax credit has a large effect on current investment. Explain.

THE DEMAND FOR MONEY

FOCUS OF THE CHAPTER

- We all hold money—either currency in our pockets or on deposit at a bank. In studying the demand for money, we try to discover exactly how much money a rational person will hold.

- Our basic goal is to find out how much money will be demanded for a known level of income and a known interest rate. (You will remember that we need this relation to form the *LM* curve, which we used in Chapter 4.)

- The evidence, both theoretical and empirical, is that higher income causes greater money demand, and higher interest rates cause lower money demand.

SECTION SUMMARIES

1. Components of the Money Stock

The most important characteristic of money is that we can use it directly to pay for things we buy. The assets in our economy that most closely fit this definition are cash and checking accounts. Together, these form $M1$. Savings accounts are good substitutes for checking accounts because you can get use of the savings deposit very quickly, even though you cannot actually make a payment by handing someone your savings passbook. Sometimes we use broader definitions of money that include time and savings deposits. The official definitions of money have been expanded to include assets that are, in an economics sense, but not legally, the same as checking accounts.

2. The Functions of Money

Money has traditionally been defined by four functions.

   a. Serving as a *medium of exchange* is far and away the most important function of money. When you buy something, you pay for it with money rather than barter for it with some other merchandise.
   b. As a *store of value,* money retains its value over time. You would hardly be willing to accept money in payment if you didn't think that someone else would accept the money from you tomorrow.
   c. Saying that money is the *unit of account* just means that prices are quoted in dollars and cents. (A grocery could post a sign showing that 3 apples cost 2 oranges.)
   d. Money serves as a *standard of deferred payment* when the amount of payment of a debt is specified in money units.

3. The Demand for Money: Theory

This section considers why people hold money. At first it seems strange to think that such a question ever needs to be asked. After all, we're all most happy to have money. The question we really need to answer is why people hold money instead of some better investment. Cash pays no interest at all, and checking and savings accounts usually pay less than is available in other safe investments. John Maynard Keynes gave three broad motives for holding money instead of some other investment:

Transactions motive
Precautionary motive
Speculative motive

The *transactions motive* arises from the cost of cashing in part of an investment each time you make a purchase. For example, it's much more sensible to draw a week's worth of pocket money at a time rather than go to the bank each morning. The most famous transactions example is contained in the *Baumol-Tobin* theory. The development of the theory has three steps.

   a. If we know how many times a month a person replenishes her cash, what will her average balance be? Suppose the person begins with $100 and is going to spend it at a steady rate. If she takes it all in cash on the first day and spends it down to zero by the end of the month, the average cash balance will be $50. Suppose, instead, she takes only $50 for the first half of the month and after using it up gets the other $50. The average will be $25. The pattern follows so that if the person begins with Y_N dollars and makes n transfers, the average cash balance is $\frac{1}{2}Y_N/n$. (The subscript N stands for "nominal.")

b. Cash doesn't earn any interest, and so the opportunity cost lost by holding money is iY_N/n. In addition, the cost of each transfer is tc. Hence,

$$\text{Total cost} = ntc + \frac{iY_N}{2n}$$

The more transfers, the higher the total costs of transactions and the less the interest lost. The best number of transfers is that which minimizes total costs. (The exact formula can be found by using calculus.)

c. Once we know the right number of transfers, we can find the average cash balance directly. The famous square-root formula turns out to be

$$M^* = \sqrt{\frac{tcY_N}{2i}}$$

This formula implies that the income elasticity of money demand is ½ and that the interest elasticity is −½, as Reviews of Technique 7, 8, 14, and 15 demonstrate.

The *precautionary motive* arises from the notion that we never know our spending plans exactly. It pays to keep a little extra money on hand in case the urge for a hot fudge sundae hits at a time when it's inconvenient to cash in an investment. The greater the uncertainty about our spending plans, the more money we would be wise to keep around just in case. Just as with the transactions motive, the higher the interest rate, the greater the cost of holding money.

The *speculative motive* states that a person might sometimes want to keep money in a savings account for investment purposes. Because other investments are risky, even though they offer higher average returns, people will hold some money as a hedge against risk. The speculative demand for money is actually a demand for a safe asset.

4. Empirical Evidence

Empirical research has settled four key points about money demand.

a. When the interest rate goes up, the demand for money goes down.
b. When income goes up, the demand for money goes up, but less than proportionately.
c. It takes time for money demand to adjust fully to changes in income and interest.
d. If the price level doubles, the number of dollars of money demanded will double.

5. The Income Velocity of Money and the Quantity Theory

Sometimes, instead of discussing the money demand equation, economists look at *velocity*. Velocity is the ratio of income to money. (You can think of it as the number of times a dollar passes from hand to hand in a year.) Higher interest rates mean lower money demand and therefore higher velocity. Higher income increases money demand but by less than the increase in income, so that velocity increases with increased income.

KEY TERMS

Real balances	Transactions demand
Money illusion	Inventory-theoretic approach
*M*1	Square-root formula
*M*2	Precautionary demand
Liquidity	Speculative demand
Store of value	Income velocity of money
Unit of account	Quantity equation
Standard of deferred payments	Hyperinflation
Medium of exchange	Goodhart's law

GRAPH IT 13

Most people find themselves ready for a relaxing exercise about halfway through the text. Graph It 13 asks you to demonstrate the essential principles of the precautionary demand for money by drawing some random wiggles (well, almost random) on the graph provided (Chart 13-1).

The idea behind the precautionary demand for money is that you want to hold enough money so that you rarely run out of money, but that you don't want to hold too much because of the opportunity cost. In Chart 13-1 we've drawn a solid wiggly line illustrating a random cash need. Now suppose your rule of thumb was that you wanted to run out of cash no more than twice during the period. We took a straightedge and drew a solid line as low as possible, but still consistent with the random wiggle's peaking over the line only twice. The solid line shows the optimal precautionary demand for money.

Now you draw in a dashed line with the same number of wiggles, but with the cash needs generally having higher peaks. Then use a straightedge to draw in a new money demand line.

REVIEW OF TECHNIQUE 13

Balance Sheets

One of the most useful devices for keeping track of changes in the economy is the *balance sheet*. A balance sheet is nothing more than a table showing both the assets and

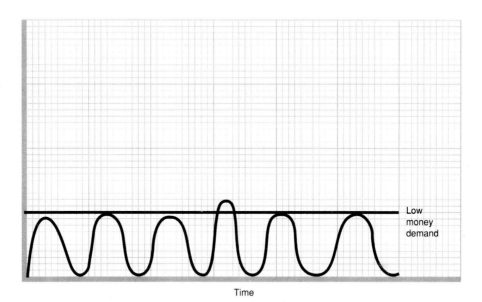

Time

CHART 13-1

liabilities of some agent in the economy. The usefulness of balance sheet analysis comes from the simple fact that changes in balance sheets must always balance. When working quickly, it is very easy to leave out some part of a transaction. By completely writing out all the balance sheet changes, one can make two special checks—for *vertical balance* and for *horizontal balance.*

For vertical balance, all the changes on a given balance sheet must balance. One possibility is that both assets and liabilities change by the same amount. The other possibility is that one asset (or liability) goes up by the same amount that another asset (or liability) goes down.

For horizontal balance, the changes in the total amount of a particular asset must add to zero when added up across every balance sheet in the economy. The reason is that one person's asset is another's liability. This should be interpreted carefully. For example, if a person withdraws money from a bank, then it is true that the total in bank accounts is less. However, this is a decrease in the *assets* of the person and a decrease in the *liabilities* of the bank.

Remember that every transaction and every combination of transactions must show both vertical and horizontal balance.

As an example, consider the following problem. Mr. A owes Professor B money. In order to pay off $15 of the debt, Mr. A gives Professor B a $20 check and Professor B gives Mr. A $5 back in cash. Professor B deposits the check in her account. The bank credits her account and debits Mr. A's. The three balance sheets on page 128 (Figure 13-1) show the transactions. Notice that we show only how the various levels change, not what their original levels were. Points 1, 2, and 3 illustrate vertical balance. Points 4 and 5 illustrate horizontal balance in cash. Points 6 and 7 show horizontal balance in IOUs. Horizontal balance in bank deposits is shown by 8, 9, 10, and 11.

Mr. A			Prof. B			Bank	
Assets	Liabilities		Assets		Liabilities	Assets	Liabilities
④ Cash +$5	⑥ –$15 IOU		⑦ IOU –$15				⑩ –$20 A's account
⑧ Deposit –$20			⑤ Cash –$5				⑪ +$20 B's account
			⑨ Deposit +$20				
① –$15	–$15		② 0		0	③ 0	0

FIGURE 13-1

FILL-IN QUESTIONS

1. The study of the demand for money is the study of the demand for _____ _____ .

2. The assets forming $M1$ are _____ .

3. The assets forming $M2$ are _____ .

4. The Baumol-Tobin theory explains the _____ motive for the demand for money.

5. The number of times a dollar is turned over per year is called _____ .

6. The ratio of income to the money stock is _____ .

7. The _____ motive explains the need to hold money against unforeseen contingencies.

8. The need to hold money because it has a safe nominal value is called the _____ _____ motive.

9. The one motive that plays little role in explaining the demand for $M1$ is the _____ _____ motive.

10. In order to find the nominal demand for money, one multiplies the real demand for money by the _____ .

TRUE-FALSE QUESTIONS

T   F   1. If the number of dollars outstanding doubles and the price level goes up one-half, then real balances have increased by one-third.

T   F   2. If GDP and the money stock both fall by 50 percent, then velocity remains constant.

T F 3. Higher inflation generally leads to higher money velocity.

T F 4. High inflation is associated with high nominal interest rates.

T F 5. In certain circumstances, M2 may be smaller than M1.

T F 6. An individual who ignores changes in the price level so long as all real variables remain constant is said to suffer from money illusion.

T F 7. According to the Baumol-Tobin theory, money demand is proportional to GDP.

T F 8. Velocity increases with real income.

T F 9. A shift of assets from checking to savings accounts increases M2.

T F 10. According to the precautionary theory of money demand, greater uncertainty about spending plans results in higher money demand.

MULTIPLE-CHOICE QUESTIONS

1. An increase in real income from 100 to 110 will, according to the Baumol-Tobin theory, cause money demand to change by a
   a. 20 percent increase
   b. 10 percent increase
   c. 5 percent increase
   d. 5 percent decrease

2. An increase in the interest rate from 5 percent per year to 6 percent per year will, according to the Baumol-Tobin theory, cause money demand to change by a
   a. 0.5 percent decrease
   b. 10 percent decrease
   c. 20 percent decrease
   d. 0.5 percent increase

3. A shift of $100 from a checking account to a savings account means
   a. M1 and M2 up
   b. M1 down, M2 up
   c. M1 down, M2 unchanged
   d. M1 and M2 down

4. The most important function of money is as a
   a. medium of exchange
   b. store of value
   c. unit of account
   d. standard of deferred payment

5. The precautionary motive leads people to hold more money when
   a. the interest rate is high
   b. uncertainty about expenses is high
   c. both the rate and uncertainty are high
   d. neither the rate nor uncertainty is high

6. The demand for money is a theory of the demand for
   a. real balances
   b. nominal balances
   c. actual balances
   d. frictional balances

7. The demand for money depends on
   a. real income and real interest rates
   b. real income and nominal interest rates
   c. nominal income and real interest rates
   d. nominal income and nominal interest rates

8. Empirical evidence indicates that the income elasticity of money demand is
   a. greater than 1   c. between 0 and ½
   b. between −½ and −1   d. less than 0

9. Empirical evidence indicates that the interest elasticity of money demand is
   a. below −1   c. between 0 and −½
   b. between −½ and −1   d. above 0

10. The amount of demand deposits relative to currency is about
    a. 10 times as great   c. equal
    b. 3 times as great   d. one-third as great

11. The size of *M2* as opposed to *M1* is about
    a. equal   c. 4 times as great
    b. 2½ times as great   d. 10 times as great

12. Money demand rises when
    a. income rises
    b. interest rates fall
    c. both income rises and interest rates fall
    d. neither income nor interest rates change

PROBLEMS

1. Assume that the Baumol-Tobin theory is true. If nominal GDP goes from $100 billion to $220 billion while the price level doubles, what is the increase in the real demand for money?

2. Suppose that we want to change the interest rate from 4 percent per year to 3 percent per year, while real GDP and the price level remain unchanged. By how much should we change the money stock if empirical investigation shows the interest elasticity to be −0.20?

3. What will happen to the demand for money and the macroeconomy, that is, GDP and the nominal interest rate, if the use of credit cards becomes more widespread? Discuss the macroeconomy using an *IS-LM* diagram.

THE FED, MONEY, AND CREDIT

FOCUS OF THE CHAPTER

- In previous chapters, the money supply has been taken to be exogenous. We now explore the process by which the Federal Reserve controls the money supply.

- We develop the connection between the monetary base, which the Federal Reserve controls directly, and the money supply.

SECTION SUMMARIES

1. Money Stock Determination: The Components

$M1$ is checkable accounts plus currency in the hands of the public. $M2$ equals $M1$ plus liquid deposits at all depository institutions. The money supply is affected by the *currency-deposit ratio* chosen by the public and by the *reserve-deposit ratio* of banks. We denote the currency-deposit ratio as *cu* and the reserve-deposit ratio as *re*. The currency-deposit ratio depends on the tastes and habits of the public. Although the ratio varies over time, treating it as a constant is convenient for illustrative purposes. The reserve-deposit ratio depends on the level of *required reserves* and of *excess reserves*. Required reserves are determined by Federal Reserve Board regulation. Banks hold excess reserves for reasons analogous to the consumer's precautionary demand for money. Excess reserves are available for making payments to other banks. Banks borrow reserves from one another at the *federal funds rate*. The higher the federal funds rate, the less excess reserves banks hold.

The Federal Deposit Insurance Corporation (FDIC) insures depositors' bank accounts up to $100,000. In addition, the FDIC usually steps in to aid failing banks with loans and other forms of assistance. The FDIC's role as an insurer of banks helps to maintain public confidence in the stability of the banking system.

The Fed directly controls the stock of *high-powered money,* also called the *monetary base, H.* High-powered money consists of currency plus reserves at the Fed.

2. The Money Multiplier

The demand for high-powered money derives from the demand for currency plus the demand for reserves against deposits. The supply of money is limited by the supply of high-powered money and the *money multiplier, mm.* The relation is given by

$$M = \left(\frac{1 + cu}{cu + re}\right) H \equiv mm \cdot H$$

The term in parentheses is the *money multiplier.* Note that this formula ignores the distinction between demand and time deposits.

A high currency-deposit ratio implies a low money multiplier, as does a high reserve-deposit ratio.

3. Controlling the Stock of High-Powered Money

High-powered money is the principal liability of the Fed. Its main asset is government bonds. The Fed creates more money through an *open market purchase,* in which it buys bonds by writing a check on itself. The amount of the check is added to the total reserves available to the public and the banking system. The Fed may buy foreign exchange for U.S. money, increasing the monetary base while engaging in *foreign exchange market intervention.* When the Federal Reserve wishes to buy foreign currency without increasing the base, it offsets its purchase of foreign exchange with an open market sale of U.S. government bonds. This operation, called *sterilization,* breaks the link between foreign exchange operations and the domestic money supply.

The *discount rate* is the interest rate the Fed charges banks for borrowing reserves. Since borrowed reserves are part of the monetary base, a high discount rate, which discourages borrowing, tends to reduce the base. In the past, the Federal Reserve used the discount rate to signal its intentions with respect to future changes in the money supply. More recently it has passively adjusted the discount rate to keep it in line with the general level of market interest rates.

It is commonly said that the government finances its deficit by printing money. When the Treasury sells bonds to the Fed rather than to the public, and receives high-powered money that the Treasury spends, the story is basically true. However, the Fed need not buy government bonds. Thus, the central bank can control the stock of high-powered money irrespective of the government budget deficit.

4. The Multiplier and the Adjustment Process

Commercial *bank credit* is the opposite side of the money supply coin. Banks are able to make credit available in the amount of their deposits minus reserves. When the base increases, banks are able to make more loans. These loans take the form of added deposits and more currency held by the public. The bank that receives the new deposits can then make more loans. This adjustment process describes the *multiple expansion of bank deposits* which, when added across all the banks in the economy, yields the money multiplier.

5. The Money Supply Function and Instruments of Monetary Control

The three main instruments of monetary control are open market operations (changes in the stock of high-powered money), the discount rate, and the required reserve ratio.

6. Equilibrium in the Money Market

Equilibrium in the money market is determined by setting money supply equal to money demand. Since the money multiplier responds to the interest rate, there is a small feedback effect, which causes the money supply to change by slightly less than a simple constant money multiplier would indicate.

7. Control of the Money Stock and Control of the Interest Rate

The Fed can control either the money supply or the interest rate, but not the two independently. The reason is that the money demand curve gives us a fixed relation between interest and the money stock.

8. Money Stock and Interest Rate Targets

In choosing between a money stock target and an interest rate target, the Fed has both economywide considerations and short-run technical considerations, the former being the more important. Consider the economywide fluctuations by looking at Figure 14-1. In panel (*a*), the *IS* curve moves around. If the interest rate is held constant, then no crowding out occurs (just as in the model of Chapter 3). On the other hand, if the Fed controls the money supply, changes in the interest rate partially counteract movements in the *IS* curve. Hence, with a volatile *IS* curve, the Fed should control the money supply rather than interest rates. In panel (*b*), changes in money demand shift the *LM* curve around. If the money supply is held constant, then money demand changes shift the *LM* curve and

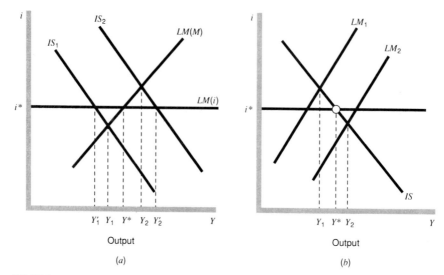

FIGURE 14-1

thus GDP. If the interest rate is held constant, the *LM* curve may shift horizontally left or right—but as long as the interest rate is constant, investment is constant, and GDP is constant. Thus, unstable money demand argues for controlling the interest rate.

In the long run, the Fed can control the money supply quite accurately. On a day-to-day basis, it is easier to set the interest rate, and the Fed frequently uses day-to-day interest rate targets even though it is targeting the money stock on a week-to-week and month-to-month basis.

Monetarists, led by Milton Friedman, are highly critical of the Fed's monetary targeting procedures. In particular, they note that the Fed's targeting procedures lead to substantial *base drift.* The data, however, indicate that the Fed's record for controlling monetary growth over the last several years has been good. "Excessive growth" in one period is usually compensated for in the following period, keeping the money growth close to the target.

9. Money, Credit, and Interest Rates

In addition to targets for *M*1 and *M*2 the Fed can target the amount of total debt in the nonfinancial sector. Proponents of credit targets argue that the Fed can better judge the impact of monetary policy on aggregate demand because there is a strong link between borrowing and spending—particularly investment spending. Conversely, interest rate targets can be unreliable indicators because of credit rationing by financial intermediaries.

10. Which Targets for the Fed?

The use of publicly announced intermediate targets by the Fed helps to give the public (households and firms) an idea of what the Fed is trying to accomplish with its policies. That is, the Fed can be accountable to the public if the public knows the Fed's goals.

There is no firm agreement, however, concerning what the Fed's targets should be. In practice, the Fed sets intermediate targets for $M1$, $M2$, $M3$, and debt growth, as well as for different interest rates.

KEY TERMS

Currency-deposit ratio
Reserve-deposit ratio
High-powered money (monetary base)
Money multiplier
Discount rate
Excess reserves
FDIC
Fan versus band

Multiple expansions of banking deposits
Money supply function
Money stock and interest rate targets
Open market purchases
Intermediate targets
Ultimate targets
Base drift
Central bank independence

GRAPH IT 14

Graph It 14 asks you to use balance sheets to illustrate the multiple expansion of deposits. We'll assume that there is only one bank and one person, Professor B. As the problem opens, Professor B has $200 on deposit. The bank is holding the $200 as reserves. The reserve requirement is 10 percent, and so $20 is required reserves and $180 is excess reserves. Table 14-1 shows the first set of balance sheets.

TABLE 14-1
FIRST BALANCE SHEET

PROFESSOR B			BANK			
Assets		Liabilities	Assets		Liabilities	
Deposit	$200	None	Reserves	$200	$200	Deposit
			(Required	20)		
			(Excess	180)		
		$200 Net worth				
	$200	$200		$200	$200	

Professor B decides to borrow as much as possible from the bank, in order to finance advanced macroeconomic research. This being a worthy cause, the bank agrees to loan the entire $180 in excess reserves. Professor B signs the loan agreement, and the bank credits her accounts with the $180 dollars. Fill in the blanks in the second set of balance sheets (Table 14-2).

Advanced macroeconomic research being as expensive as it is, Professor B decides to go for another loan. The bank again agrees to loan all its excess reserves. The bank increases the size of Professor B's loan balance and credits Professor B's account. Fill out the details in the third set of balance sheets (Table 14-3).

TABLE 14-2
SECOND BALANCE SHEET

PROFESSOR B		BANK	
Assets	Liabilities	Assets	Liabilities
Deposit $_____	$180 Loan	Reserves $200	$_____ Deposit
		(Required _____)	
		(Excess _____)	
	$_____ Net worth		
$_____	$_____	$_____	$_____

TABLE 14-3
THIRD BALANCE SHEET

PROFESSOR B		BANK	
Assets	Liabilities	Assets	Liabilities
Deposit $_____	$_____ Loan	Reserves $_____	$_____ Deposit
		(Required _____)	
		(Excess _____)	
	$_____ Net worth		
$_____	$_____	$_____	$_____

TABLE 14-4
FINAL BALANCE SHEET

PROFESSOR B		BANK	
Assets	Liabilities	Assets	Liabilities
Deposit $_____	$_____ Loan	Reserves $_____	$_____ Deposit
		(Required _____)	
		(Excess 0)	
	$_____ Net worth		
$_____	$_____	$_____	$_____

Clearly, this process could go on for a long time. Using what you've learned about the money multiplier, in Table 14-4 fill out a final set of balance sheets reflecting the final multiple expansion of deposits and zero excess reserves.

REVIEW OF TECHNIQUE 14

Percentage Change

Looking at fluctuations in economic variables in terms of percentage changes is easy and convenient. Here we quickly review the calculations of percentage changes in preparation for Review Technique 15.

Percentage change is defined as the amount of the change in a variable divided by its original level. (For ease of expression, we generally multiply the change by 100.) The percentage change in X is

$$100 \cdot \frac{\Delta X}{X}$$

If X goes from 100 to 120, the percentage change is 20/100, or 20 percent. If X goes from 100 to 80, the change is −20/100, or minus 20 percent. Notice that if X goes back from 80 to 100, the change is 20/80, or 25 percent. For small changes in X, it doesn't matter whether we use the original level or the new level as a base. For example, if X drops from 100 to 99, the change is minus 1 percent. If it returns from 99 to 100, the percentage change is 1/99, or 1.01 percent.

FILL-IN QUESTIONS

1. Currency plus bank reserves form _____ or _____.
2. Total reserves of a bank are _____ reserves plus _____ reserves.
3. The interest rate charged by the Federal Reserve to member banks is the _____ _____.
4. The interest rate charged by one bank to another for loans of deposits at the Fed is the _____.
5. The Federal Reserve lowers its holdings of bonds and decreases the money supply through a(n) _____.
6. The ratio of the money supply to high-powered money is the _____.
7. _____ is the operation by which the Fed offsets the effects of foreign exchange operations.
8. In order to avoid disrupting the money supply process, the Treasury does most of its business through _____ _____ accounts at commercial banks.
9. Public portfolio preferences affect the money supply through changes in the _____.
10. The principal asset of the Federal Reserve is _____.

TRUE-FALSE QUESTIONS

T F 1. An increase in high-powered money increases the money supply.
T F 2. An increase in the public's preferences for currency vis-à-vis deposits increases the money supply.
T F 3. An increase in reserve requirements increases the money supply.
T F 4. An increase in bank preferences for excess reserves increases the money supply.
T F 5. An increase in income increases the money supply.
T F 6. The Federal Reserve increases the money supply when it buys foreign currency.
T F 7. After accounting for induced changes in the money multiplier, an increase in high-powered money works through money demand to lower the interest rate.
T F 8. An increase in bank borrowing from the Fed increases the money supply.
T F 9. For a given stock of high-powered money, higher interest rates increase the money supply.

MULTIPLE-CHOICE QUESTIONS

1. The money multiplier is
    a. negative
    b. between 0 and 1
    c. exactly 1
    d. greater than 1

2. The Federal Reserve does *not* set by regulation
    a. the federal funds rate
    b. the discount rate
    c. the rate on bank deposits
    d. a, b, or c

3. Repeated errors by the Federal Reserve might lead to an upward spiral of the money supply under the
    a. band
    b. fan
    c. both
    d. neither

4. If the currency-deposit ratio is one-half and the reserve-deposit ratio is 10 percent, the money multiplier is
    a. −0.75
    b. 0.75
    c. 1
    d. 2.5

5. The money multiplier reaches a maximum when the currency-deposit ratio equals
    a. 0
    b. ½
    c. 1
    d. infinity

6. The money multiplier reaches a maximum when the reserve-deposit ratio equals
    a. 0
    b. ½
    c. 1
    d. infinity

7. The money multiplier reaches a maximum when excess reserves
    a. equal required reserves
    b. become negative
    c. equal 0
    d. approach infinity

8. Deposits of commercial banks are insured by
    a. the Federal Reserve
    b. the Treasury
    c. the FDIC
    d. neither a nor b nor c

9. Bank credit will increase following an increase in
    a. the reserve requirement
    b. the monetary base
    c. the discount rate
    d. a, b, and c

PROBLEMS

1. Suppose that the only deposits requiring reserves are checkable deposits, that the reserve requirement on checkable deposits is 10 percent, and that people always hold 40 percent as much in currency as they hold in checkable deposits.
   a. If high-powered money equals $100 billion, what is the level of $M1$?
   b. If high-powered money is increased by $50 billion, by how much do checkable deposits increase?

2. Suppose that, in addition to the original conditions in problem 1, a 4 percent reserve requirement is put on time deposits, and that consumers always hold 2½ times as much in time deposits as in checkable deposits.
   a. What is the level of $M2$?
   b. What is the level of $M1$?

3. The demand functions for currency and checkable deposits are given below. The reserve requirement on checkable deposits is 10 percent, and no other assets require reserves. High-powered money equals $1,150; GDP equals $2,000. What is the interest rate?

$$CU = 0.5Y - 495i$$
$$D = Y - 50i$$

4. Suppose the public becomes suspicious of the financial stability of the banking system and decides to hold a greater fraction of its money balances in the form of cash. How will the money supply and the macroeconomy by affected by the shift from demand deposits to cash? Discuss using *IS-LM* analysis.

STABILIZATION POLICY: PROSPECTS AND PROBLEMS

FOCUS OF THE CHAPTER

- The preceding chapters developed a macroeconomic model that would appear to solve the problems of economic policy making. Once we know our national goals and all the appropriate policy multipliers, we need only perform a few calculations to discover the best economic policy. The world is far more complicated than this. The controversy over what caused the great depression (the controversy is discussed in the first three sections of Chapter 15) is evidence of how complicated macroeconomic theorizing and policy making can be. In this chapter we discuss the three *handicaps of policy making:*

  1. *Lags* in the effects of policy
  2. The role of *expectations* in determining private sector responses to policy
  3. *Uncertainty* about the effects of policy

SECTION SUMMARIES

1. The Great Depression

During the early part of the great depression (1929–1933) the money stock fell rapidly; its composition changed as well, with the currency-deposit ratio rising from 18.5 percent in March 1931 to 40.7 percent two years later. Large-scale bank failures resulted in the destruction of deposits, and banks that remained open increased their reserve holdings. The money multiplier fell, reducing the money stock as a result. The Fed did little to prevent bank failures and increase the money supply.

Although fiscal policy was stimulative prior to 1932, the presidential candidates of 1932 advocated a balanced federal budget. Federal, state, and local fiscal policies were contractionary throughout the mid-1930s.

During the period 1933 to 1937, the federal government created the Federal Deposit Insurance Corporation (FDIC), the Securities and Exchange Commission, and the Social Security Administration. These institutions were viewed as potentially stabilizing forces in the economy.

2. The Great Depression: The Issues and Ideas

Early Keynesians believed that the depression was a consequence of contractionary fiscal policy. They pointed to the fact that the full-employment budget was in surplus during the early 1930s. They argued that expansionary monetary policy would not have produced an economic recovery because interest rates were already close to zero.

Monetarists, notably Milton Friedman and Anna Schwartz, claimed that it was precisely the Fed's failure to help struggling banks and its failure to increase the money stock that prolonged the depression.

3. The New Economics

Activism became the trademark of U.S. macroeconomic policy making during the 1960s. The approach was dubbed the *New Economics.*

Beginning in the Kennedy administration, the Council of Economic Advisers (CEA) advocated the active use of tax incentives and other fiscal policy tools as means of encouraging economic growth. The performance of the U.S. economy during the 1960s seemed to be testimony to the potency of fiscal policy. The 1964 tax cut was a major stimulus to economic growth. The U.S. economy did not experience a recession during the period 1961 to 1969.

4. Lags in the Effects of Policy

The first difficulty in responding to a disturbance is determining whether the disturbance is permanent or temporary. If it is temporary, the disturbance will likely have passed before policy changes can become effective. If the timing of a policy is poor, it may actually *destabilize* the economy.

Policy changes take time to become effective. This time is divided into the *inside lag,* the time necessary to undertake a policy change, and the *outside lag,* the time necessary for the policy action to take effect. The inside lag is subdivided into the *recognition lag,* the *decision lag,* and the *action lag.* The recognition lag is the time required for policy makers to realize that a problem exists. The decision lag is the time spent between discovering the problem and deciding what to do about it. The action lag is the time needed to put decisions into effect. The recognition lag is the same for monetary and fiscal policy. Decision and action lags are generally much larger for fiscal than for monetary policy. Of course, *automatic stabilizers* have no inside lag at all.

The outside lag arises from the gradual response of the economy to policy changes. The *dynamic multipliers* of Chapter 11 are a prime example. The outside lag is a *distributed lag;* that is, its effects are spread out over time. Fiscal policy generally has a shorter outside lag than does monetary policy.

5. Expectations and Reactions

Expectations of future economic conditions are critical in economic models. These expectations are extremely difficult to model accurately. Most econometric models approximate expectations by including an average of past variables. This approach leads to serious errors when people know about the future impact of some event rather than having to rely solely on previous experience. In addition, expectations themselves depend on policy. Finding consistent models of expectations and policy rules is currently a major research problem. Lucas's *econometric policy evaluation critique* points out that many of today's macromodels lack this consistency.

6. Uncertainty and Economic Policy

There are three major sources of uncertainty in economic models. First, some events are unpredictable, such as natural disasters and simple changes in consumer tastes. Second, we recognize that we never know whether our models are exactly correct. Third, the true empirical values of the coefficients in our models are all uncertain.

7. Activist Policy

Proponents of activist policy argue that we should use the tools of macroeconomics to reduce economic fluctuations. While some economists have argued against the use of activist policy entirely, active policy is appropriate so long as we recognize all the lags and uncertainty involved and are careful to be as modest as necessary in our attempts to offset disturbances. Critics of activist policies have argued that the monetary authority should be forced to follow policy rules rather than being able to use discretionary activist policies.

KEY TERMS

Economic disturbances	New Economics
Political business cycle	Econometric policy evaluation critique
Econometric models	Multiplier uncertainty
Macroeconomic models	Activist policy
Inside lag	Fine-tuning
Recognition lag	Rules versus discretion
Decision lag	Dynamic consistency
Action lag	Policy rule
Outside lag	Automatic stabilizers
New Deal	

GRAPH IT 15

Economists make much of the distinction between stocks and flows. Capital, wealth, and the money supply are examples of stocks. Investment, GDP, and interest payments are examples of flows. A very much analogous distinction is made in business and in accounting between a balance sheet and an income statement. This Graph It gives you a balance sheet showing the stocks of assets and liabilities at a bank (Table 15-1). You are then asked to prepare an income statement showing the bank's income and expense flows over the year and a new balance sheet showing the stocks at the beginning of the next year.

Assume that the bank receives no interest on reserves, 9.5 percent interest on Treasury bills, and 14 percent interest on loans. The bank pays 5.5 percent on deposits and pays a 20 percent dividend on paid-in capital. Any profits left over after paying dividends are called retained earnings and are added to the paid-in capital account. Fill in the details of the income and expense statement (Table 15-2).

Assume that the bank invests its profits entirely in Treasury bills and that depositors withdraw all their interest. Show how the balance sheet looks at the beginning of the second year (Table 15-3).

TABLE 15-1
BANK BALANCE SHEET 1

Assets		Liabilities	
Reserves	$ 200	$2,000	Deposits
Treasury bills	400		
Loans	1,600	200	Paid-in capital
	$2,200	$2,200	

TABLE 15-2
BANK INCOME STATEMENT

Income		Expenses	
Interest on reserves	$ 0	$ _____	Deposit interest
Interest on Treasury bills	_____	_____	Stockholders' dividends
Interest on loans	_____	_____	Retained earnings
	$ _____	$ _____	

TABLE 15-3
BANK BALANCE SHEET 2

Assets		Liabilities	
Reserves	$ _____	$ _____	Deposits
Treasury bills	_____	_____	Paid-in capital
Loans	_____		
	$ _____	$ _____	

REVIEW OF TECHNIQUE 15

Definition of Elasticity

The *elasticity* of X with respect to Y is the percentage change in X that results from a percentage change in Y. This can be written several ways:

$$\frac{\text{Percentage change in } X}{\text{Percentage change in } Y}$$

$$\frac{\frac{\Delta X}{X}}{\frac{\Delta Y}{Y}} \qquad\qquad \frac{\Delta X}{\Delta Y} \cdot \frac{Y}{X}$$

The elasticity of a given relation is independent of the units of measurement of the variables.

It is worth noting that if X is proportional to Y, then X has unit elasticity with respect to Y, that is, the elasticity is 1. This is true irrespective of the constant of proportionality. This is proved as follows: Suppose $X = aY$. If Y changes by ΔY, then X changes by $a\Delta Y$. The percentage change in X is $a\Delta Y/aY$, which equals $\Delta Y/Y$. The ratio of the percentage change in X to the percentage change in Y is $(\Delta X/X)/(\Delta Y/Y) = (a\Delta Y/aY)/(\Delta Y/Y) = (\Delta Y/Y)/(\Delta Y/Y)$, which, of course, equals 1.

FILL-IN QUESTIONS

1. The time required for policy makers to counteract an economic disturbance is the

    _____.

2. The time required for a new policy to produce a change in the economy is the

    _____.

3. The three handicaps of policy making are _____, _____, and _____.

4. The _____ is the period between the time when a new policy is chosen and the time when the policy is first put into effect.

5. The time required for an economic disturbance to be discovered is the _____ _____.

6. The time necessary for policy makers to choose a new policy is called the _____ _____.

7. A policy that requires no direct action on the part of policy makers is called a(n) _____.

8. Economists who believe policy should be used to counteract economic disturbances are called _____.

9. The _____ lag is much longer for fiscal than for monetary policy.

10. The _____ lag is shorter for fiscal than for monetary policy.

PROBLEM

1. The U.S. economy has operated near its potential level of GDP since the time of its recovery from the recession of 1981–1982. However, the federal budget has been in deficit throughout this most recent period. To combat the federal deficit, Congress passed the Gramm-Rudman budget law, which mandates across-the-board cuts in federal spending if yearly deficit reduction targets cannot be met through the appropriations process. Assuming that maintaining GDP near its potential is a goal of policy, what would be the policy response if mandatory Gramm-Rudman budget cuts were invoked? Analyze the problem within the *IS-LM* framework and consider two cases: In one, the *LM* curve is vertical; in the other, the *LM* curve is positively sloped.

part four

INFLATION, UNEMPLOYMENT, BUDGET DEFICITS, AND INTERNATIONAL ADJUSTMENT

THE DYNAMICS OF INFLATION AND UNEMPLOYMENT

FOCUS OF THE CHAPTER

- Modified to take account of inflationary expectations, the Phillips curve becomes a dynamic aggregate supply curve. When the expected inflation rate is equal to the actual inflation rate, output is at its full-employment level. For a *given* rate of expected inflation, the dynamic aggregate supply curve implies a tradeoff between output and inflation. In the long run, the tradeoff cannot persist because inflationary expectations will "catch up" with the actual inflation rate.

- Together with the dynamic aggregate supply curve, the dynamic aggregate demand curve determines the equilibrium level of output and inflation. In the short run, adaptive expectations imply that output may deviate from full employment as a result of monetary, fiscal, and other forms of shocks. In the long run, inflation is mainly a monetary phenomenon. Rational inflationary expectations imply that anticipated monetary and fiscal policy has no real effects.

SECTION SUMMARIES

1. Inflation, Expectations, and the Aggregate Supply Curve

The aggregate supply curve

$$P = P_{-1}[1 + \lambda(Y - Y^*)]$$

is derived by combining the Phillips curve (the inverse relationship between the unemployment rate and the level of output) and the markup pricing rule of firms. An implication of markup pricing is that firms pass wage increases on to consumers directly. Thus, in our model, wages and prices always rise or fall at the same rate.

Using the aggregate supply curve we can write the wage-Phillips curve as

$$\frac{W - W_{-1}}{W_{-1}} - g_w = \lambda(Y - Y^*)$$

Friedman and Phelps argued that the simple wage-Phillips curve incorrectly ignores the effect of expected inflation on wage rates. At the very least, workers will demand periodic wage increases to compensate for expected inflation. Workers care about real wages, not nominal wages. To take account of the role of expected (price) inflation on wage changes, we write the expectations-augmented wage-Phillips curve:

$$g_w = \pi^e + \lambda(Y - Y^*)$$

When Y is equal to Y^*, wages rise at the expected rate of inflation. When Y is below (above) Y^*, wages rise at a rate below (above) the expected rate of inflation.

Since π, the actual inflation rate, is assumed to be equal to g_w, the rate of wage inflation, we can substitute π for g_w in the expectations-augmented wage-Phillips curve to derive the dynamic aggregate supply curve:

$$\pi = \pi^e + \lambda(Y - Y^*)$$

2. Short- and Long-Run Aggregate Supply Curves

There is a short-run (dynamic) aggregate supply curve corresponding to every level of expected inflation. For example, at an expected inflation rate of 5 percent (Figure 16-1), the dynamic aggregate supply curve is *SAS*. At $Y = Y^*$, the actual inflation rate equals the expected inflation rate (5 percent), as should be the case. If expected inflation were to jump to 10 percent, the new short-run aggregate supply curve would be *SAS'*. Along each short-run aggregate supply curve, there is a tradeoff between inflation and unemployment.

The short-run dynamic aggregate supply curve appeared to shift in the late 1960s as the public began to expect higher inflation rates. Higher actual inflation rates became associated with each level of GDP.

If the actual inflation rate remains stable for a long period of time, the public will begin to anticipate that particular level of inflation. The only level of output consistent with $\pi = \pi^e$ is full employment. When the economy is resting at full employment, prices and wages are rising at the rate expected by the public; the long-run aggregate supply curve is vertical.

It is not clear whether wage adjustments required by labor contracts reflect compensation for past inflation or expectations of current and future inflation. The fact that many adjustments are based on last period's inflation rate gives wage changes the

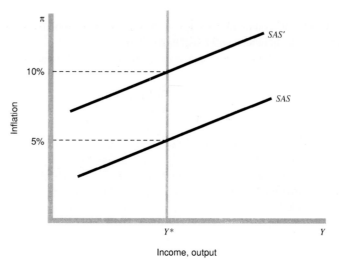

FIGURE 16-1

THE DYNAMIC AGGREGATE SUPPLY CURVE

appearance of being compensation for past inflation. If wage adjustments are based on last period's inflation rate, wages and prices change only gradually over time.

Anticipated inflation based on the past behavior of inflation is called adaptive expectations. For example, inflationary expectations are adaptive when

$$\pi^e = \pi_{-1}$$

According to the rational expectations hypothesis, people use all the relevant and (economically) available information to forecast the future behavior of the price level. The rational expectations hypothesis implies that the public does not make systematic mistakes in forecasting the inflation rate. The dynamic aggregate supply curve under the adaptive expectations hypothesis is

$$\pi = \pi_{-1} + \lambda(Y - Y^*)$$

3. Dynamic Aggregate Demand

The dynamic aggregate demand curve shows the relationship between the rate of inflation and the rate of change in aggregate demand for a fixed level of nominal money supply growth and a fixed rate of fiscal expansion. It is

$$Y = Y_{-1} + \varphi(m - \pi) + \sigma \cdot f$$

where φ and σ are positive constraints, $m - \pi$ is the rate of change of real money balances, and f is the rate of fiscal expansion. The dynamic aggregate demand curve says that the rate of change in aggregate demand, $Y - Y_{-1}$, is positively related to the growth of real money balances and fiscal expansion.

We write the dynamic aggregate demand curve (derived from a simplified *IS-LM* model) as

$$\pi = m - \frac{1}{\varphi}(Y - Y_{-1})$$

to highlight the relationship between actual inflation, the rate of growth of the nominal money stock, and the change in aggregate demand (assuming, for simplicity, that f is zero). Plotting π against Y (for a given m and Y_{-1}), the dynamic aggregate demand curve is downward-sloping, as in Figure 16-2. Holding the rate of growth of the nominal money stock fixed, a reduction in π causes real balances to grow more rapidly and spending to increase.

An increase (decrease) in the nominal growth rate of money causes the dynamic aggregate demand curve to shift up (down).

4. Inflation and Output

The equilibrium inflation rate and level of output are determined by the intersection of the dynamic aggregate supply curve with the dynamic aggregate demand curve. In the short run, holding the expected inflation rate constant, an increase in the growth rate of the nominal money stock will shift the dynamic aggregate demand curve rightward, raising the level of output. The inflation rate will increase, but not by as much as the growth rate of the money stock. An exogenous increase in expected inflation will reduce output in the short run. Actual inflation will rise, but not by as much as the expected inflation rate.

FIGURE 16-2
THE DYNAMIC AGGREGATE DEMAND CURVE

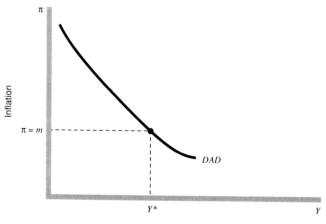

Output, income

When the economy is resting at full employment and the nominal money stock is growing at a positive rate (f assumed to be zero), the expected inflation rate, the actual inflation rate, and the growth rate of the nominal money stock are all equal. In the long run ("steady state"), the inflation rate is determined solely by the growth rate of the money stock. In reality, the economy never reaches a steady state. However, macroeconomists would expect the average behavior of the economy over a long period of time to approximate the steady-state behavior predicted by our model.

5. The Adjustment Process

We consider the dynamic adjustment of the inflation rate and the level of output to a permanent increase in the growth rate of the money stock under the assumption that inflationary expectations are adaptive. The economy is initially at point E in Figure 16-3, where money growth rate is m_0 and the inflation rate is π_0. An increase in the growth rate of money to m_1 shifts the aggregate demand curve upward; the inflation rate is now π_1 and the level of output is Y_1 (point E_1). Expected inflation is still last period's actual level of inflation, π_0.

Because output has increased from its initial level, the dynamic aggregate demand curve shifts again. The aggregate supply curve shifts up now, as expected inflation rises to π_1; the economy moves to point E_2. The actual inflation rate has already risen above its eventual steady-state level, π_1. At some point output will decrease to Y^* and inflation will have increased by exactly the increase in money growth.

FIGURE 16-3
DYNAMIC ADJUSTMENT TO A PERMANENT INCREASE IN THE GROWTH RATE
OF THE MONEY STOCK

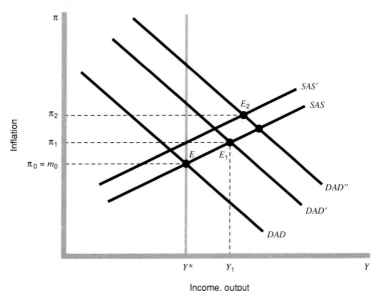

6. Expectations and Sluggish Adjustment

During the process of adjustment to an increase in the growth rate of money, the economy exhibits a period of *stagflation* and *overshooting*.

With perfect-foresight inflationary expectations—the equivalent of rational expectations when there is no uncertainty—π equals π^e and the economy is at full employment always. Under rational expectations, unexpected changes in the growth rate of the money supply may cause temporary deviations of output from its full-employment level, but readjustment to full employment will occur within one period.

A permanent fiscal expansion will temporarily raise output and increase the inflation rate. With an unchanged money supply growth rate, the economy must eventually return to its initial equilibrium, at which $Y = Y^*$, and $\pi = m_0$. During the adjustment process the economy exhibits overshooting—a recession—and since government spending exceeds its old level in the new equilibrium, some private spending has been permanently crowded out.

7. Dynamic Adjustment Done More Formally

We now take a more formal look at dynamic adjustment in the scenarios graphed in Figure 16-4a. The arrows indicate the direction in which aggregate demand rises (falls) when nominal money growth is greater (less) than inflation.

The aggregate supply curve is

$$\pi = \pi^e + \lambda(Y - Y^*)$$

If we assume adaptive expectations such as $\pi^e = \pi_{-1}$, then

$$\pi - \pi^e \equiv \pi - \pi_{-1} \equiv \Delta\pi = \lambda(Y - Y^*)$$

The inflation rate will be rising if the level of output, Y, exceeds the full-employment rate of output, Y^*, and will be falling if the opposite is true. These scenarios are pictured in Figure 16-4b, where the arrows indicate the direction in which the inflation rate is moving at the specified level of output.

We combine aggregate demand (Figure 16-4a) and aggregate supply (Figure 16-4b) into one figure (Figure 16-5a) that describes the dynamics of inflation and output. In region I, both output and inflation are rising; in region II, inflation is rising and output is falling; in region III, both inflation and output are falling; and in region IV, output is rising and inflation is falling. In Figure 16-5b, we graph the *IS* schedule for a given level of autonomous spending. Figures 16-5a and b permit us to keep track of the real interest rate, the actual inflation rate and level of output, and the dynamics of inflation and output, all at once.

A permanent increase in the growth rate of the money stock from m_0 to m' shifts the long-run equilibrium from E to E' as in Figure 16-6a. With adaptive expectations, the expected inflation rate is last period's inflation rate, so that the equilibrium real interest

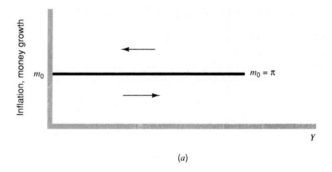

(a)

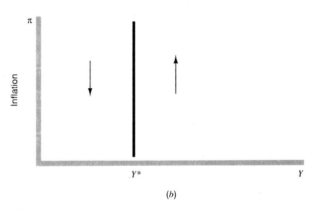

(b)

FIGURE 16-4

rate initially falls. With output above its full-employment level, the inflation rate rises. Output eventually returns to Y^*, the real interest rate returns to r^*, and the inflation rate rises to its new level, m', which is the new growth rate of the money stock.

8. Interest Rates and Inflation: The Fisher Equation

The Fisher equation

$$r^* = i - \pi^*$$

helps us track the nominal interest rate during the adjustment of the economy to a new equilibrium. If inflationary expectations are adaptive, the nominal interest rate adjusts slowly to changes in the growth rate of the money stock. If, for example, there is a permanent increase in the growth rate of the money stock, the nominal interest rate will initially fall by the same amount as the initial decline in the real rate but will eventually rise above its initial level by the amount of the increase in the steady-state inflation rate.

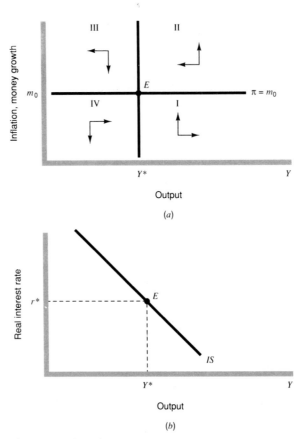

FIGURE 16-5

The declining phase of the nominal interest rate adjustment path is called the *liquidity effect* to denote the impact of increased real balances on the interest rate. The income effect—which causes the nominal and real interest rates to begin to rise—results from the fact that increased nominal income causes the real demand for money to rise. The Fisher, or expectations, effect denotes the adjustment of the nominal interest rate to changing inflationary expectations.

A sustained increase in the growth rate of the money stock must eventually reduce real money balances. In order for this to occur, there must be a period during the adjustment to the increase in which the price level rises more rapidly than the money stock.

KEY TERMS

Expectations-augmented aggregate
    supply curve
Short-run aggregate supply curve
Long-run aggregate supply curve
Adaptive expectations

Rational expectations
Stagflation
Overshooting
Dynamic aggregate demand curve
Inflationary inertia

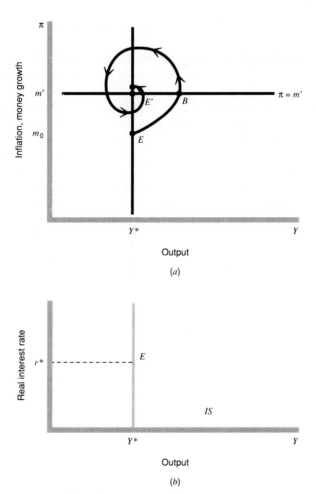

FIGURE 16-6

Credibility   Expectations effect
Wage and price controls   Liquidity effect
Fisher equation   Income effect

GRAPH IT 16

Graph It 16 asks you to calculate the opportunity cost differences between money, bonds, and capital. The purpose of this exercise is to determine when you should look at the nominal interest rate and when you should look at the real interest rate.

Assume that money pays no interest. Bonds pay the nominal interest rate. Capital takes the form of seed corn. Every bushel of seed corn you have at the beginning of the year grows into 1.1 bushels by the end of the year. Initially, the general price level equals

1.0, and a bushel of corn costs $1. You start with $100 in money, $100 in bonds, and 100 bushels of corn.

Fill out Table 16-1 on the basis of the assumptions that the price level of corn and everything else rises to 1.02 by the end of the year and that the nominal interest rate is 7 percent.

Fill out Table 16-2 on the basis of the new assumptions that the price level rises to 1.12 by the end of the year and that the nominal interest rate is 17 percent.

You should be able to see that in both tables the opportunity cost of money (versus bonds) is approximately the nominal interest rate—whether the cost is measured by the real difference or the dollar difference. The opportunity cost of capital (seed corn) is approximately the real interest rate in both cases. At low inflation rates (such as in Table 16-1), the real and nominal interest rates are approximately the same, and so it doesn't matter much which one we look at. At high inflation rates (such as in Table 16-2), the difference is crucial.

TABLE 16-1

Asset	Beginning value	End dollar value	End real value	Dollar difference	Real difference
Money	$100	$100.00	$ 98.04		
Bonds	$100	$107.00	$104.90	$7	_____
Corn	$100	$112.20	$110.00	_____	_____

TABLE 16-2

Asset	Beginning value	End dollar value	End real value	Dollar difference	Real difference
Money	$100	$_____	$_____		
Bonds	$100	_____	_____	$_____	$_____
Corn	$100	_____	_____	_____	_____

REVIEW OF TECHNIQUE 16

Infinite Geometric Series

Infinite geometric series have been used at least twice in the text. They were first used when we discussed the simple consumption function and multiplier, and second when we considered the multiple expansion of bank deposits. We now demonstrate how to calculate the sum of an infinite series. Suppose that c is a fraction between 0 and 1 and that S is the sum of the following series.

$$S = 1 + c + c^2 + c^3 + c^4 + \ldots$$

Notice then that

$$cS = c + c^2 + c^3 + c^4 + c^5 + \ldots$$

If we subtract the second line from the first, we get

$$S - cS \ = 1 + (c - c) + (c^2 - c^2) + (c^3 - c^3) + \ldots$$
$$S - cS \ = 1 + 0 + 0 + 0 + \ldots = 1$$
$$S(1 - c) = 1$$
$$S = \frac{1}{1 - c}$$

Notice that if c happens to be the marginal propensity to consume, then S is the simple multiplier.

FILL-IN QUESTIONS

1. _____ occurs when the inflation rate rises above or below its steady-state level during the adjustment to a disturbance.

2. So long as people do not make systematic errors in predicting the future of the economy, they are said to have _____.

3. In order to explain inflation, the _____ curve takes into account not only the current state of the economy but also people's expectations about future price changes.

4. The theory that in the long run the economy must return to full employment is shown by the long-run _____ curve.

5. Simultaneous high inflation and high unemployment is called _____.

6. A(n) _____ government policy pronouncement is one that the public believes the government will act upon.

7. People are said to have _____ expectations when there is no uncertainty and they know the actual inflation rate precisely.

8. A provision in a wage contract that ties the wage rate to the inflation rate is called a(n) _____ clause.

9. An increase in the money supply moves the *LM* curve and thus initially lowers the interest rate through the _____.

10. As nominal income starts to rise, interest rates start to rise because of the _____ _____.

TRUE-FALSE QUESTIONS

T F 1. Rational expectations theory says that GDP always equals potential GDP.

T F 2. Income policies have been mostly unsuccessful in the United States.

T F 3. We can think of the Phillips curve as being vertical when expected inflation and actual inflation are equal.

T F 4. Inflation is increased by high expectations of inflation.

T F 5. Increased inflationary expectations lower the nominal interest rate.

MULTIPLE-CHOICE QUESTIONS

1. Initially, the general price level is 100. If, 6 months later, the general price level is 102, the annual inflation rate has been
   a. 2 percent
   b. 4 percent
   c. 5 percent
   d. 12 percent

2. If expected inflation rises by one percentage point, in the short run the nominal interest rate will
   a. remain constant
   b. rise by less than one point
   c. rise by one point
   d. rise by more than one point

3. If expected inflation rises by one percentage point, in the long run the nominal interest rate will
   a. remain constant
   b. rise by less than one point
   c. rise by one point
   d. rise by more than one point

4. If expected inflation rises by one percentage point, in the short run the expected real interest rate will
   a. remain constant
   b. fall by less than one point
   c. fall by one point
   d. fall by more than one point

5. If expected inflation rises by one percentage point, in the long run the expected real interest rate will
   a. remain constant
   b. fall by less than one point
   c. fall by one point
   d. fall by more than one point

6. Assuming that real GDP grows at 3 percent per year and the money supply grows at 6 percent per year, then, if the income elasticity of the demand for money is ½, long-run inflation will be
   a. 3 percent
   b. 4½ percent
   c. 6 percent
   d. 7½ percent

7. An increase of 1 percent per year in the rate of growth of the money supply will increase inflation in the long run by
   a. 0
   b. 0.5 percent
   c. 1 percent
   d. more than 1 percent

8. A permanent increase in the rate of growth of money of 1 percent will permanently increase GDP by
   a. 0
   b. 0.5 percent
   c. 1 percent
   d. more than 1 percent

9. A permanent increase in government spending will generate
   a. temporarily increased inflation
   b. permanently increased inflation
   c. no change in inflation
   d. temporarily decreased inflation

10. A permanent increase in the level of the money stock, with no change in the rate of growth, will generate
    a. temporarily increased inflation
    b. permanently increased inflation
    c. no change in inflation
    d. temporarily decreased inflation

PROBLEMS

Use the following equations for questions 1 through 3.

$$Y = Y_{-1} + 2f + 2{,}000(m_{-1} - \pi_{-1}) + 1{,}000\,\Delta\pi^e \qquad \text{Dynamic aggregate demand}$$

$$\pi = \pi^e + 0.8\left(\frac{Y - Y*}{Y*}\right) \qquad \text{Expectations-augmented Phillips curve}$$

$$\pi^e = \pi_{-1} \qquad \text{Inflationary expectations}$$

Initially, GDP equals 4,000, as does potential GDP. Initial $\bar{A}(f=0)$ is 1,000, and both inflation and inflationary expectations have been zero for some time. The rate of growth of the money supply, m, is also initially zero.

1. Suppose the government permanently increases spending by 500. What is the level of GDP in the year of the increase? What is the inflation rate? What inflation rate will people expect for the next year? What actually happens to GDP and inflation the following year? The year after?

2. Suppose, instead, that the money supply is temporarily increased by 50 percent, so that m equals 0.5 and then returns to 0 in the following year. Obviously, aggregate demand is not changed the first year, since money only affects income with a lag. What happens to GDP and inflation the next year? The year after? The year after that?

3. Suppose the government lets the money supply grow at 50 percent per year permanently. What happens to GDP and inflation in years 2, 3, 4, and 5 of the new policy?

4. The term "structure of interest rates" is a relationship that links the yields to maturity of bonds of different terms. For example,

$$R_{4,93} \cong \frac{R_{1,93} + R^e_{1,94} + R^e_{1,95} + R^e_{1,96}}{4}$$

tells us that the current (1993) interest rate on a four-year bond can be approximately equated to an equally weighted average of current and expected future interest rates on one-year bonds. Consider, then, in a dynamic *AD-AS rational expectations* framework, how an *unanticipated* increase in the rate of monetary growth will, in general, affect the nominal term structure of interest rates. Illustrate using the yield curve.

THE TRADEOFFS BETWEEN INFLATION AND UNEMPLOYMENT

FOCUS OF THE CHAPTER

- After reviewing the available tradeoffs between unemployment and inflation, we study their relative costs.

- We study the *anatomy of unemployment,* its distribution among different groups in society, and the determination of the natural rate.

- We then look at the costs of inflation, with special emphasis on the difference between *anticipated* and *unanticipated inflation.*

- We conclude with a look at the politics of inflation and unemployment.

SECTION SUMMARIES

1. The Anatomy of Unemployment

There are three central facts about unemployment in the United States. These facts help us to understand who bears the cost of unemployment.

    a. There are substantial flows in and out of unemployment each month, and most people who become unemployed return to work very quickly.

    b. Much of the total number of unemployed persons is made up of people who are unemployed for long periods.

    c. Different groups in society have very different unemployment rates. Teenagers are unemployed more than adults. African Americans are unemployed more than whites.

2. Full Employment

The *full-employment level of unemployment,* also called the natural rate of unemployment, is the unemployment rate at which flows in and out of unemployment just balance *and* at which expectations about prices and wages are correct. The natural rate of unemployment changes over time. Since the overall natural rate is a weighted average of natural rates of different groups in society, the natural rate has risen as groups with higher unemployment have become a larger part of the labor force.

3. The Costs of Unemployment

Okun's law suggests that a one-percentage-point increase in the unemployment rate for 1 year costs society about 2.25 percent of GDP. The burden of unemployment is not spread evenly over society. Most of it is borne by the individuals who find themselves out of work.

4. The Costs of Inflation

In determining the costs of inflation, we make a critical distinction between *perfectly anticipated* and *imperfectly anticipated* inflation. If everyone knew how much inflation there would be, all agreements and contracts would be written to reflect this inflation. The only costs of anticipated inflation are those that arise because the interest rate on currency cannot be adjusted to inflation (since there is no interest on currency) and because people have to spend a lot of time remarking price tags. Both costs are trivial. When inflation is *unanticipated* or *imperfectly anticipated,* people who owe nominal debts repay them with cheaper dollars and people who are creditors are paid off in cheaper dollars. Thus debtors benefit and creditors lose. Of course, most people are both debtors and creditors. Unanticipated inflation helps some individuals and hurts others. The effect of unanticipated inflation is mostly *distributional.*

5. Inflation and Indexation: Inflation-Proofing the Economy

The major areas in which unanticipated inflation redistributes income are long-term nominal loans and long-term wage contracts. For example, most homeowners found their homes to be good investments in the 1960s and 1970s because the increase in house prices was as great as the mortgage interest rate. The homeowners effectively paid zero interest. Long-term wage contracts fix nominal wages over a period of several years. In order to avoid too great a change in the real wage should inflation differ from the rate expected when the contract was signed, many contracts include cost-of-living adjustments (COLAs), which index the wage rate to the rate of inflation.

6.   The Political Economy of Inflation and Unemployment

After a shock, policy makers must choose the adjustment path that will return the economy to full employment. They can increase aggregate demand rapidly at the expense of high prices, or they can fight inflation at the expense of a slow recovery. In a perfect society, political leaders would weigh the costs and benefits involved. It has been suggested that politicians actually manipulate the economy (thus generating the so-called *political business cycle*) in order to aid their own reelection.

KEY TERMS

Unemployment pool

Layoffs

Involuntary quits

Accessions

Separations

Durations of spells of unemployment

Natural rate of unemployment

Targeted programs

Costs of cyclical unemployment

Okun's law

Anticipated inflation

Redistribution of wealth

Fisher equation

Indexation

COLA

Extended Phillips curve

Political business cycle

Quits

Replacement ratio

Frequency of unemployment

Zero inflation target

Central bank independence

Structural unemployment

Cyclical unemployment

GRAPH IT 17

As you know, statistics can be misleading. When a statistic is a weighted average of underlying data, changes in the weights can easily lead us to guess wrong about what is going on in the economy. Graph It 17 illustrates this by looking at changes in the natural rate of unemployment.

The underlying information for Table 17-1 is the unemployment rate for adults and teenagers and the number of adults and teenagers in the labor force. From these figures we calculated the number employed. Then we added up the total labor force and the total employed and worked backward to get the overall unemployment rate, 3.67 percent $[3.67 = 1 - (1,156/1,200)]$.

Now you fill in Table 17-2 and answer the following two questions. Has the overall unemployment rate risen? If so, which group is unemployed more?

TABLE 17-1
"THE OLD DAYS"

	Unemployment rate	Number in labor force	Number employed
Adults	3.00	1,000	970
Teenagers	7.00	200	186
Total	3.67	1,200	1,156

TABLE 17-2
"THE NEW DAYS"

	Unemployment rate	Number in labor force	Number employed
Adults	2.80	1,000	___
Teenagers	5.50	800	___
Total	___	___	___

REVIEW OF TECHNIQUE 17

Constant Returns to Scale

A production function is said to *exhibit constant returns to scale* if whenever we double all inputs, the amount of output doubles. Notice that we emphasize that *all* inputs must be increased in a balanced way, not increasing just one while the other inputs stay constant.

We can prove that the Cobb-Douglas production function has constant returns to scale. We need only show that for any combination of capital and labor, if we multiply both K and N by any arbitrary constant, b, and then plug these new levels into the production function, output Y will have been multiplied by the same b.

$$Y = AK^a N^{1-a}$$
$$? = A(bK)^a(bN)^{1-a}$$
$$? = Ab^a K^a b^{1-a} N^{1-a} = AK^a N^{1-a}(b^a b^{1-a}) = AK^a N^{1-a}(b)$$
$$! = bY$$

FILL-IN QUESTIONS

1. The problem of stabilization policy concerns the tradeoff between _____ and _____.

2. The _____ is the permanently sustainable rate of unemployment.

3. Contracts can be adjusted in advance for _____ inflation.

4. Unforeseen inflation is called _____ or _____.

5. The effects of unforeseen inflation are mostly _____.

6. The short-run relation between unemployment and GDP is described by _____ _____.

7. An unforeseen increase in prices benefits _____.

8. This group benefits at the expense of _____.

TRUE-FALSE QUESTIONS

T F 1. The natural rate of employment is determined by long-run aggregate demand policies.

T F 2. The effects of unanticipated employment are mostly distributional.

T F 3. The effects of unanticipated inflation are mostly distributional.

T F 4. The effects of anticipated unemployment are very large.

T F 5. The effects of anticipated inflation are trivial.

T F 6. Most people who become unemployed return to work quickly.

T F 7. Most unemployment is accounted for by people who are only briefly unemployed.

T F 8. Optimally, the unemployment rate would be zero.

T F 9. The natural rate of unemployment cannot be changed by government economic policies.

T F 10. Aggregate demand policies cannot be used to change inflation in the long run.

MULTIPLE-CHOICE QUESTIONS

1. The natural rate of unemployment is currently estimated at around
    a. 0
    b. 2 to 3 percent
    c. 5 to 6 percent
    d. 8 to 9 percent

2. Compared with white unemployment among groups of the same age and sex, African American unemployment is
   a. less
   b. roughly the same
   c. 1½ to 2 times as great
   d. nearly 4 times as great

3. The typical person who becomes unemployed either finds a new job or leaves the labor force in about
   a. a week
   b. a month
   c. 6 months
   d. a year

4. The natural rate of unemployment is the level at which
   a. entry and exit from the unemployment pool balance
   b. expectations about wages and prices are correct
   c. neither a nor b occurs
   d. both a and b occur

5. The natural rate of unemployment changes in response to
   a. labor market policies
   b. the composition of the labor force
   c. neither a nor b
   d. both a and b

6. Inflation could be brought to an abrupt halt by
   a. a deep, short recession
   b. a shallow, short recession
   c. a big boom
   d. none of the above

7. Inflation could be brought to a gradual halt by
   a. a deep, long recession
   b. a shallow, long recession
   c. a big boom
   d. none of the above

8. If the government commands total credibility, and prices and wages are fully flexible, inflation
   a. can be stopped instantly, but with high unemployment
   b. can be stopped instantly, with no unemployment
   c. can be stopped gradually, with no unemployment
   d. cannot be stopped

9. Anticipated inflation largely transfers wealth from
   a. debtors to creditors
   b. creditors to debtors
   c. poor to rich
   d. none of the above

10. Unanticipated inflation largely transfers wealth from
    a. young to old
    b. poor to rich
    c. creditors to debtors
    d. none of the above

PROBLEMS

1. Suppose that the natural rate of unemployment is 5 percent for adults and 8 percent for teenagers. If teenagers are 40 percent of the labor force, what is the overall natural rate? What would the natural rate be if the number of working teenagers increased until teenagers made up 50 percent of the labor force? Would full-employment GDP be higher or lower at this new natural rate?

2. Suppose that in a typical month, four people out of every hundred leave their jobs. If two of these people are out of work for 1 month, one is out of work for 2 months, and one is out of work for a year, what is the average duration of unemployment? What is the employment rate?

3. Assume you buy a 1-year bond at $100 with a 7 percent nominal interest rate and that over the year the inflation rate is 10 percent. What is your real gain over the next year?

4. Assume people expect the inflation rate to be 10 percent. What nominal interest rate will they charge to obtain a 2 percent real return?

5. Suppose you own a piece of real estate that is gaining in value at 2 percent per year plus the inflation rate. If the inflation rate is 10 percent and the capital gains tax rate is 25 percent, what is your real after-tax return if you sell after 2 years?

6. The following equations describe the economy.

$$m + v = p + y \qquad\qquad \text{Money demand}$$

$$p = 1 + \frac{3}{4}(Y - Y^p) \qquad \text{Short-run aggregate supply}$$

(Note that the equations are in logarithmic form and that Y^p represents potential GDP.)

Calculate the effect on GDP and the price level of a 10 percent increase in the money supply. What does this form of the money demand equation imply about the effectiveness of monetary policy?

MONEY, DEFICITS, AND INFLATION: EVIDENCE AND POLICY ISSUES

FOCUS OF THE CHAPTER

- Very high inflation rates are due primarily to excessive money growth, but the link between money and inflation at low inflation rates is much weaker.

- We look at whether money growth raises or lowers interest rates.

- Budget deficits may generate money growth, but whether or not they actually do depends on Federal Reserve policy.

- We examine the relationship between hyperinflations and money growth.

SECTION SUMMARIES

1. Money, Inflation, and Interest Rates

The monetarist claim that monetary growth affects the price level, but not real variables, is essentially correct in the long run. In the short run, monetary and nonmonetary forces influence both the inflation rate and real variables.

In the model developed in Chapter 16, we found that growth in aggregate demand, $\Delta Y = Y - Y_{-1}$, depends on the rate of growth of real money balances, and the rate of growth of real money balances equals the difference between nominal money growth and inflation.

$$\Delta Y = f(m - \pi)$$

Aggregate demand rises (falls) when nominal money growth is greater (less) than inflation. Chapter 16 also used the Fisher equation

$$r = i - \pi$$

to explain the relationship between money growth, inflation, and interest rates.

2. Empirical Evidence

Empirical evidence suggests that changes in the monetary growth rate are associated with changes in the inflation rate, though with a lag. The length of the lag is not constant but may range anywhere from a few months to several years.

In all likelihood, shifts in the position of the money demand function have played an important role in determining the relationship between π and m. Furthermore, supply shocks may temporarily sever the link between inflation and money growth.

The nominal interest rate and the actual inflation rate tend to move together over time, but the relationship is not one for one. The actual real rate is not constant over time.

3. Alternative Strategies to Reduce Inflation

In fighting inflation, we choose between *gradualism,* in which we have a small recession for a long time, and *cold turkey policies,* in which we have a shorter, deeper recession. The choice is difficult. However, the cold turkey policies have the advantage of being *credible.* If people believe the government is going to reduce inflation, then π^e falls. For every point π^e falls, we get rid of one point of inflation without having to pay the unemployment price.

Two policies that have been suggested to reduce inflation without paying an unemployment price are *incomes policy* and *TIP* (tax incentive policy). Incomes policy means either formal or informal wage or price controls. TIP provides tax subsidies to companies that hold down price and wage increases in order to try to accomplish the same result as wage and price controls without the need for as much regulation. Both policies face two problems. First, relative price changes are necessary for efficient allocation of economic resources, and controls greatly interfere with the market's ability to change prices. Second, governments try to use those policies instead of controlling aggregate demand rather than using the policies together with actions to control aggregate demand.

4. Deficits, Money Growth, and the Inflation Tax

The government's budget constraint states that

Budget deficit = sales of bonds + increase in the money base

The Fed is said to *monetize* the deficit when it purchases a part of any new Treasury issues of debt to finance the deficit. The Fed faces a dilemma in deciding whether or not to monetize the deficit. Fiscal expansion unaccompanied by a monetary accommodation will have the undesirable effect of raising interest rates. On the other hand, excessive monetary accommodation will have the longer-term effect of raising the inflation rate. Moreover, monetary accommodation can stabilize interest rates only temporarily. Evidence on whether or not the Federal Reserve partially monetizes deficits is mixed.

The creation of high-powered money serves as an alternative to taxation in financing a deficit. "Tax" revenue obtained by money creation is known as *seigniorage*. The government collects seigniorage by creating high-powered money that is used to pay for the government's purchases of goods and services.

The amount collected through the inflation tax is

$$\text{Inflation tax revenue} = \text{inflation rate} \times \text{real money base}$$

The government cannot collect inflation tax revenue at arbitrarily high rates of inflation. Eventually, as the money growth rate becomes large, the real money stock will fall to zero. In practice, the amount of inflation tax revenue collected by governments in developed countries is small, although there have been situations in which as much as 10 percent of GDP was collected through seigniorage.

5. Hyperinflation

A rough characterization of a hyperinflation economy would be one for which the animal inflation rate was 1,000 percent per year or more. All hyperinflation economies suffer from large budget deficits and rapid monetary growth. Usually the tax-collecting system has broken down, and the government has restored to the collection of seigniorage. Countries that have been able to stop a hyperinflation have done so by balancing the government budget and (eventually) reducing the growth rate of the money supply.

Increasing nominal interest rates increases the size of the measured deficit, but the measured deficit gives a distorted picture of its true size. A better measure is the inflation-corrected deficit, which accounts for the fact that the real value of the government's outstanding debt falls with inflation.

KEY TERMS

Fisher effect	Seigniorage
TIP	Inflation-corrected deficit
Expectations effect	Heterodox programs
Monetization of Deficits	Sacrifice ratio
Hyperinflation	Cold turkey
Inflation tax	Gradualism
Incomes policies	

GRAPH IT 18

Graph It 18 gives you the opportunity to investigate the relationship between the level of (and change in) the U.S. government's inflation tax revenues and the size of (and change in) the U.S. budget deficit. Use the data in Table 18-1 to compute the federal government's annual inflation tax revenues for the period 1965 to 1991. Since Table 18-1 reports only $M1$, not the monetary base, you will need to compute the monetary base on

TABLE 18-1

Year	Deficit, $ billions	M1, $ billions	Price level, index: 1982–1984 = 100	Inflation tax revenue, $ billions	Change in budget deficit	Change in inflation tax
1964	2.6	160.4	31			
1965	–1.3	167.9	31.5	0.90	–3.9	
1966	1.4	172.1	32.4	1.64	2.7	0.74
1967	12.7	183.3	33.4	_____	_____	_____
1968	4.7	197.5	34.8	_____	_____	_____
1969	–8.5	204	36.7	_____	_____	_____
1970	13.3	214.5	38.8	_____	_____	_____
1971	21.7	228.4	40.5	_____	_____	_____
1972	17.3	249.3	41.8	_____	_____	_____
1973	6.6	262.9	44.4	_____	_____	_____
1974	11.6	274.4	49.3	_____	_____	_____
1975	69.4	287.6	53.8	_____	_____	_____
1976	52.9	306.4	56.9	_____	_____	_____
1977	42.4	331.3	60.6	_____	_____	_____
1978	28.1	358.4	65.2	_____	_____	_____
1979	15.7	382.8	72.6	_____	_____	_____
1980	60.1	408.8	82.4	_____	_____	_____
1981	58.8	436.4	90.9	_____	_____	_____
1982	135.5	474.4	96.5	_____	_____	_____
1983	180.1	521.2	99.6	_____	_____	_____
1984	166.9	552.2	103.9	_____	_____	_____
1985	181.4	619.9	107.6	_____	_____	_____
1986	201.1	724.3	109.6	_____	_____	_____
1987	151.8	749.7	113.6	_____	_____	_____
1988	136.6	786.4	118.3	_____	_____	_____
1989	124.2	793.6	124	_____	_____	_____
1990	165.3	825.4	130.7	_____	_____	_____
1991	200.7	896.7	136.2	_____	_____	_____

your own. In your computations, assume that the money multiplier is equal to 3.00. (You should ask yourself how the value of the money multiplier affects the amount of inflation tax collected.) Now, on Chart 18-1*a*, graph the amount of inflation tax revenue against the budget deficit. On Chart 18-1*b*, plot the change in the inflation tax revenue against the change in the budget deficit; the first two points are plotted for you in each diagram. Can you draw any conclusions from these two diagrams?

REVIEW OF TECHNIQUE 18

Compound Interest

You may have heard of the "miracle of compound interest." When the interest on a debt is allowed to accumulate, together with the interest on the interest, and the interest on the interest on the interest, and so on, the total mounts up quickly. If you start off with P

CHART 18-1*a*

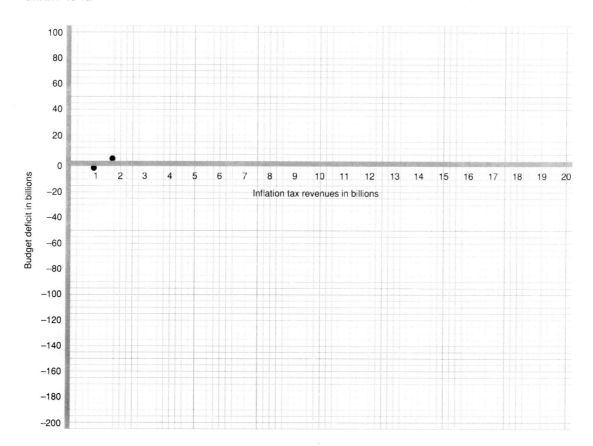

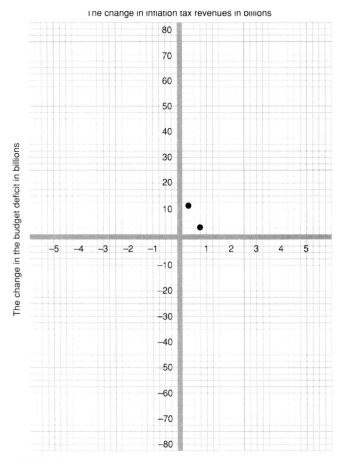

The change in inflation tax revenues in billions

CHART 18-1*b*

dollars and invest them at interest rate *r* for *t* years, you end up with a final value *FV* given by the formula

$$FV = P(1 + r)^t$$

For example, $1.00 invested at 5 percent for 1 year will give you back $1.00 × 1.05 = $1.05. Invested for 2 years, it would yield $1.00 × 1.05 × 1.05 = $1.1025. If you didn't receive the interest on the interest, then after 2 years you'd have received 10 cents in interest, rather than 10¼ cents. (This is called "simple interest.") A fourth of a cent doesn't seem worth making much of a fuss about compound interest, but if you held the investment for 30 years, simple interest would return your dollar plus $1.50 in interest while compound interest returns your dollar plus $3.32 in interest.

Sometimes you would like to know how long your money will take to double when invested at compound interest. A good rule of thumb is the "rule of 72s." The approximate number of years required for an investment to double is found by dividing 72 by the interest rate. For example, at 5 percent an investment doubles in about 14½ years; at 10 percent, in just over 7.

FILL-IN QUESTIONS

1. An extremely rapid inflation is called a(n) _____.

2. Government revenue from printing money results in what is sometimes called a(n) _____.

3. The revenue the government receives from printing money is also known as ____ _____.

4. Official deficit figures can be adjusted for the drop in the value of the national debt due to inflation to obtain the _____.

5. The _____ describes the connection between the nominal interest rate, the real interest rate, and the expected inflation rate.

6. The Federal Reserve has the discretion to _____ if it wishes.

7. Another name for the Fisher effect is the _____.

TRUE-FALSE QUESTIONS

T   F   1.   In the long run, growth of the money supply has a major effect on the price level.

T   F   2.   In the long run, growth of the money supply has a major effect on real output.

T   F   3.   In the long run, growth of the money supply has a major effect on nominal GDP.

T   F   4.   In the long run, growth of the money supply has a major effect on nominal interest rate.

T   F   5.   In the long run, growth of the money supply has a major effect on the real interest rate.

T   F   6.   Hyperinflations are always caused by very rapid money growth.

T   F   7.   Hyperinflations are usually accompanied by very large budget deficits.

T   F   8.   The U.S. budget deficit is financed largely by the Federal Reserve's "printing money."

T   F   9.   The economy responds to money growth with a lag of uncertain length.

T   F   10.   The nominal interest rate and the inflation rate are tightly linked.

MULTIPLE-CHOICE QUESTIONS

1. If the nominal money supply is growing at 6 percent a year while the real money supply is constant at $100 billion, then the "inflation tax" is
   a. $100 billion   c. $6 billion
   b. $60 billion   d. 0

2. When the rate of inflation is greater than the rate of money growth, the real money supply
   a. rises   c. remains constant
   b. falls   d. may do any of a, b, or c

3. A hyperinflation usually ends with
   a. a reduction of the budget deficit
   b. a reduction in the growth of the money supply
   c. a currency reform
   d. all of the above

4. An increase in the rate of growth of the money supply
   a. raises interest rates
   b. lowers interest rates
   c. first lowers, then raises interest rates
   d. first raises, then lowers interest rates

5. The Federal Reserve is likely to monetize the debt if it targets
   a. interest rates   c. either a or b
   b. the money supply   d. neither a nor b

6. The United States came close to suffering a hyperinflation
   a. in 1933   c. in 1979
   b. in 1945   d. never

7. As the inflation rate rises, the revenue from the "inflation tax"
   a. rises
   b. falls
   c. rises, but eventually starts to fall
   d. falls, but eventually starts to rise

8. An increase in the rate of money growth will eventually cause the real money supply to
   a. be higher
   b. be lower
   c. remain constant
   d. do any of a, b, or c, depending on the country

9. In the United States, at high inflation rates, we might expect the "inflation tax" as a fraction of GDP to be around
   a. 0.5 percent
   b. 5 percent
   c. 25 percent
   d. 50 percent

10. Compared with the speed of movement of the economy under adaptive expectations, the speed under rational expectations is
    a. faster
    b. slower
    c. faster, but adjustment is incomplete
    d. slower, but adjustment is more complete

PROBLEMS

1. What rate of money growth can the United States sustain without any inflation?

2. If the annual rate of inflation is 1,000 percent, what is the monthly rate of inflation? If the annual rate of inflation is 19,000 percent, what is the daily rate of inflation?

3. Suppose that the nominal interest rate is 50 percent per year, and the inflation rate is 48 percent per year. If you invest $100 today, what will be the real value of your investment in 10 years?

BUDGET DEFICITS AND THE PUBLIC DEBT

FOCUS OF THE CHAPTER

- The budget deficit became a major economic and political problem in the mid-1980s as the national debt grew more rapidly than GDP ever has during peacetime.

SECTION SUMMARIES

1. Federal Government Finances: Facts and Issues

Government expenditures consist of *mandatory* and *discretionary outlays*. Mandatory outlays, consisting mainly of entitlement programs, have doubled as a percentage of GDP since 1965. Discretionary expenditures, including defense outlays, have declined over the same period. Net interest payments have risen from 1.3 percent of GDP in 1965 to 3.1 percent in 1991. Federal government spending as a percentage of GDP has continually increased, reaching 25 percent in 1991.

Transfer payments, such as unemployment compensation, are not included in the definition of government purchases of goods and services, *G,* but do affect aggregate demand indirectly by altering household disposable income.

Most of the federal government's revenues are obtained from the personal income tax and from social insurance taxes on wage earners. As a source of revenue, the corporate income tax has declined in importance over time. Examination of government spending and revenue data over time indicates that our current deficit problem is a consequence of rising outlays, not falling revenues.

High and persistent budget deficits were a fact of economic life in the United States during the 1970s and 1980s. The deficit is composed of cyclical and structural components. The cyclical component represents the effects of the business cycle on the difference between government spending and revenues. Recessions are usually associated with an increase in the budget deficit as tax revenues fall in relation to spending. A rule of thumb is that each one-percentage-point increase in the unemployment rate is associated with a $25 billion to $30 billion increase in the budget deficit.

Taxes were cut below spending in the early 1980s, resulting in massive deficits. *Supply-siders* had argued that tax cuts could cause so large an incentive to work that the work force would increase greatly and income would rise sharply. Therefore tax collections would actually be higher at the low tax rates than at the high tax rates. Supply-side cuts do not appear to have raised work effort or saving; they have unquestionably increased the deficit. A political argument was also made that spending could be controlled only be controlling tax revenues.

The 1985 Gramm-Rudman-Hollings Act imposed maximum deficit ceilings with the intention of reducing the federal deficit to zero by 1991. In early 1989 it became apparent that the goals of the Gramm-Rudman-Hollings Act would not be achieved. More recently the Budget Enforcement Act of 1990 attempted to curtail spending and raise taxes. Our continuing experience with large deficits suggests these attempts have been unsuccessful.

2. The Mechanics of Financing the Budget

The *budget deficit* is the difference between government spending and tax receipts. The U.S. Treasury can finance the deficit in either of two ways:

    a. It can sell government bonds to the public.
    b. It can borrow from the central bank by selling bonds to the Fed.

When the government borrows from the Fed, the Fed lends newly "printed" high-powered money. Deficit financing through sale of bonds to the public does not affect the money stock. Financing through borrowing from the Fed increases high-powered money by the amount borrowed from the Fed. For this reason, deficit financing through sale of the debt to the Fed is called *monetizing the debt.* In the United States, the Fed independently decides on how much of the national debt it wishes to buy up; this is called accommodation. Therefore, there is no necessary connection between the government deficit and the money supply.

3. The Dynamics of Deficits and Debts

To highlight the significance of interest payments in generating a budget deficit, we decompose the total deficit into the *primary deficit*—noninterest outlays minus total government revenues—and interest payments. Since 1960, interest payments as a fraction of GDP have continued to rise, and since 1975, the noninterest budget has been in deficit. With a noninterest budget deficit, the total budget deficit will continue to grow as the government accumulates more debt just to pay the interest on previously outstanding bonds.

A useful measure of the magnitude of the debt relative to the size of the economy is the debt-GDP ratio. The debt-GDP ratio is growing, remaining constant, or shrinking as $b(r - y) + x$ is greater than, equal to, or less than zero. In the equation, b is the debt-income ratio, r is the real interest rate, y is the growth rate of real GDP, and x is the noninterest budget surplus measured as a fraction of nominal income. The debt-income ratio cannot continue to rise indefinitely without special actions, such as tax increases, or a large unanticipated inflation that wipes out the real value of the debt. In 1992 the United States was not in a position in which such drastic actions needed to be taken.

4. Economic Effects of Debt-Financed Deficits

Deficits can be either transitory or permanent and money-financed or debt-financed. Money-financed deficits cause a higher price level if transitory and a higher inflation rate if permanent. Transitory debt-financed deficits (which are more common in the United States than transitory money-financed deficits) partially crowd out private borrowing. A permanent real deficit cannot be financed purely by debt because interest payments would eventually become larger than GDP (unless the economy is growing faster than the debt).

One important question about debt financing is whether people regard government bonds as net wealth. Government bonds are certainly wealth to an individual, but consumers as a whole may feel their wealth is reduced by the future taxes they will have to pay to repay the debt. This latter idea is the basis of the *Barro-Ricardo equivalence* hypothesis, which states that a debt-financed tax cut cannot have any real effects on the economy.

5. The Burden of the Debt

The national debt, well over $4 trillion, seems like a great burden. However, as a nation, we owe a large portion of it to ourselves. (A growing portion of the debt is borrowed from people in other countries.) We also tend to forget that a significant fraction of the debt is offset by government assets, such as buildings and dams. The debt is an indirect burden if it results in a lower investment and thus lower long-term growth.

KEY TERMS

Budget deficit	Laffer curve
Public debt	Gramm-Rudman-Hollings Act
Debt financing	Barro-Ricardo equivalence
Entitlement spending	Discretionary spending
Debt-income ratio	Bracket creep

Tax indexation	Burden of the debt
Transfers	Money financing
Primary deficit	Intergenerational accounting
Noninterest deficit	

GRAPH IT 19

In the 1980s interest payments on the national debt became a substantial portion of federal government spending. Because a large part of the nominal interest payments go to cover inflation, rather than the real cost of interest, it can be hard to see how big the debt really is. Graph It 19 asks you to do a little inflation accounting to get a handle on this problem.

Tables 19-1 and 19-2 track the debt, using five rows of information. The row "Spending deficit" shows how much the government spent on goods and services in excess of its revenues. (Assume the government does all its spending on the first day of the year.) The row "Beginning debt" is last year's beginning debt plus last year's interest plus this year's spending deficit. The "Interest" row shows the interest due on the beginning debt plus the spending deficit. "Price level" records the price at the end of the year.

TABLE 19-1

Year	1	2	3	4	5
Spending deficit	$100.00	$100.00	$100.00	$100.00	$100.00
Beginning debt	100.00	202.00	_____	_____	_____
Interest	2.00	4.04	_____	_____	_____
Price level, end of year	1.00	1.00	_____	_____	_____
Real debt, end of year	102.00	206.04	_____	_____	_____

TABLE 19-2

Year	1	2	3	4	5
Spending deficit	$100.00	$110.00	$121.00	$133.10	$146.41
Beginning debt	100.00	222.00	_____	_____	_____
Interest	12.00	26.64	_____	_____	_____
Price level, end of year	1.10	1.21	_____	_____	_____
Real debt, end of year	101.82	205.49	_____	_____	_____

"Real debt" equals the spending deficit plus beginning debt plus interest, all deflated by the price level.

We want to know what difference inflation makes. Fill out the remainder of Table 19-1, which is based on zero inflation and a 2 percent interest rate. Then fill out Table 19-2, which is based on 10 percent inflation and a 12 percent interest rate. (Notice that the real spending deficit is the same in both cases.) What is the dollar difference in what the government owes by the end of year 5? How large is the difference?

REVIEW OF TECHNIQUE 19

Marginal Product

You will remember from your introductory economics course that *marginal product* is the amount of extra output that can be produced with one *extra* unit of input. In general, there are two ways to calculate a marginal product. One way is to calculate output for the production function you are given, add one more unit of input, and recalculate. Alternatively, if you are at home with calculus, you can take the derivative of production with respect to the input. In this review, we illustrate a simple way to use our previous work on logarithms to find the marginal product of capital for the Cobb-Douglas production function. Suppose we have the function

$$Y = AK^a N^{1-a} \qquad A = 1{,}000 \qquad a = 0.25$$

First, we directly calculate the marginal product for the case $K = 256$, $N = 81$. Initially, we calculate output.

$$Y = 1{,}000 \cdot (256)^{.25}(81)^{.75} = 1{,}000 \cdot (4) \cdot (27) = 108{,}000$$

Now, using a calculator, we recalculate with $K = 257$, and obtain

$$Y = 1{,}000 \cdot (4.004) \cdot (27) = 108{,}105$$

Thus the marginal product of capital is 105 (108, 105 − 108,000).

We can calculate this much more generally by using a couple of tricks with logarithms. Taking natural logs of both sides of the Cobb-Douglas function, we have

$$\ln Y = \ln A + a \ln K + (1 - a) \ln N$$

Now take the change in the logs of both sides:

$$\Delta \ln Y = a \Delta \ln K$$

We know that a change in a log is a percentage change, so that for any variable X,

$$\Delta \ln X = \frac{\Delta X}{X}$$

In this case,

$$\frac{\Delta Y}{Y} = \frac{a\Delta K}{K} \qquad \text{or} \qquad \frac{\Delta Y}{\Delta K} \equiv MPK = \frac{aY}{K}$$

Note that 0.25 (108,000)/256 equals 105.

FILL-IN QUESTIONS

1. The _____ is the difference between government expenditures and receipts.

2. The _____ is the net accumulation over the years of the difference between government expenditures and receipts.

3. The sale of government bonds by the Treasury to the Fed is called _____ _____ .

4. The method of government financing through sales of debt to the public is called _____ .

5. The method of government financing through sales of debt to the Fed is called _____ .

6. The part of the deficit not including interest payments is called the _____ or _____ .

7. In an attempt to reduce deficits in the second half of the 1980s, Congress passed the _____ .

8. The notion that the average person in the United States is responsible for $16,000 in government debt is known as _____ .

TRUE-FALSE QUESTIONS

T   F   1. A budget surplus is a negative budget deficit.

T   F   2. The government budget deficit is a flow.

T   F   3. The national debt is a stock.

T   F   4. A deficit necessarily leads to an increase in the money supply.

T   F   5. The Fed buys bonds from the Treasury by "printing" more $M1$.

T   F   6.   Interest payments on the debt themselves increase the current deficit.

T   F   7.   State and local governments, like the federal government, can finance their deficits either by issuing bonds or by having the Fed print more money.

MULTIPLE-CHOICE QUESTIONS

1. The deficit is $35 billion per year with an initial national debt of $700 billion. If no money is printed, what will the level of the national debt be in 3 years?
    a. $105 billion
    b. $700 billion
    c. $735 billion
    d. $805 billion

2. The federal government is mostly paid for by
    a. the individual income tax
    b. the Fed
    c. the corporate income tax
    d. the Social Security tax

3. If the budget surplus is $100 billion and the government sells $10 billion in bonds to the public, high-powered money
    a. increases by $100 billion
    b. remains constant
    c. falls by $100 billion
    d. falls by $110 billion

4. Since the 1960s, federal revenues as a fraction of GDP have
    a. fallen slightly
    b. remained about fixed
    c. risen slightly
    d. risen sharply

5. Since the 1960s, state and local expenditures as a fraction of GDP have
    a. fallen slightly
    b. remained fixed
    c. risen slightly
    d. risen sharply

6. Total federal expenditure as a fraction of GDP is about
    a. 10 percent
    b. 25 percent
    c. 40 percent
    d. 60 percent

7. The largest slice of the federal budget goes for
    a. defense
    b. benefit payments to individuals
    c. grants to state and local governments
    d. interest payments on the national debt

8. The most rapidly growing source of federal revenue has been
    a. the individual income tax
    b. the corporate income tax
    c. tariff revenue
    d. Social Security and similar taxes

9. Since World War II, the national debt as a fraction of GDP has
   a. dropped drastically, but has recently started to rise
   b. remained roughly constant
   c. risen drastically, then leveled off
   d. been level, but has recently risen rapidly

PROBLEMS

1. Since the U.S economy is growing, some level of primary deficit is sustainable without causing the ratio of debt to national income to rise. Assume that over some long period of time the real interest rate in the United States is about 2 percent per year and that the rate of GDP growth is about 2.7 percent per year. How large a primary deficit (as a fraction of GDP) can the government run without an increase in the debt-to-income ratio?

2. Suppose that the government ran a budget deficit of $200 billion one year. Rather than paying it off the following year, the government borrows enough extra to pay the interest on the debt. The government keeps up this policy for 10 years and then pays off the entire accumulated debt. How much will it owe if it has been paying 2 percent interest per year? (*Hint:* See Review of Technique 18 on compound interest problems.)

3. Consider a simple macroeconomic model of the kind encountered in Chapter 3.

$$C = 80 + 0.9YD$$
$$YD = Y + TA - TR$$
$$Y = C + I + G$$

where $I = 600$ and G, TA, and TR are initially zero.

   a. Determine GDP and consumption.
   b. Suppose that the government conducts a one-year road construction program that costs 50 and is financed entirely by tax collections. Calculate GDP for this and all future years.
   c. Now suppose that the government issues 10 percent Consols instead of raising taxes. The interest on such bonds is paid forever, while the principal is never repaid. Calculate GDP and consumption for this and all future years.
   d. What is the difference between the policies in a and b in terms of their effects on current and future GDP and consumption? Is behavior in this model consistent with Ricardian equivalence? Explain.

INTERNATIONAL ADJUSTMENT AND INTERDEPENDENCE

FOCUS OF THE CHAPTER

- Exchange rates have been allowed to float since 1973. This chapter analyzes the workings of the domestic and world economies when exchange rates are determined by supply and demand.

  1. The model of Chapter 6 is extended to emphasize the role of money.
  2. We look at a world in which all prices are flexible in order to study the determinants of the exchange rate itself.

- Later sections extend these results and consider some of the practical consequences. We explore the role of exchange rate expectations and the relations between interest rates in different countries. We also look at the interdependence between countries and the role of exchange rate intervention by central banks.

SECTION SUMMARIES

1. Adjustments under Fixed Exchange Rates

With a fixed exchange rate and a fixed foreign price level, an increase (decrease) in the domestic price level reduces (increases) foreign demand for domestically produced goods and increases (reduces) the domestic demand for imports.

Aggregate demand is the sum of domestic aggregate demand, A, and the net exports, NX. The trade balance schedule, $NX = 0$, is downward sloping when drawn against the domestic price level and domestic income (Figure 20-1). To the right (left) of the trade balance schedule there exists a current account deficit (surplus).

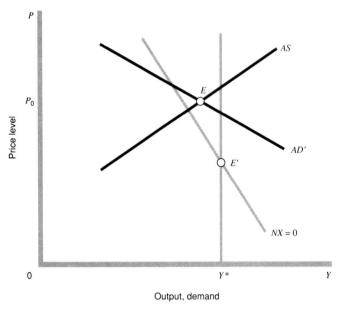

FIGURE 20-1

The short-run equilibrium (point E) in Figure 20-1 shows a situation in which the current account is in deficit and the economy is below full employment. With a fixed exchange rate, a current account deficit means that the central bank is depleting its reserves of foreign exchange. This situation cannot persist. A cut in aggregate demand coupled with an increase in aggregate supply can move the economy to full employment and trade balance at the point E'.

Without policy intervention, automatic adjustment mechanisms will move the economy from E to E'. On the aggregate demand side, the central bank's policy of pegging the exchange rate while the economy is running a current account deficit leads to a reduction in the domestic money supply. The result is a leftward shift of the aggregate demand curve. As prices fall, wages fall, and the aggregate supply curve shifts down. The automatic nature of this adjustment process gives it the name *classical adjustment process*.

Sometimes conflicts exist between the goal of achieving domestic full employment (internal balance) and the goal of achieving a trade (external) balance. Figure 20-2 shows the trade balance schedule and a vertical line at full employment. The two lines divide the quadrant into four regions, each region corresponding to some combination of recession/boom and trade surplus/deficit. At point A, policy makers face a policy dilemma. Any policy that shifts aggregate demand and cuts through A moves the economy closer to external (internal) balance at the expense of internal (external) balance. The government must find policies to shift the trade balance schedule rightward—for example, by levying tariffs on imported goods or by devaluing the home currency. These are expenditure-switching polices. Whatever the solution chosen, policy dilemmas cannot be solved using one policy instrument. As a rule, policy makers need as many policy instruments as they have targets in order to achieve their goals.

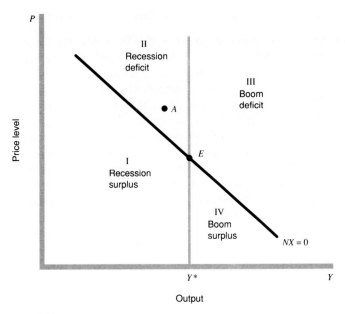

FIGURE 20-2

2. Exchange Rate Changes and Trade Adjustment: Empirical Issues

If real wages are sticky, as they may be in economies with substantial wage indexation, the adjustment mechanisms intended to bring an economy into equilibrium may break down. Another important qualification to the model of this chapter is the *J curve*. When our currency depreciates, we import fewer goods, but we pay more for each good. Thus, in dollar terms, total imports may increase. The empirical evidence is quite strong that, in fact, in the short run the total value of imports does increase, but in the long run the volume effect is more important and imports do decrease.

3. The Monetary Approach to the Balance of Payments

The monetary approach to the balance of payments is based on the belief that balance of payments deficits are mainly a result of excessive monetary growth. Proponents of the monetary approach charge that central banks often respond to the contractionary effects of a balance of payments deficit (under fixed exchange rates) with a sterilization policy. Sterilization leads to persistent balance of payment deficits.

The monetary approach prescribes a contraction of domestic credit to reduce the balance of payments deficit. Such a policy has a short-run cost of higher domestic interest rates and lower domestic income.

4. Flexible Exchange Rates, Money, and Prices

In this section, we allow for long-run price flexibility. We also assume that there is perfect capital mobility. This means that in the short run, the economy can be away from potential GDP. We are always on the *BB* schedule.

We are used to a monetary expansion increasing GDP through a decreased interest rate. The mechanism here is a little different. Since capital is perfectly mobile, the domestic interest rate is fixed equal to the world interest rate. When the money supply increases now, the exchange rate immediately depreciates until the *IS* curve has moved enough so that it crosses the new *LM* curve on the *BB* schedule, as in Figure 20-3. In the long run, prices rise just enough to return the real money supply to its initial level. This increase in the price level also offsets the depreciation of the exchange rate so that competitiveness, *eP**/*P*, returns to its initial level. GDP returns to potential. Because exchange rates adjust rapidly and prices adjust slowly, the adjustment to long-run equilibrium involves great variations in relative prices and competitiveness.

The concept of *purchasing power parity* (PPP) suggests that the terms of trade, *eP**/*P*, should remain constant. Consider the price of German-made and U.S.-made Volkswagens. If the two cars are identical, they ought to sell for the same price. We should have *eP**/*P* equal 1. If the two cars are truly different, then the relative price might persist at 1.2:1. Purchasing power parity asserts that the terms of trade depend on the true relative values of domestic and foreign goods, not on monetary changes. Purchasing power parity is quite appealing in the long run, but there are substantial deviations from PPP in the short-run.

FIGURE 20-3

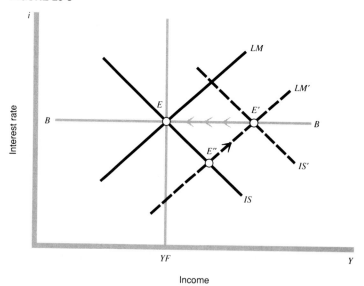

5. Interest Differentials and Exchange Rate Expectations

Interest rates in different countries are often quite different. This disparity is due to expectations of exchange rate changes. Suppose the U.S. interest rate is 10 percent and the German interest rate is 8 percent, while the dollar is expected to depreciate by 2 percent over the coming year. Investors could invest money in the United States and earn 10 percent directly. Alternatively, they could buy deutsche marks, make a German investment, and earn 8 percent. But now, when the marks are turned back into dollars, they cost 2 percent less, so investors get 2 percent more dollars. The 8 percent plus the 2 percent gives the same 10 percent dollar yield.

6. Exchange Rate Fluctuations and Interdependence

In practice, the present system of foreign exchange is one of *dirty floating*. Central banks *intervene* from time to time in order to influence the exchange rate. It is often argued that governments ought to intervene to smooth out temporary fluctuations; unfortunately, it is nearly impossible to know whether an exchange rate fluctuation is temporary or permanent.

It used to be argued that floating exchange rates allowed nations to pursue totally independent macroeconomic policies. We now know that *spillover* effects are caused by the changes in a nation's competitive position. Thus *interdependence* suggests that countries can benefit from coordination of macroeconomic policies.

KEY TERMS

Real exchange rate
Expenditure-switching policies
Expenditure-reducing policies
Policy dilemmas
Monetary approach
Sterilization
Devaluation
Competitiveness
Policy coordination

Exchange rate overshooting
Exchange rate expectations
Purchasing power parity
J curve
Intervention
Dirty float
Interdependence
Crawling peg
Synchronization

GRAPH IT 20

The text tells us that imports rise when GDP rises or when the value of the dollar rises. In this Graph It, we ask you to see whether that is true—but we don't want you to draw a graph. Instead, we ask you to use the computer to examine the relation between imports, GDP, and the value of the dollar. Since you can't draw a three-dimensional graph, we ask you to run regressions on a computer, using the data in Table 20-1. (If you don't have easy access to a computer with a regression program, just flip to the answer section.)

TABLE 20-1

BILLIONS OF 1987 DOLLARS

Year	GDP	Exports	Imports	Value of dollar
1967	2,690.3	130.0	153.7	120.0
1968	2,801.0	140.2	177.7	122.1
1969	2,877.1	147.8	189.2	122.4
1970	2,875.8	161.3	196.4	121.1
1971	2,965.1	161.9	207.8	117.8
1972	3,107.1	173.7	230.2	109.1
1973	3,268.6	210.3	244.4	99.1
1974	3,248.1	234.4	238.4	101.4
1975	3,221.7	232.9	209.9	98.5
1976	3,380.8	243.4	249.7	105.6
1977	3,533.2	246.9	274.7	103.3
1978	3,703.5	270.2	300.1	92.4
1979	3,796.8	293.5	304.1	88.1

SOURCE: *Economic Report of the President*

Estimate the following three relations:

$$\text{Imports} = \text{constant} + aY$$
$$\text{Imports} = \text{constant} + b \times \text{value of the dollar}$$
$$\text{Imports} = \text{constant} + aY + b \times \text{value of the dollar}$$

What values do you find for *a* and *b?*

REVIEW OF TECHNIQUE 20

Triangular Arbitrage

We always quote bilateral exchange rates in terms of the dollar; 60 cents per mark and 20 cents per franc, for example. What is the mark-franc exchange rate? Obviously, it must be 3 francs per mark. Suppose it is only 2 francs per mark. You could then take $1 and buy 5 francs. You could take the 5 francs and get 2½ marks. These marks could be turned into $1.50. Now you could take the $1.50 and go around the triangle again and make even more profit. This is called *triangular arbitrage.* If the franc were worth 4 marks, a profit could be made by going around the triangle in the other direction. The only mark-franc exchange rate that prevents infinite arbitrage profits is 3 francs per mark.

FILL-IN QUESTIONS

1. Proponents of the monetary approach to the balance of payments believe that _____ has been a major cause of chronic balance of payments deficits in a number of countries.

2. A(n) _____ exists when a government's goals of internal and external balance are in conflict with each other.

3. It is possible for _____ to improve the performance of a group of interdependent economies.

4. _____ consists of the monetary authority's claims on the public and private sectors.

5. If the relative prices of goods in two countries, adjusted for the exchange rate, are constant, we say there is _____.

6. The _____ shows the response over time of imports to a devaluation.

7. The value of the dollar relative to its purchasing power in other countries is the _____.

8. The important linkages between countries cause _____, or _____, effects.

9. A policy that aims to encourage consumption of domestic goods and discourage imports is called a(n) _____.

TRUE-FALSE QUESTIONS

T F 1. Exchange rates adjust in order to keep the relative price of imports and domestically produced goods from changing.

T F 2. If the dollar appreciates, with prices of domestic goods fixed both in the United States and in Germany, German goods become more expensive in the United States.

T F 3. An increase in the exchange rate increases domestic aggregate demand.

T F 4. An increase in German prices increases U.S. aggregate demand.

T F 5. An increase in world interest rates causes U.S. interest rates to rise.

T F 6. With perfect capital mobility, U.S. interest rates must equal world interest rates.

T F 7. With perfect capital mobility, GDP must equal potential GDP.

T F 8. If purchasing power parity holds between two countries, then changes in exchange rates just offset the difference in the inflation experienced in the two countries.

T   F   9. Given enough time, the economy will reach full employment and bal-
             ance of trade equilibrium without direct government intervention.

MULTIPLE-CHOICE QUESTIONS

1. If the typical German good cost 1,000 marks and the typical U.S. good cost $250,
   and if the exchange rate is 25 cents, the terms of trade are
   a. 4 to 1   c. 1 to 1
   b. 1 to 4   d. 16 to 1

2. If German prices increase 10 percent while the dollar depreciates by 10 percent,
   constant U.S. prices would imply that relative prices
   a. increased 10 percent   c. remained constant
   b. increased 20 percent   d. fell 20 percent

3. If the value of the yen increases and the value of the mark decreases, then the effective exchange rate of the dollar
   a. increases
   b. remains unchanged
   c. decreases
   d. cannot be determined from the information given

4. If purchasing power parity always holds, and if the current exchange rate is 25 cents
   per mark, and if the exchange rate in the next year is also expected to be 25 cents,
   German inflation over the year must be expected to be _____
   U.S. inflation.
   a. greater than
   b. the same as
   c. less than
   d. indeterminable because of insufficient information

5. Empirical evidence shows that following a devaluation, the dollar value of imports
   a. rises, then falls   c. remains unchanged
   b. falls, then rises   d. rises

6. Capital flows into the United States when the U.S. interest rate (adjusted for expected changes in the exchange rate) is _____ foreign inter-
   est rates.
   a. greater than
   b. equal to
   c. less than
   d. capital never flows into the United States

7. With flexible prices and perfect capital mobility, the economy
   a. is always at potential GDP and has a current account balance
   b. is always at potential GDP and need not have a current account balance
   c. need not be at potential GDP and must have a current account balance
   d. need not be at potential GDP or have a current account balance

8. If the economy is initially in a recession and is running a trade deficit, the economy will eventually return to both internal and external balance without government intervention and with
   a. higher prices
   b. unchanged prices
   c. lower prices
   d. higher imports

PROBLEMS

1. The interest rate in Germany is 10 percent, and the interest rate in the United States is 12 percent. If the current value of the mark is 50 cents, what is the exchange rate expected to be in a year?

2. Assume the dollar per pound exchange rate is quoted at 1.5 and the dollar per mark at 0.4. Is there an opportunity for triangular arbitrage if the mark per pound exchange rate is quoted at 2? Refer to Review of Technique for this chapter.

ANSWERS TO QUESTIONS AND PROBLEMS

CHAPTER 1

Graph It 1

CHART 1-1
PERCENTAGE CHANGE IN GDP

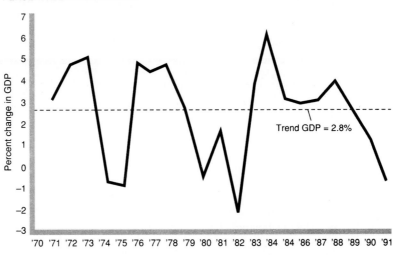

TABLE 1-1

Year	GDP	Percent change from previous year
1970	2,875.8	
1971	2,965.1	3.11
1972	3,107.1	4.79
1973	3,268.6	5.20
1974	3,248.1	−0.63
1975	3,221.7	−0.81
1976	3,380.8	4.94
1977	3,533.2	4.51
1978	3,703.5	4.82
1979	3,796.8	2.52
1980	3,776.3	−0.54
1981	3,843.1	1.77
1982	3,760.3	−2.15
1983	3,906.6	3.89
1984	4,148.5	6.19
1985	4,279.8	3.16
1986	4,405.5	2.94
1987	4,540.0	3.05
1988	4,718.6	3.93
1989	4,836.9	2.51
1990	4,884.9	0.99
1991	4,848.4	−0.75

Fill-In Questions

1. potential output
2. output gap
3. trough
4. fiscal
5. monetary
6. stabilization policies
7. Okun's law
8. recovery or expansion
9. recessions
10. aggregate demand

True-False Questions

1. False. Okun's law says that when GDP goes up, employment goes down.
2. True.
3. False. It's a "forest" chapter.

CHAPTER 2

Graph It 2

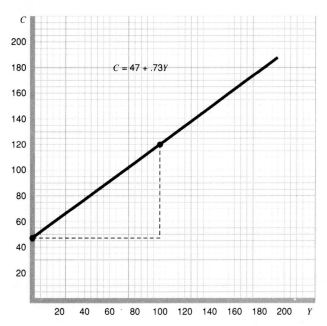

CHART 2-2

Fill-In Questions

1. gross domestic product (GDP)
2. depreciation (capital consumption allowance)
3. market prices, factor costs
4. consumed, saved
5. transfers, taxes
6. measure of economic welfare (MEW)
7. GDP deflator
8. assets, liabilities
9. the budget deficit, the foreign trade surplus
10. exports, imports

True-False Questions

1. False. Investment equals private savings plus the government budget surplus minus net exports.
2. False. Sale of a home just transfers assets from one person to another. No *new* production is added.
3. True.
4. True.
5. False. An individual can't spend the part of production that is needed to replace worn-out machines.
6. False. By "investment" we mean buying new productive equipment, not financial investment.
7. True.
8. False. Net national worth represents ownership of assets, wherever located.
9. True.
10. True.

Multiple-Choice Questions

1. b   2. d   3. b   4. a   5. d   6. a   7. d   8. d   9. b   10. c

Worked-Out Problems

1. $BD = G + TR - TA = 0$; therefore $G = TA - TR = 300$
   $YD = C + S = 1,000 + 100 = 1,100$
   $YD = Y - TA + TR = 1,100 = Y - 300$
   Therefore, GDP equals $1,400.

2. $TA - TR - G = I - S + NX$
   $-50 = I - 200 - 10$
   $I = \$160$

3. $I = Y - C - G - NX = 150$
   $S = BD + NX + I = 290$
   Therefore, $YD = C + S = 790$

4. $YD = Y + TR - TA = 520$
   $S = YD - C = 170$
   Therefore, $NX = S - I - BD = -100$
   Net national worth will fall as the economy sells off assets to pay for the persistent trade deficit. Disposable income will fall, since foreigners rather than domestic residents receive the interest payments from a positive foreign asset position.

CHAPTER 3

Graph It 3

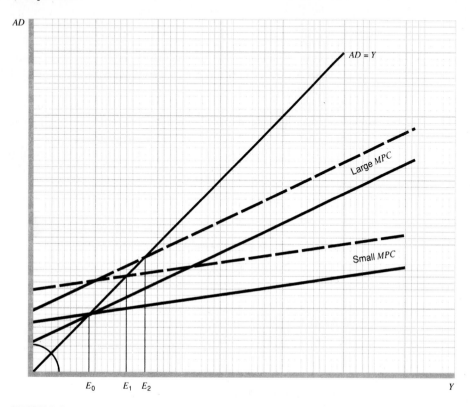

CHART 3-1

Fill-In Questions

1. equilibrium
2. the consumption function
3. marginal propensity to consume (*MPC*)
4. marginal propensity to save (*MPS*)
5. multiplier
6. budget deficit (*BD*)
7. automatic stabilizer
8. full-employment budget surplus (*BS**)
9. 1
10. planned saving, actual investment

True-False Questions

1. True.
2. False. More taxes mean lower disposable income, less consumption, and thus lower GDP.
3. True.
4. True.
5. False. The budget surplus increases because GDP and thus taxes rise. However, potential GDP doesn't change, and so the full-employment budget surplus doesn't change.
6. False.
7. False. The higher MPC means a larger multiplier and thus higher GDP.
8. True.
9. False. GDP will go up by $1/[1 - c(1 - t)] \cdot \Delta G$ because of the increase in G and down by $c/[1 - c(1 - t)] \cdot \Delta G$ because of the drop in TR. Thus the net effect is an increase of $(1 - c)/(1 - c + ct) \cdot \Delta G$.
10. False. This is just the opposite of having a high MPC.

Multiple-Choice Questions

1. c   2. a   3. b   4. b   5. a   6. b   7. c   8. a   9. d   10. b

Worked-Out Problems

1. $C = C + cY_d$
   $Y_d = Y - TA$

   Combining the two equations yields
   $C = C + c(Y - TA)$
   $Y \equiv C + I + G$

   Combining the two equations yields
   $Y = C + c(Y - TA) + I + G$
   $Y - cY = C - cTA + I + G$

   $$Y = \frac{1}{1 - c}(C + I + G) - \frac{c}{1 - c} TA$$

   $$= \frac{1}{1 - 0.9}(100 + 200 + 500) - \frac{0.9}{1 - 0.9} 400$$

   $$= \$4,400$$

2. First, we need to calculate the appropriate multiplier. The income tax is $TA = tY$. Disposable income is $Y - tY$, or $(1 - t)Y$. Thus the consumption function is

   $$C = C + c(1 - t)Y$$

Combining this with the aggregate demand identity gives us

$$Y = C + c(1 - t)Y + I + G$$
$$Y[1 - c(1 - t)] = C + I + G$$
$$Y = \frac{1}{1 - c(1 - t)}(C + I + G)$$

Since autonomous consumption and investment do not change in this problem, we can rewrite the equation as

$$\Delta Y = \frac{1}{1 - c(1 - t)} \Delta G$$

The value of the multiplier is $\dfrac{1}{1 - 0.9(\frac{2}{3})} = \dfrac{1}{1 - 0.6} = 2.5$

$$\Delta Y = 2.5\Delta G$$
$$750 = 2.5\Delta G$$
$$\Delta G = 750/2.5 = \$300$$

The change in the budget deficit is the change in government spending minus the change in tax collections. Government spending goes up $300. Since income goes up $750 and the marginal tax rate is 33 percent, tax collections go up by $250. The budget deficit goes up by $50.

3. This problem essentially needs to be worked backward. We start by analyzing the sources of change in the budget deficit.

$$BD = G - TA$$
$$\Delta BD = \Delta G - \Delta TA$$

In question 3a, investment changes. This changes income and tax collections. Government spending does not change.

$$\Delta BD = 0 - \Delta TA$$
$$TA = tY \quad \text{so} \quad \Delta TA = \Delta tY = t\Delta Y$$
$$\Delta BD = t\Delta Y$$
$$15 = \frac{1}{3}Y$$

We see that a $15 increase in the budget deficit implies that GDP fell by $45. The only remaining step is to see how large a change in investment would cause a $45 drop in income. From the previous problem, we know that the multiplier on investment is 2.5. Therefore, the change in investment must have been −45/2.5. Investment dropped by $18.

In b, both government spending and tax collection are changing.

$$\Delta BD = \Delta G - t\Delta Y$$

We know from the preceding problem that $\Delta Y = 2.5\Delta G$.

$\Delta BD = G - (\frac{1}{3})2.5\Delta G = [1 - (\frac{1}{3})2.5]\Delta G = \frac{1}{6}\Delta G$
$\Delta G = 6\Delta BD = 6(15) = \$90$

This illustrates one of the fundamental findings of macroeconomics. An increase in the budget deficit can result from either a dropoff in economic activity or an increase in government spending.

4. $NX = 20 - 0.1Y = 0$ implies that $Y = 200$.
$\quad Y = 200 = C + \bar{I} + \bar{G}$
$\qquad\quad = 60 + 150(1 + t)$
$\quad t = \frac{1}{15}$
$\quad BS = (\frac{1}{15})(200) - 15 = -1.67$

CHAPTER 4

Graph It 4

Chart 4-1 and the accompanying Table 4-1 clearly show that loose money is associated with low unemployment, and vice versa.

TABLE 4-1

Year	Unemployment	M1	CPI	M1/P
1980	7.1	408.8	82.4	4.96
1981	7.6	436.4	90.9	4.80
1982	9.7	474.4	96.5	4.92
1983	9.6	521.2	99.6	5.23
1984	7.5	552.2	103.9	5.31
1985	7.2	619.9	107.6	5.76
1986	7.0	724.3	109.6	6.61
1987	6.2	749.7	113.6	6.60
1988	5.5	786.4	118.3	6.65
1989	5.3	793.6	124.0	6.40
1990	5.5	825.4	130.7	6.32
1991	6.7	896.7	136.2	6.58

SOURCE: *Economic Report of the President*, 1991.

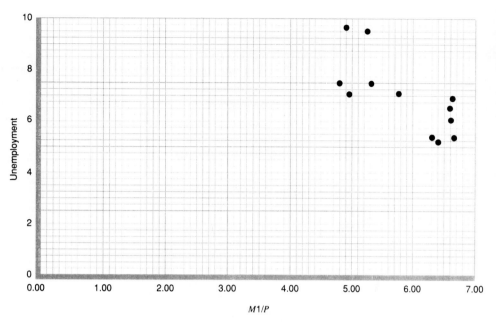

CHART 4-1

Fill-In Questions

1. income, interest rate
2. goods
3. assets, or money
4. open market purchase
5. demand for
6. investment
7. real balances
8. equilibrium
9. fiscal policy multiplier
10. monetary policy multiplier

True-False Questions

1. True.
2. True.
3. True.
4. False. The *IS* curve has a negative slope.
5. False.

6. False. Interest rates go up, and so investment goes down.
7. False. Transfers change A by less than government purchases change A, and so the *IS* curve is moved farther to the right by G than by *TR*.
8. False. Tax rates enter the multiplier and thus affect the slope of the *IS* curve.
9. False.
10. False. The fiscal policy multiplier determines this.

Multiple-Choice Questions

1. c   2. b   3. b   4. a   5. c   6. b   7. c   8. b   9. b   10. a

Worked-Out Problems

1. a. *IS:* $Y = 100 + 0.8(Y - 500) = \bar{I} - 1{,}000i + 550$
    $Y(1 - 0.8) = 250 + \bar{I} - 1{,}000i$
    $Y = 1{,}250 + 5\bar{I} - 5{,}000i$

    Note that we use I in place of 200 because autonomous investment changes in part c of this question.
    LM: $M/P = Y - 1{,}000i$

    b. Substituting the *IS* curve into the *LM* curve,

    $M/P = 1{,}250 + 5\bar{I} - 5{,}000i - 10{,}000i$
    $i = [1{,}250 + 5\bar{I} - (M/P)]/15{,}000$
    $= 0.09$

    Substituting the equation for the interest rate back into the *IS* curve,

    $Y = 1{,}250 + 5\bar{I} - 5{,}000[1{,}250 + 5\bar{I} - (M/P)]/15{,}000$
    $= (\frac{2}{3})(1{,}250 + 5\bar{I}) + (M/P)/3$
    $= \$1{,}800$

    Disposable income equals $\$1{,}800 - \$500$, or $\$1{,}300$. Inserting this into the consumption function, we can calculate that consumption is $\$1{,}140$. Putting the interest rate into the investment function, we find that investment is $\$110$. Note that we now have a check on our calculations: $C + I + G = 1{,}100 + 110 + 550 = 1{,}800 = Y$, as it should.

    c. Using the formulas derived in solving part b, we see that the fiscal policy multiplier is 10/3. Therefore, GDP drops by $\$300$. The interest rate multiplier of autonomous spending is 1/3,000, and so the interest rate drops by 3 percent. This increases investment by $\$30$. The induced increase of $\$30$ plus the autonomous drop of $\$90$ mean the overall investment drops by $\$60$.

d. We need to increase Y by $300. The monetary policy multiplier is 1/3. Therefore, we need to increase the money supply by $900. Using the equation for the interest rate, we see that this will decrease the interest rate by an additional 6 percent.

e. See Figures *a, b, c.*

FIGURES *a, b, c*

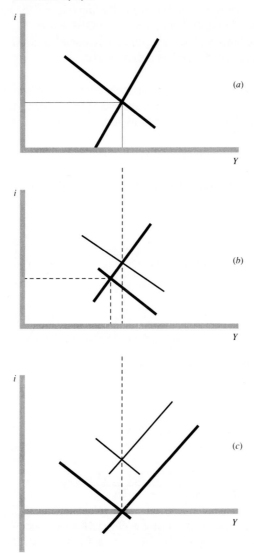

2. a. The consumption function is $C = 100 + 0.9(Y - Y/3) = 100 = 0.6Y$
    The *IS* curve is $Y = 2,500 - 2,500i$

    The equilibrium equations for interest and income are

    $i = 0.20 - 0.00008(M/P)$
    $Y = 2,000 + 0.2 \ (M/P)$

    The initial interest rate is 16 percent. Putting this into the investment function, we find that investment equals $40 and GDP equals $2,100. Taxes are one-third of income, and so tax collections come to $700. Since government spending is $710, the budget deficit is $10.

    b. In order to balance the budget, tax collections would have to rise by $10. This implies that GDP would have to rise by $30. Since the monetary policy multiplier is 0.2, the money supply must increase by $150.

3. Solve the model using the traditional specification of money demand.

    IS: $Y = \bar{C} + c(1 - t)Y + \bar{I} - bi + \bar{G}$
    $\quad = (\bar{C} + \bar{I} + \bar{G}) + c(1 - t)Y - bi$

    Solve for *i*:

    $$i = \frac{\bar{C} + \bar{I} + \bar{G}}{b} - \frac{[1 - c(1 - t)]Y}{b}$$

    LM: $= \frac{\bar{M}}{\bar{P}} = kY - hi$

    $$i = \frac{k}{h} Y - \frac{1}{h} \frac{\bar{M}}{\bar{P}}$$

    Substituting the *IS* curve into the *LM* curve,

    $$\frac{\bar{C} + \bar{I} + \bar{G}}{b} - \frac{[1 - c(1 - t)]Y}{b} = \frac{k}{h} Y - \frac{1}{h} \frac{\bar{M}}{\bar{P}}$$

    $$\left[\frac{k}{h} + \frac{1 - c(1 - t)}{b}\right] Y = \frac{kb + h[1 - c(1 - t)]}{kb} Y$$

    $$= \frac{\bar{C} + \bar{I} + \bar{G}}{b} - \frac{1}{h} \frac{\bar{M}}{\bar{P}}$$

$$Y = \frac{k(\bar{C} + \bar{I} + \bar{G})}{kb + h[1 - c(1 - t)]} + \frac{b\bar{M}/\bar{P}}{kb + h[1 - c(1 - t)]}$$

where

$$\frac{k}{kb + h[1 - c(1 - t)]} \quad \text{and} \quad \frac{b}{kb + h[1 - c(1 - t)]}$$

are the fiscal and monetary policy multipliers, respectively.
Next, solve the model using the special specification for money demand.
The *IS* curve is unchanged:

$$i = \frac{\bar{C} + \bar{I} + \bar{G}}{b} - \frac{[1 - c(1 - t)]Y}{b}$$

$$LM: \frac{\bar{M}}{\bar{P}} = kC - hi = k[\bar{C} + c(1 - t)Y] - hi$$

$$= k\bar{C} + kc(1 - t)Y - hi$$

Solve for *i*:

$$i = \frac{k}{h}\bar{C} + \frac{kc(1 - t)}{h}Y - \frac{1}{h}\frac{\bar{M}}{\bar{P}}$$

Substituting the *IS* curve into the *LM* curve,

$$\frac{\bar{C} + \bar{I} + \bar{G}}{b} - \frac{[1 - c(1 - t)]Y}{b} = \frac{k}{h}\bar{C} + \frac{kc(1 - t)}{h}Y - \frac{1}{h}\frac{\bar{M}}{\bar{P}}$$

$$\left[\frac{1 - c(1 - t)}{b} + \frac{kc(1 - t)}{h}\right]Y = \frac{\{k[1 - c(1 - t)] + kbc(1 - t)\}Y}{bk}$$

$$= \frac{\bar{C} + \bar{I} + \bar{G}}{b} - \frac{k\bar{C}}{h} - \frac{1}{h}\frac{\bar{M}}{\bar{P}}$$

$$Y = \frac{\bar{C}(h - kb) + k(\bar{I} + \bar{G})}{kbc(1 - t) + h[1 - c(1 - t)]} + \frac{b\bar{M}/\bar{P}}{kbc(1 - t) + h[1 - c(1 - t)]}$$

where

$$\frac{k}{kbc(1 - t) + h[1 - c(1 - t)]} \quad \text{and} \quad \frac{b}{kbc(1 - t) + h[1 - c(1 - t)]}$$

are the fiscal and monetary policy multipliers, respectively, for an economy with consumption as an argument in the money demand function. Since $c(1 - t) < 1$, both multipliers are larger with consumption than with income as an argument in the money demand function. Fiscal policy is more powerful because replacing GDP with consumption in the money demand function effectively lowers the income elasticity of money demand and thus makes the *LM* curve flatter. The flatter the *LM* curve, the weaker the crowding-out effect following an increase in government spending. Monetary policy is more powerful in the special case because the lower the effective income elasticity of money demand, the greater the increase in income needed to offset an increase in money supply to clear the money market. Note that the horizontal shift of the *LM* curve is greater than in the traditional model:

$$\frac{\bar{M}/\bar{P}}{kc(1 - t)} > \frac{\bar{M}/\bar{P}}{k}$$

CHAPTER 5

Graph It 5

See Chart 5-1.

Fill-In Questions

1. monetary policy multiplier
2. fiscal policy multiplier
3. crowding out
4. monetary accommodation
5. monetary-fiscal policy mix, composition of output
6. liquidity trap
7. classical case

True-False Questions

1. False. The effectiveness of monetary policy depends on the movement of the *LM* curve and the slope of the *IS* curve.
2. False. The effectiveness of fiscal policy depends on the movement of the *IS* curve and the slope of the *LM* curve.
3. True.
4. True.
5. False. At higher GDP, tax collections are higher and thus the budget deficit is lower.

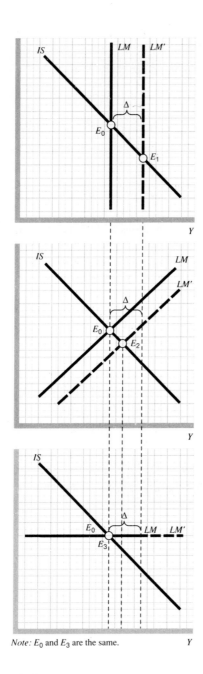

Note: E_0 and E_3 are the same.

CHART 5-1

Multiple-Choice Questions

1. b   2. d   3. c   4. b   5. a   6. d   7. c   8. b   9. a   10. c

Worked-Out Problems

1. We know that the multiplier on autonomous spending, A, is given by

$$\frac{h\alpha}{h + kb\alpha}$$

All we need figure out is what happens to A. Transfers enter A through the consumption function and are multiplied by the marginal propensity to consume. A goes up by c dollars for each dollar increase in transfers in part a of the question and by $c(1 - t)$ dollars for each dollar increase in transfers in part b. Thus, the transfer policy multipliers are

a. $\dfrac{ch\alpha}{h + kb\alpha}$ b. $\dfrac{c(1 - t)h\alpha}{h + kb\alpha}$

2. a. The increase in government purchases increases GDP by the fiscal policy multiplier. The decrease in transfers cuts GDP by the transfer policy multiplier found in question 1a above. The net increase is 1 billion times

$$(1 - c) \cdot \frac{h\alpha}{h + kb\alpha}$$

   b. Total government spending doesn't change, but tax collections and the budget surplus rise by t times the amount found in 1a.

3. a. The inflation rate over 1985 was $(327.4 - 315.5)/315.5 \times 100 = 3.8$ percent.
   b. The real interest rate is the nominal interest rate minus the actual inflation rate, or approximately 3.7 percent.

4. IS: $Y = C + I = (\bar{C} + \bar{I}) + cY - br$

$$= \frac{(\bar{C} + \bar{I})}{1 - c} - \frac{br}{1 - c}$$

LM: $\dfrac{\bar{M}}{\bar{P}} = kY - h(r + \pi^e)$

Substituting the *IS* curve into the *LM* curve:

$$\frac{\bar{M}}{\bar{P}} = \frac{k(\bar{C} + \bar{I})}{1 - c} - \frac{kbr}{1 - c} - h(r + \pi^e)$$

Holding money and autonomous spending constant,

$$\frac{kb}{1 - c}\Delta r + h\Delta r = -h\Delta\pi^e$$

$$\frac{kb - (1 - c)h}{1 - c}\Delta r = -h\Delta\pi^e$$

$$\frac{\Delta r}{\Delta\pi^e} = \frac{(1 - c)h}{kb + (1 - c)h}$$

Since $\dfrac{\Delta i}{\Delta\pi^e} = \dfrac{\Delta r}{\Delta\pi^e} + 1$

the earlier equation can be written as

$$\frac{\Delta i}{\Delta\pi^e} = \frac{-(1 - c)h}{kb + (1 - c)h} + 1 = \frac{kb}{kb + (1 - c)h} < 1$$

Substituting $\Delta r/\pi^e$ into the *IS* curve,

$$\frac{\Delta Y}{\pi^e} = \frac{bh}{kb(1 - c)h}$$

An increase in expected inflation is not fully reflected in the nominal interest rate for the fixed-price *IS-LM* model. The real interest rate falls, stimulating investment spending and GDP.

5. *IS:* $Y = \bar{A} + c(1 - t)Y + d(Y^P - Y) - bi$

$$[1 - c(1 - t) + d]Y = \bar{A} + dY^P - bi$$

$$i = -\frac{[1 - c(1 - t) + d]Y}{b} + \frac{\bar{A}}{b} + \frac{dY^P}{b}$$

Compared with the standard model, the *IS* curve is steeper.

$$LM: \quad i = \frac{k}{h}Y - \frac{1}{h}\frac{\bar{M}}{\bar{P}}$$

as in the standard model. Substituting the *IS* curve into the *LM* curve,

$$\frac{k}{h}Y + \frac{1 - c(1 - t) + d}{b}Y = \frac{\bar{A}}{b} + \frac{dY^P}{b} + \frac{1}{h}\frac{\bar{M}}{\bar{P}}$$

$$\frac{kb + h[1 - c(1 - t) + d]}{hb}Y = \frac{\bar{A}}{b} + \frac{dY^P}{b} + \frac{1}{h}\frac{\bar{M}}{\bar{P}}$$

$$Y = \frac{h\bar{A}}{kb + h[1 - c(1 - t) + d]} + \frac{hdY^P}{kb + h[1 - c(1 - t) + d]}$$

$$+ \frac{b\bar{M}/\bar{P}}{kb + h[1 - c(1 - t) + d]}$$

Thus, since $d > 0$, the monetary policy multiplier is smaller when government spending responds negatively to deviations of Y and Y^P. If the economy starts from a position of full employment and a monetary expansion takes place, then the rise in GDP is mitigated by the induced fiscal contraction.

CHAPTER 6

Graph It 6

Chart 6-1 shows the relation of exports to the value of the dollar. A 1 percent increase in the exchange rate cuts exports by about 3 billion 1987 dollars.

Fill-In Questions

1. exchange rate
2. current account
3. capital account
4. balance of payments
5. fixed exchange rate regime, floating exchange rate regime
6. dirty or managed float
7. depreciation
8. devaluation
9. endogenous
10. balance of payments

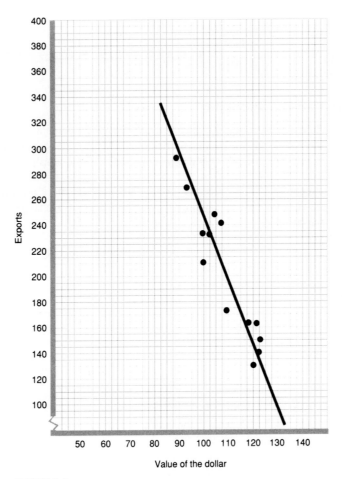

CHART 6-1

True-False Questions

1. False. Expansionary policy increases imports, increasing the trade deficit.
2. False. Interest rates are lower, and so capital leaves the country.
3. True.
4. True.
5. True.
6. False. Our imports rise. German imports and then GDP rise as well.
7. True.
8. True.
9. False. Eventually the bank will run out of reserves.

Multiple-Choice Questions

1. b   2. a   3. a   4. c   5. a   6. a   7. b   8. b   9. d

Worked-Out Problems

1. Initially, there are 4 marks to the dollar. A 50 percent devaluation results in an exchange rate of 2 marks to the dollar. Another 20 percent devaluation results in a rate of 1.6 marks per dollar. One mark is now worth 62.5 cents.

2. Negative. The coefficient b is certainly positive, and Y increases with an increase in R, so a (which captures the partial effect of a change in R on Q) *must* be negative.

3. $Y = C + I + G + NX = C + 0.9Y + I + G + X - (Q + 0.1Y)$
$Y(1 - 0.9 + 0.1) = (C + I + G + X - Q)$
The multiplier is thus $I/(I - 0.9 + 0.1) = 1/0.2 = 5$.

4. The essential thing is to recognize that our imports are German exports and vice versa. Variables without a subscript are for the United States.

$Y = C + I + G + NX$
$\quad = C + 0.9Y + I + G + (Q_G + 0.2Y_G) - (Q + 0.1Y)$
$Y(1 - 0.9 + 0.1) = (C + I + G + Q_G - Q) + 0.2Y_G$
$Y = 5(C + I + G + Q_G - Q) + Y_G$
$Y_G = C_G + I_G + G_G + NX_G$
$\quad = C_G + 0.8Y_G + I_G + G_G + (Q + 0.1Y) - (Q_G + 0.2Y_G)$
$Y_G(1 - 0.8 + 0.2) = (C_G + I_G + G_G + Q - Q_G) + 0.1Y$
$Y_G = 2.5(C_G + I_G + G_G + Q - Q_G) + 0.25Y$

To conserve on notation, call autonomous U.S. and German spending A and A_G, respectively. Thus several substitutions show that

$Y = 5A + Y_G$
$Y_G = 2.5A_G + 0.25Y$
$Y = 5A + 2.5A_G + 0.25Y$
$Y(1 - 0.25) = 5A + 2.5A_G$
$Y = 4/3(5A + 2.5A_G)$ and also that
$Y_G = 2.5A_G + 0.25(4/3)(5A + 2.5A_G) = 5/3A + 10/3A_G$

So, the multiplier of the U.S. government's spending on U.S. GDP is 20/3, and the multiplier on German GDP is 5/3. Notice that including all repercussion effects, the estimate of the multiplier rose from 5.0 in question 2 to 6.67 in question 3.

5. The increase in the money stock is not necessary in order to maintain the interest rate. Although the increase in G will temporarily raise the interest rate, the money

stock will increase automatically as the monetary authority buys foreign exchange and sells dollars in order to maintain the exchange rate. Output, of course, rises.

6. The interest rate falls, the demand for the dollar falls, exports increase (as dollars become cheaper), and imports fall as foreign currency becomes more expensive. That is, the *IS* curve shifts rightward.

7. The shift in world income to high-savings-propensity OPEC countries reduces world aggregate demand and hence income. This is represented by the downward shift in the *IS* curve from IS_1 to IS_2. The real money supply falls because of the rise in the price of oil, given the constancy of the nominal money supply. This is represented by the downward shift in the *LM* curve from LM_1 to LM_2. As drawn in Figure *d*, the shift in the *IS* curve dominates the shift in the *LM* curve. This results in a lower real rate at a lower level of world income. World monetary authorities could restore the original level of income by increasing the nominal money stock to a level that would compensate for the higher savings propensity and for the rise in oil prices. This requires a higher real money supply and a lower real interest rate than were obtained prior to the oil price increase. This policy would shift the *LM* curve to LM_3. Fiscal policy could also restore the original level of income. Given a constant nominal money stock, such a fiscal expansion would result in a rise in the real rate. It is represented by the shift in the *IS* curve to IS_3.

FIGURE *d*

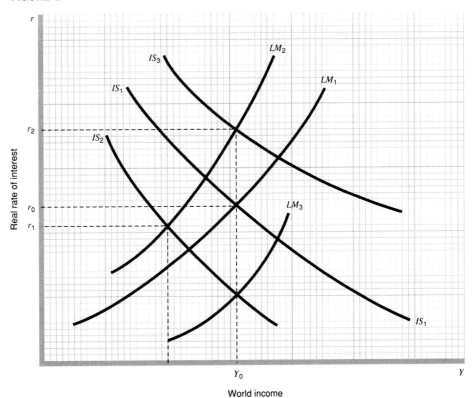

World income

CHAPTER 7

Graph It 7

CHART 7-1

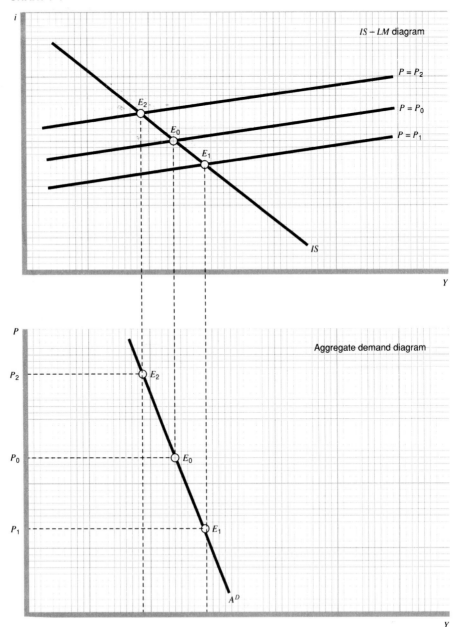

Fill-In Questions

1. autonomous spending
2. the money supply
3. *IS-LM*
4. crowding out
5. neutrality
6. aggregate supply
7. aggregate demand
8. horizontal
9. vertical

True-False Questions

1. False. Higher prices mean lower real balances. The *LM* curve moves left, increasing interest rates.
2. False. A low monetary policy multiplier means a steep aggregate demand curve.
3. True.
4. False. Same as question 2.
5. True.
6. False. The aggregate demand curve.
7. True.
8. True.
9. True.
10. False. Prices rise in proportion to the increased money supply, so that real balances are unchanged and the position of the *LM* curve is changed.

Multiple-Choice Questions

1. c 2. c 3. b 4. a 5. a 6. d 7. b 8. d 9. b 10. c

Worked-Out Problems

1. $Y = 2(1,500) + 4(50,000/P_{-1}) = 5,000$
   $P = P_{-1}[0.2 + 0.8(5,000/4,000)] = 120$

   Next year:

   $Y = 3,000 + 4(50,000/120) = 4,667$
   $P = 120[0.2 + 8(4,667/4,000)] = 136$

   Year after:

   $Y = 3,000 + 4(50,000/136) = 4,471$
   $P = 136[0.2 + 0.8(4,471/4,000)] = 148.8$

ANSWERS TO QUESTIONS AND PROBLEMS

2. In the long run, $P = P_{-1}$, and so $Y = Y_p = 4{,}000$
   $4{,}000 = 3{,}000 + 4(50{,}000/P)$
   $1/P = 1{,}000/200{,}000 \qquad P = 200$

   Y is at its original level. Consumption must also be at its original level. Since $Y = C + I + G$, if G is up 500, investment must be down 500. Therefore, the interest rate must be up 0.25.

3. $4{,}000 = 2{,}000 + 4(100{,}000/P)$
   $1/P = 2{,}000/400{,}000 \quad P = 200$

   Investment and the interest rate are unchanged!

CHAPTER 8

Graph It 8

See Chart 8-1.

Fill-In Questions

1. long-term labor market relations
2. inflation
3. Phillips curve
4. labor productivity
5. markup
6. supply shocks

True-False Questions

1. True.
2. False. Adding a unit of labor increases output, although each additional unit adds less than the previous unit.
3. True.
4. True.
5. True.
6. True.
7. False. You cannot undo the effects of a shock that permanently lowers potential GDP.

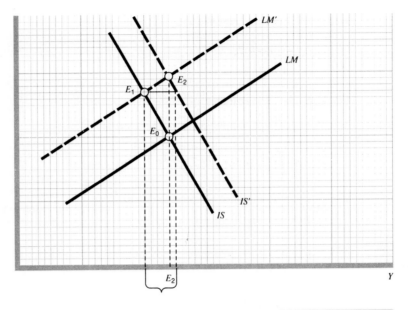

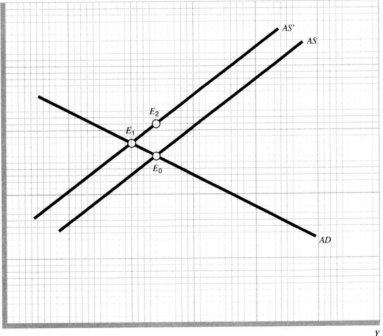

CHART 8-1

Multiple-Choice Questions

1. c   2. c   3. a   4. a   5. c

Worked-Out Problems

1. The aggregate supply curve in this case is

$$P = P_{-1}\left[1 - 2(0.4) \cdot \frac{Y_P - 1.1Y_P}{Y_P}\right] = P_{-1}(1.08)$$

Since the initial price level is 100, the price level after 1 year is 108. In the second year, P_{-1} is therefore 108, and so the second year's price level is 116.6.

2. The aggregate supply curve is given above. No inflation means $P = P_{-1}$. Therefore, the term in square brackets must equal 1, and so we must have $Y = Y_P$.

3. In percentage changes the equation can be written
   $$\%\Delta M - \%\Delta P = 0.555\%\Delta Y - 0.185\%\Delta i \quad \text{or}$$
   $$\pi = \%\Delta M - 0.555\%\Delta Y + 0.185\%\Delta i$$

   a. $\pi = 0.03 - 0.555(0.02) + 0.185(0)$ or $\pi = 1.89\%$

   b. An increase in money growth will cause an increase in inflation, which will cause the nominal interest rate to rise. Since money growth is three percentage points higher than in part a, long-run inflation will also be three percentage points higher, so in the long run $\pi = 4.9$ percent. The nominal interest rate will also be three percentage points higher, or $i = 8$ percent. The change from 5 percent to 8 percent is a 60 percent change [$(8 - 5)/5 = 0.6$], so money demand in the long run will drop by about $0.185(0.6) = 11.1$ percent. Over the adjustment period, inflation must be greater than 4.9 percent, so that the excess over 4.9 percent cumulatively lifts the price level by an extra 11.1 percent. See Figure e.

CHAPTER 9

Graph It 9

Chart 9-1 clearly shows that in the case of a vertical aggregate supply curve an increase in the money stock immediately results in higher prices with no increase in output.

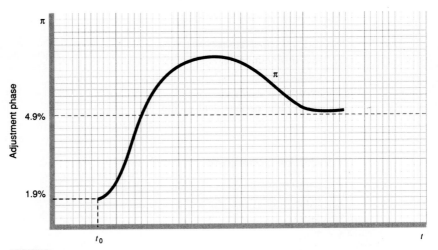

FIGURE *e*

CHART 9-1

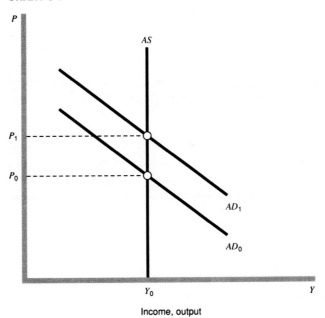

Income, output

Fill-In Questions

1. rational expectations
2. real business cycle
3. intertemporal substitution of leisure
4. vertical
5. frictionless neoclassical model

True-False Questions

1. False. Unanticipated changes.
2. False. It does not allow for systematic errors.
3. True.
4. True.
5. True.
6. False.
7. True.

Multiple-Choice Questions

1. b   2. b   3. d   4. d   5. a

CHAPTER 10

Graph It 10

TABLE 10-1
SHORT- AND LONG-RUN INCREASE IN AGGREGATE DEMAND

BILLIONS OF DOLLARS

(1) 1979 investment	480.2
(2) 20% increase	96
(3) Increase in GDP [2 × (2)]	192
(4) Actual 1979 GDP	2,488.6

TABLE 10-2
SHORT- AND LONG-RUN DECREASES IN AGGREGATE SUPPLY

BILLIONS OF DOLLARS

	1 Year	5 Years
(1) Increase in annual investment	$ 96	$ 96
(2) Cumulative increase in capital	96	480
(3) Total capital (roughly 3 × GDP)	7,466	7,466
(4) As percent of total capital	1.29%	6.43%
(5) Relative increase in production		
[¼ × (4)]	0.32%	1.61%
(6) Increase in AS [GDP × (5)]	$ 8	$ 40
(7) As fraction of AD increase		
[100 × (6)/(3) from Table 10-1]	4.2%	20.8%

You can see from Table 10-1 that the aggregate supply effects of an increase in investment take many years to catch up with the aggregate demand effects.

Fill-In Questions

1. potential
2. per capita
3. productivity
4. production function
5. marginal product of capital
6. capital's share of output
7. constant returns to scale
8. steady state
9. technological change

True-False Questions

1. True.
2. False. Eventually, the additional capital stock gets depreciated away unless the saving rate rises.
3. False. It takes time for a higher saving rate to add to the capital stock.
4. True.
5. False. The growth rate depends only on technological change.
6. False. It takes time for the population to grow.

7. True.
8. False. More people, more output, although less output per person.
9. True.
10. True.

Multiple-Choice Questions

1. a   2. b   3. b   4. d   5. a   6. b   7. c   8. c   9. b   10. c

Worked-Out Problems

1. GDP per capita is $x = Y/N$. Capital per worker is $k = K/N$.
   $$Y = AK^a N^{1-a}$$
   $$Y/N = AK^a N^{1-a} N^{-1} = AK^a N^{1-a-1} = AK^a N^{-a} = A(K/N)^a$$
   $$x = AK^a$$

2. Look at Review of Technique 19. You will see that there one can prove directly that the marginal product of labor is $(1 - a)Y/N$. Total payments to labor are the marginal product of labor times the total amount of labor $[(1 - a)Y/N] \cdot N$. To find out what share of total GDP this represents, we divide by total GDP:
   $$\{[(1 - a)Y/N] \cdot N\}/Y = 1 - a = 1 - 0.25 = 0.75$$

3. Apply the formula

   $$\frac{\Delta Y}{Y} = \theta \frac{\Delta K}{K} + (1 - \theta)\frac{\Delta N}{N}$$

   where θ is capital's share, 0.25. In this case, $0.25(0.2) + 0.75(0.1)$ yields a 12.5 percent growth in GDP. Since population has grown 10 percent, per capita GDP grows by 2.5 percent.

4. Applying the formula for the growth rate of the capital-labor ratio, $\Delta k/k = sx/k - (n + d)$, yields $0.1 = 0.3k^{1/4}/k - (0.1 + 0.05)$. Solving for k yields $k^{-3/4} = 0.25/0.3$, or $k = 1.275$. In the steady state, $sx/k = (n + d)$; so $0.3k^{-3/4} = 0.15$, or $k = 2.52$. The capital-labor ratio nearly doubles in the transition to the steady state.

5. The path of per capita GDP is illustrated in Figures $f(1)$ and $f(2)$. $k = K/N$ falls to half its original value. Per capita GDP drops down to the dashed line and then gradually returns to the steady state.

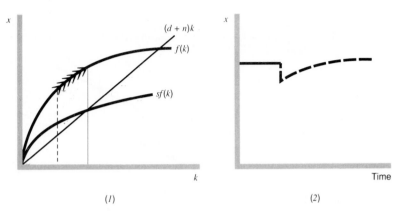

FIGURE f

6. The path of per capita GDP is illustrated in Figures $g(1)$ and $g(2)$. The new saving curve is shown by the dashed curve. Per capita GDP gradually rises from the old steady state to the new steady state.

FIGURE g

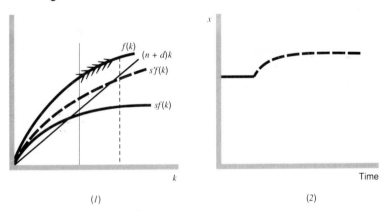

CHAPTER 11

Graph It 11

The completed graph appears below. You should have found the short-run *MPC* to be about 0.7 and the long-run *MPC* to be about 0.9. We made up the data by applying the following equation to each group of three points.

$$C_i = 0.4[(Y_1 + Y_2 + Y_3)/3] + 0.5Y_i \quad \text{for } i = 1, 2, \text{ or } 3$$

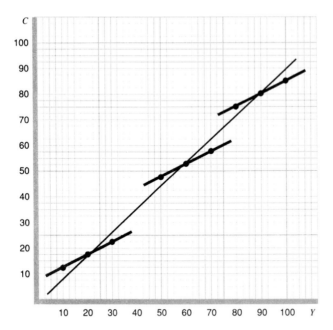

CHART 11-1

Fill-In Questions

1. life-cycle
2. permanent
3. dissaving
4. 0.90
5. 0.90
6. short-run
7. long-run
8. working, retirement
9. distributed

True-False Questions

1. False. It's just the other way around.
2. True.
3. True.
4. True.
5. True.
6. True.
7. True.

8. False. You have to save in order to have a bequest to leave, and so you reduce current consumption.

9. True.

10. True.

Multiple-Choice Questions

1. b   2. a   3. c   4. b   5. c   6. a   7. c   8. c   9. c   10. a

Worked-Out Problems

1. Total resources are the sum of disposable income over the next 40 years. These resources must be spread out evenly over a 50-year period. A $100 tax cut that is permanent increases disposable lifetime income by a total of 40 times $100, or $4,000. Spread over 50 years, this cut increases consumption by $80 each year. A cut that lasts only 1 year increases lifetime disposable income by $100, and so consumption increases by $2. A cut that is not in effect this year but is in effect for the next 39 years yields a total increase of $3,900. Consumption increases $78 each year including the current one.

2. $\Delta C = 0.8(0.75\Delta YD + 0.25\Delta YD_{-1})$

   a. $\Delta C = 0.8[0.75(100) + 0.25(0)] = 60$
      $\Delta C = 0.8[0.75(100) + 0.25(100)] = 80$

   b. $\Delta C = 0.8[0.75(100) + 0.25(0)] = 60$
      $\Delta C = 0.8[0.75(0) + 0.25(100)] = 20$

3. Substituting the consumer's estimate of permanent income into the consumption function yields
   $C = c(1 - t)\theta Y + c(1 - t)(1 - \theta)Y_{-1}$
   Substituting the consumption and investment into the national income identity yields
   $Y = c(1 - t)\theta Y + c(1 - t)(1 - \theta)Y_{-1} - br + \bar{I} + \bar{G}$
   which can be written as the *IS* curve. Substituting the *LM* curve for *r*,

   $$r = \frac{k}{h}Y - \frac{1}{h}\frac{\bar{M}}{P}$$

   will yield the reduced form for GDP in terms of the fiscal and monetary policy multipliers, that is

$$Y = c(1 - t)\theta Y + c(1 - t)(1 - \theta)Y_{-1} - \frac{kb}{h}Y + \frac{b}{h}\frac{\bar{M}}{P} + \bar{I} + \bar{G}$$

$$Y\left[\frac{h - hc(1 - t)\theta + kb}{h}\right] = c(1 - t)(1 - \theta)Y_{-1} + \frac{b}{h}\frac{\bar{M}}{P} + \bar{G} + \bar{I}$$

Solving for Y yields

$$Y = \frac{hc(1 - t)(1 - \theta)Y_{-1}}{h - hc(1 - t)\theta + kb} + \frac{b\bar{M}/P}{h - hc(1 - t)\theta + kb}$$

$$+ \frac{h(\bar{G} + \bar{I})}{h - hc(1 - t)\theta + kb}$$

Therefore, both the fiscal and the monetary policy multiplier are smaller for the case in which consumption depends on a weighted average of current and lagged income ($\theta < 1$). If $\theta < 1$, then the marginal propensity to consume out of current income is smaller, which in turn implies a steeper *IS* curve and weaker fiscal and monetary policy.

4. $C = 0.8(0.5)Y^P = 0.4Y^P = 0.24Y + 0.16Y_{-1}$

Substitute consumption and investment into the national income identity.

$Y = 0.24Y + 0.16Y_{-1} + 0.1(Y - Y_{-1}) - 1,000r + G$

Solving for Y yields the *IS* curve.

$Y = 0.091Y_{-1} - 1,515.2r + 1.52G$

Since prices are fixed, $i = r$. Solve the *LM* curve for r; then substitute the result into the *IS* curve and solve for *Y*.

$r = 0.0004Y - 0.0005(M/P)$
$Y = 0.0567Y_{-1} + 0.472(M/P) + 0.946G$

The initial effect of a unit increase in G is $\Delta Y = 0.964(1.0)$. Since tax collections rise by only half the increase in income, the budget deficit increases by $1.0 - (0.5)0.964 = 0.527$.

In the long run, income equals permanent income. We could solve the entire problem over again, substituting Y for Y^P. However, it's easier to just take the final short-run solution, set $Y = Y_{-1}$, and solve from there.

$Y(1 - 0.0567) = 0.472M/P + 0.946G$

Carrying answers to only three places has left a little round-off error. The exact answer is $Y = 0.5M/P + 1.0G$. So the long-run multiplier is 1.0 and the long-run change in the budget deficit is 0.5.

CHAPTER 12

Graph It 12

TABLE 12-1

Year	GDP	I	$Y_t - Y_{t-1}$	$I_t - I_{t-1}$
1980	3,776.3	594.4		
1981	3,843.1	631.1	66.8	36.7
1982	3,760.3	540.5	−82.8	−90.6
1983	3,906.6	599.5	146.3	59.0
1984	4,148.5	757.5	241.9	158.0
1985	4,279.8	745.9	131.3	−11.6
1986	4,405.5	735.1	125.7	−10.8
1987	4,540.0	749.3	134.5	14.2
1988	4,718.6	773.4	178.6	24.1
1989	4,836.9	789.2	118.3	15.8
1990	4,884.9	744.5	48.0	−44.7
1991	4,848.4	672.6	−36.5	−71.9

Also see Charts 12-1 and 12-2 on pages 234 and 235.

Fill-In Questions

1. business fixed, residential housing, inventory
2. flow, stock
3. marginal product of capital
4. rental or user cost of capital
5. expected future
6. investment tax credit
7. depreciation
8. disintermediation
9. inventory cycle

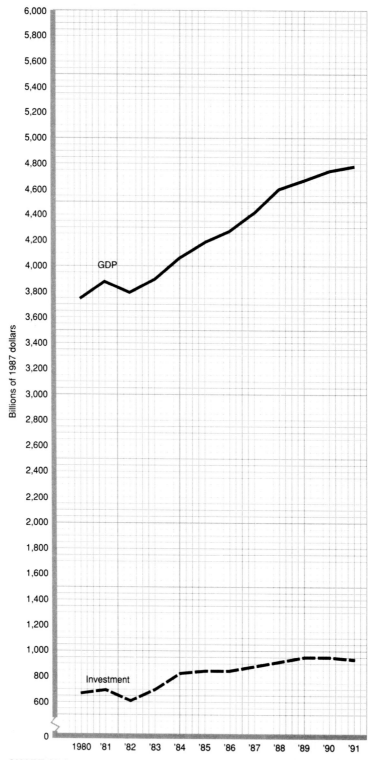

CHART 12-1

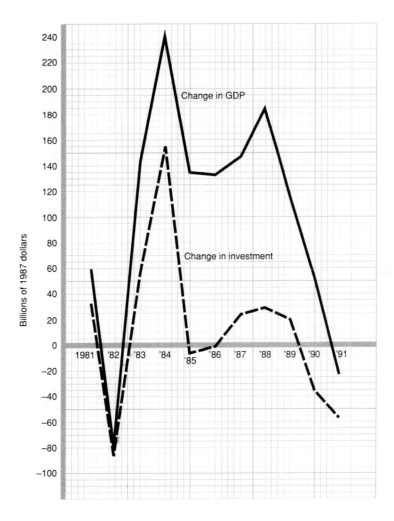

CHART 12-2

True-False Questions

1.   False. High interest rates make capital more expensive and thus lower investment.
2.   True.
3.   False. If the government pays for part of your equipment, you want to buy more.
4.   False. If mortgage rates are high, people's monthly house payments will be high. People will buy less housing, lowering residential investment.
5.   True.
6.   True.
7.   False. If you expect sales to rise, you will need to have more goods on hand, increasing inventory.
8.   False. It's the level of investment that's proportional to changes in income.

9. True.
10. True.

Multiple-Choice Questions

1. d 2. b 3. b 4. c 5. d 6. c 7. a 8. c 9. b 10. a 11. b

Worked-Out Problems

1. $rc = i - \pi + d = 0.12 - 0.06 + 0.10 = 0.16$

   a. $K^* = 0.25(16,000)/0.16 = 25,000$
   b. $K^* = 0.25(32,000)/0.16 = 50,000$
   c. $I_{net} = (K^* - K_{-1}) = 50,000 - 25,000 = 25,000$
      $I_{gross} = I_{net} + dK_{-1} = 25,000 + 0.1(25,000) = 27,500$

2. $I_{net} = K - K_{-1} = 0.5(K^* - K_{-1})$

   Year 1: $I_{net} = 0.5(3,600 - 2,000) = 800$ $I_{gross} = 800 + 0.1(2,000) = 1,000$
   Year 2: $I_{net} = 0.5(3,600 - 2,800) = 400$ $I_{gross} = 400 + 0.1(2,800) = 680$
   Year 3: $I_{net} = 0.5(3,600 - 3,200) = 200$ $I_{gross} = 200 + 0.1(3,200) = 520$

   Notice that each year's net investment is added to the capital stock to determine the following year's capital stock.

3. A "fair" loan is one in which the amount of the loan equals the present discounted value of the payment.

   $$1.000 = \frac{220}{1.1} + \frac{Q_2}{1.1^2}$$

   $Q_2 = 1.1^2(1,000 - 200) = \$968$

4. A temporary cut in the personal income tax has a small effect on consumers' lifetime wealth. Assuming that consumers follow the life-cycle hypothesis, the benefits of this increase are spread over current and future years. The increase in consumption in any one year is quite small. In the same way, a temporary increase in the investment tax credit does not change long-run desired capital. However, it causes a large increase in current investment because any investment done today receives the government subsidy which will not be available in subsequent years. Indeed, firms may "move up" investment scheduled for the future in order to take advantage of the temporarily higher tax credit.

CHAPTER 13

Graph It 13

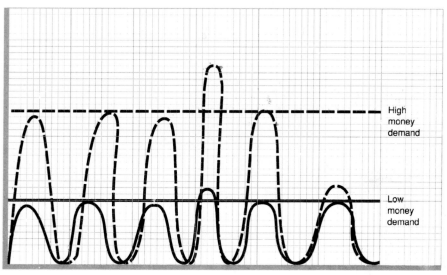

Time

CHART 13-1

Fill-In Questions

1. real balances
2. currency and demand deposits
3. $M1$ plus time and savings deposits
4. transactions
5. velocity
6. velocity
7. precautionary
8. speculative
9. speculative
10. price level

True-False Questions

1. True.
2. True.
3. True.

4. True.
5. False. $M1$ is a strict subset of $M2$.
6. False. To do otherwise would show money illusion.
7. False. The Baumol-Tobin theory says money demand is proportional to the square root of GDP.
8. True.
9. False. This is just a switch between different components of $M2$.
10. True.

Multiple-Choice Questions

1. c   2. b   3. c   4. a   5. b   6. a   7. b   8. b   9. c   10. b   11. b   12. c

Worked-Out Problems

1. Since the price level doubles, the $220 billion is worth only $110 billion in real (constant-dollar) terms. The change from $100 billion to $110 billion is a 10 percent increase. Since the Baumol-Tobin theory says that the income elasticity is one-half, real money demand will rise by 5 percent.

2. This problem has to be worked backward. We know the amount by which we want the interest rate to change. We assume that interest changes by the amount given, and we find the amount of change in the money stock that this implies. If we change the money stock by the latter amount, the desired change in the interest rate will result.

   The interest rate is to go from 4 percent to 3 percent. This is a drop of 25 percent. (The change is 1 percent; 1 percent over 4 percent is one-fourth, or 25 percent. A very common error is to think the change is 1 percent. The change is one percentage point of annual interest, not 1 percent.) We are told that the interest elasticity is –0.20, and one-fifth of one-fourth is 5 percent. Thus, a 5 percent *increase* in the money stock will produce the desired interest rate change.

3. An increase in the use of credit cards will imply a fall in the demand for money. If the stock of money is held constant by the Fed, then the nominal interest rate will have to fall to maintain money market equilibrium. This can be represented by an outward movement of the *LM* curve, which leads to an increase in GDP. (A decrease in money demand shifts the *LM* curve in the same way as an increase in the money supply.) See Figure *h.*

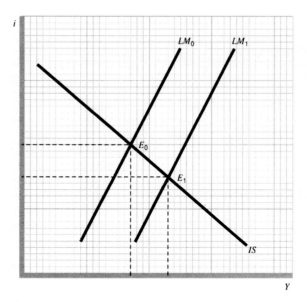

FIGURE *h*

CHAPTER 14

Graph It 14

TABLE 14-1
FIRST BALANCE SHEETS

PROFESSOR B			BANK		
Assets		Liabilities	Assets		Liabilities
Deposit	$200	None	Reserves	$200	$200 Deposit
			(Required	20)	
			(Excess	180)	
		$200 Net worth			
	$200	$200		$200	$200

TABLE 14-2
SECOND BALANCE SHEETS

	PROFESSOR B				BANK		
Assets		**Liabilities**		**Assets**		**Liabilities**	
Deposit	$380	$180	Loan	Reserves	$200	$380	Deposit
				(Required	38)		
				(Excess	162)		
		$200	Net worth	Loan	$180		
	$380	$380				$380	$380

TABLE 14-3
THIRD BALANCE SHEETS

	PROFESSOR B				BANK		
Assets		**Liabilities**		**Assets**		**Liabilities**	
Deposit	$542	$342	Loan	Reserves	$200	$542	Deposit
				(Required	54.2)		
				(Excess	145.8)		
		$200	Net worth	Loan	$342		
	$542	$542				$542	$542

TABLE 14-4
FINAL BALANCE SHEETS

	PROFESSOR B				BANK		
Assets		**Liabilities**		**Assets**		**Liabilities**	
Deposit	$2,000	$1,800	Loan	Reserves	$ 200	$2,000	Deposit
				(Required	200)		
				(Excess	0)		
		$ 200	Net worth	Loan	$1,800		
	$2,000	$2,000				$2,000	$2,000

Fill-In Questions

1. high-powered money, the monetary base
2. required, excess
3. discount rate
4. federal funds rate
5. open market sale
6. money multiplier
7. sterilization
8. tax and loan
9. currency-deposit ratio
10. government bonds

True-False Questions

1. True.
2. False. A higher currency-deposit ratio means a lower money multiplier and so a lower money supply.
3. False. A reserve requirement means a lower money multiplier and so a lower money supply.
4. False. This also lowers re and thus the money multiplier.
5. False. Income has nothing to do with the money supply.
6. True.
7. True.
8. True.
9. True.

Multiple-Choice Questions

1. d   2. a   3. c   4. d   5. a   6. a   7. c   8. c   9. b

Worked-Out Problems

1. $CU = 0.4D$
$M1 = CU + D = 0.4D + D = 1.4D$
$H = CU + 0.1D = 0.4D + 0.1 = 0.5D$

   a. $M1/H = 1.4D/0.5D$
   $M1 = 2.8H = 2.8(100) = \$280$ billion
   b. $H = 0.5D;\ \Delta D = 2\Delta H = 2(50) = \$100$ billion

2. $M2 = CU + D + T = 0.4D + 2.5D = 3.9D$
    $H = CU + 0.1D + 0.04T = 0.4D + 0.1D + 0.04(2.5)D = 0.6D$

  a. $M2 = (3.90/0.6)H = 6.5(100) = \$650$ billion
  b. $M1 = [0.4 + (1/0.6)]H = (1.4/6)100 = \$233$ billion

3. $H = CU + 0.1D = (0.5Y - 495i) + 0.1(Y - 50i) = 0.6Y - 500i$
    $i = (0.6Y - H)/500 = [0.6(2,000) - 1,150]/500 = 50/500 = 10\%$

4. The money supply will fall because a rise in the currency–deposit ratio will decrease the money multiplier, $(1 + cu)/(cu + re)$, and hence the money supply for a given monetary base. The LM curve moves left, yielding a higher nominal interest rate and a lower level of GDP. See Figure i, where $cu_1 > cu_0$.

FIGURE i

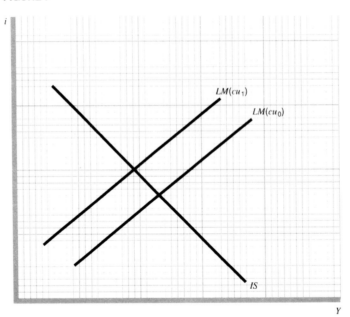

CHAPTER 15

Graph It 15

TABLE 15-1
BANK BALANCE SHEET 1

Assets		Liabilities	
Reserves	$ 200	$2,000	Deposits
Treasury bills	400		
Loans	1,600	200	Paid-in capital
	$2,200	$2,200	

TABLE 15-2
BANK INCOME STATEMENT

Income		Expenses	
Interest on reserves	$ 0	$110	Deposit interest
Interest on Treasury bills	38	40	Stockholders' dividends
Interest on loans	224	112	Retained earnings
	$262	$262	

TABLE 15-3
BANK BALANCE SHEET 2

Assets		Liabilities	
Reserves	$ 200	$2,000	Deposits
Treasury bills	512		
Loans	1,600	312	Paid-in capital
	$2,312	$2,312	

Fill-In Questions

1. inside lag
2. outside lag
3. lags, expectations, uncertainty
4. action lag
5. recognition lag
6. decision lag
7. automatic stabilizer
8. activists
9. decision
10. outside

Worked-Out Problems

1. A drop in government spending will move the *IS* curve to the left. If the *LM* curve is vertical, as in Figure *j,* then interest rates will drop sufficiently so that investment "crowding-in" will completely replace the decrease in government spending. GDP will remain at potential GDP. In the more likely case that the *LM* curve is positively sloped, as in Figure *k,* the contractionary fiscal policy would reduce GDP. Expansionary monetary policy, increasing the money supply to move the *LM* curve to the right, could be used to maintain GDP at potential.

FIGURE *j*

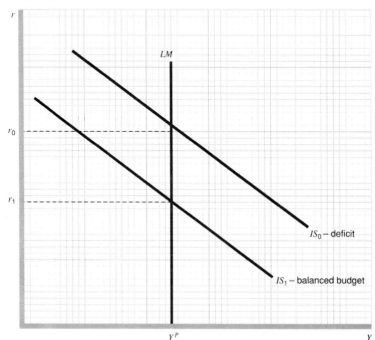

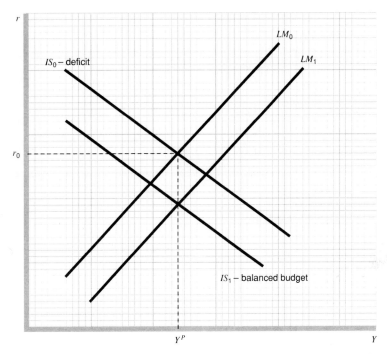

FIGURE *k*

CHAPTER 16

Graph It 16

TABLE 16-1

Asset	Beginning value	End dollar value	End real value	Dollar difference	Real difference
Money	$100	$100.00	$ 98.04		
				$7.00	$6.86
Bonds	$100	$107.00	$104.90		
				$5.20	$5.10
Corn	$100	$112.20	$110.00		

TABLE 16-2

Asset	Beginning value	End dollar value	End real value	Dollar difference	Real difference
Money	$100	$100.00	$ 89.29		
				$17.00	$15.17
Bonds	$100	$117.00	$104.46		
				$ 6.20	$ 5.54
Corn	$100	$123.20	$110.00		

Fill-In Questions

1. overshooting
2. rational expectations
3. expectations-augmented aggregate supply
4. Phillips
5. stagflation
6. credible
7. perfect foresight
8. index
9. liquidity effect
10. income effect

True-False Questions

1. False. Rational expectations theory says only that *predictable* events don't move GDP away from potential.
2. True.
3. True.
4. True.
5. False. Just the opposite.

Multiple-Choice Questions

1. b   2. b   3. c   4. b   5. a   6. b   7. c   8. a   9. a   10. a

Worked-Out Problems

1. $f = 500$ $m_{-1} = 0, \pi_{-1} = 0$ $\Delta\pi^e = 0$
    $Y = 4,000 + 2(500) = 5,000$

$$\pi = 0 + 0.8\frac{5,000 - 4,000}{4,000} = 0.2 \quad \text{or 20\% per year}$$

Next period's expected inflation is this period's actual inflation, 0.2.

Next Year:

$f = 0$
$Y = 5,000 + 0 + 2,000(0 - 0.2) + 1,000(0.2 - 0) = 4,800$

$\pi = 0.2 + 0.8\dfrac{4,800 - 4,000}{4,000} = 0.36$ or 36% per year

Year after next:

$Y = 4,800 + 0 + 2,000(0 - 0.36) + 1,000(0.36 - 0.2) = 4,240$

$\pi = 0.36 + 0.8\dfrac{4,240 - 4,000}{4,000} = 0.408$ or 40.8% per year

2. $f = 0$ $m_{-1} = 0.5$ $\Delta \pi^e = 0$
$Y = 4,000 + 2,000(0.5 - 0) = 5,000$
The rest of the answers are identical to those for problem 1.

3. Year 2:
$Y = 4,000 + 2,000(0.5 - 0) = 5,000$

$\pi = 0 + 0.8\dfrac{5,000 - 4,000}{4,000} = 0.20$ or 20% per year

Year 3:
$Y = 5,000 + 2,000(0.5 - 0.2) + 1,000(0.2 - 0) = 5,800$

$\pi = 0.2 + 0.8\dfrac{5,800 - 4,000}{4,000} = 0.56$ or 56% per year

Year 4:
$Y = 5,800 + 2,000(0.5 - 0.56) + 1,000(0.56 - 0.2) = 6,040$

$\pi = 0.56 + 0.8\dfrac{6,040 - 4,000}{4,000} = 0.968$ or 96.8% per year

Year 5:
$Y = 6,040 + 2,000(0.5 - 0.968) + 1,000(0.968 - 0.56) = 5,512$

$\pi = 0.968 + 0.8\dfrac{5,512 - 4,000}{4,000} = 1.27$ or 127% per year

4. The answer is "it depends." Since an unanticipated increase in money moves the *LM* curve out and lowers the nominal interest rate, we know that the current short-run rate falls. What happens to the current long-run rate depends on what people expect to happen to short rates in the future. In the long run, increased money growth leads to higher inflation and increased short-term nominal interest rates. As soon as people realize this will happen, the current long rate will rise. Until then, nothing much happens to the long rate. Assuming that people catch on pretty quickly, but that prices don't move as quickly as people catch on, short rates will fall and the long rate will rise. The yield curve will become steeper. (See Figure *l.*)

FIGURE *l*

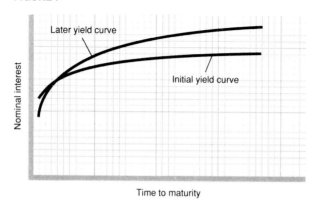

CHAPTER 17

Graph It 17

TABLE 17-2
"THE NEW DAYS"

	Unemployment rate	Number in labor force	Number employed
Adults	2.80	1,000	972
Teenagers	5.50	800	756
Total	4.00	1,800	1,728

The "average" unemployment rate has risen, even though the typical individual, adult or teenager, is less likely to be unemployed.

Fill-In Questions

1. unemployment, inflation
2. natural rate
3. perfectly anticipated
4. imperfectly anticipated, unanticipated
5. distributional
6. Okun's law
7. borrowers
8. lenders

True-False Questions

1. False. Aggregate demand policies have no effect on the natural rate.
2. False. Lost output is gone forever.
3. True.
4. True.
5. True.
6. True.
7. False. Those who are unemployed for a long time make up a large part of the overall average.
8. False. It makes sense for people to spend time looking around for jobs.
9. False. Job creation programs may lower the natural rate, and unemployment insurance programs definitely raise the natural rate.
10. False. Print enough money and you can get as much inflation as you'd like!

Multiple-Choice Questions

1. c   2. c   3. b   4. d   5. d   6. a   7. b   8. b   9. d   10. c

Worked-Out Problems

1. Originally, $u = 0.6(0.05) + 0.4(0.08) = 6.2$ percent. Later, $u = 0.5(0.05) + 0.5(0.08) = 6.5$ percent. Of course, GDP will be much higher in the latter case, since so many more teenagers are working!

2. The average duration of unemployment is $(2 \cdot 1 + 2 + 12)/4 = 4$ months. In any given month, there will be two people undergoing a 1-month unemployment span,

two people with a 2-month unemployment span, and twelve people with a 1-year stretch. Thus, 16 percent of the labor force will be unemployed.

3. At the end of the year you have $107. The price level is now 1.1, and so the real value is 107/1.1 = $97.27. In real terms, you have lost $3.

4. In order to gain a 2 percent real return, you need $100(1 + i)/1.1 = 102$, or $102(1.1)/100 = 1.222$; that is, i is approximately 12 percent.

5. The price of your property will be rising 12 percent per year, so that after 2 years, when you will sell it, you will receive $1.25 on the dollar, although it takes $1.21 to equal one constant dollar. Your nominal gain is $0.25. The tax on this is approximately $0.06, so that you are left with $1.10, which is worth $0.98 in real terms. Your 4 percent before-tax gain has turned into a 2 percent after-tax real loss.

6. Substitute the money demand function into the short-run aggregate supply curve and solve for the price level.

$$p = 1 + \frac{3}{4}(m + v - p - y^P)$$

$$p\left(1 + \frac{3}{4}\right) = 1 + \frac{3}{4}(m + v - y^P)$$

$$p = \frac{4}{7} + \frac{3}{7}(m + v - y^P)$$

If the money supply goes up by 10 percent, the price level goes up by 30/7 percent, or 4.3 percent. To determine GDP, substitute the expression for the price level back into the money demand function.

$$y = m + v - \frac{4}{7} - \frac{3}{7}(m + v - y^P)$$

$$= -\frac{4}{7} + \frac{4}{7}(m + v) + \frac{3}{7}y^P$$

If $\Delta m = 10$ percent, then $\Delta Y = 40/7$ percent or 5.7 percent. Since money demand obeys the strict quantity theory, the *LM* curve is vertical. Monetary policy is most effective in this case. The initial increase in the money supply causes an increase in the price level (by moving the aggregate demand curve across the aggregate supply curve). The price increase moves the *LM* curve partway back toward its initial position (from LM_1 to LM_2).

CHAPTER 18

Graph It 18

Charts 18-1*a* (p. 252) and 18-1*b* (p. 254) show the budget deficit and the change in the budget deficit plotted against inflation tax revenue and the change in inflation tax revenues. Inflation tax revenues are computed by multiplying the high-powered money stock by the inflation rate between year *t* and *t* − 1. The high-powered money stock is computed by dividing the level of *M*1 by the money multiplier (check the discussion in Chapter 13 if you have forgotten how to compute the stock of high-powered money). It is clear from the charts that there is little association between the size or change in budget deficits and the amount or change in the amount of inflation tax revenues collected.

Fill-In Questions

1. hyperinflation
2. inflation tax
3. seigniorage
4. inflation-corrected deficit
5. Fisher effect
6. monetize
7. expectations effect

True-False Questions

1. True.
2. False. In the long run, GDP pretty much stays at potential GDP.
3. True.
4. True.
5. False. The nominal interest rate adjusts to expected inflation, and the real rate is unaffected.
6. True.
7. True.
8. False. The vast bulk of the deficit is financed by selling government bonds to the public.
9. True.
10. False, although they do tend to move together over long periods of time.

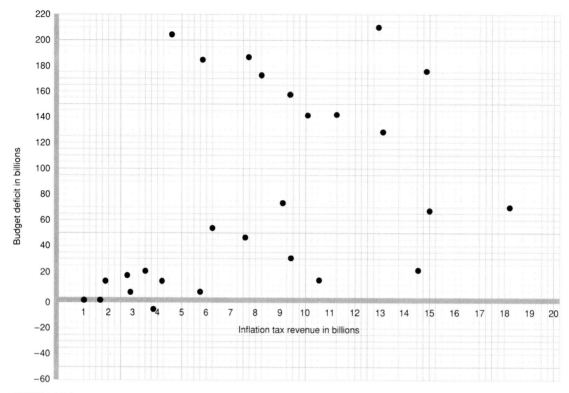

CHART 18-1a

Multiple-Choice Questions

1. c   2. b   3. d   4. c   5. a   6. d   7. c   8. b   9. a   10. a

Worked-Out Problems

1. The inflation will equal the rate of money supply growth less the rate of growth in money demand due to increased GDP. Inflation will be zero if the rate of money growth, m, equals the income elasticity of money demand, η, times the rate of growth of potential GDP, g^*. A good estimate of the income elasticity (from Chapter 14) is 0.7, with a range of between 0.5 and 1.0. A reasonable estimate for potential GDP growth is 3.0 percent, with a range of about 2.5 to 3.5 percent. So our best estimate of noninflationary money growth is 2.1 percent per year (0.7×3.0) with a range of 1.25 (that is, 0.5×2.5) to 3.5 (that is, 1.0×3.5) percent per year.

TABLE 18-1a

Year	Deficit, $ billions	Inflation tax revenue, $ billions
1964	2.6	
1965	−1.3	0.90
1966	1.4	1.64
1967	12.7	1.89
1968	4.7	2.76
1969	−8.5	3.71
1970	13.3	4.09
1971	21.7	3.34
1972	17.3	2.67
1973	6.6	5.45
1974	11.6	10.09
1975	69.4	8.75
1976	52.9	5.89
1977	42.4	7.18
1978	28.1	9.07
1979	15.7	14.48
1980	60.1	18.39
1981	58.8	15.01
1982	135.5	9.74
1983	180.1	5.58
1984	166.9	7.95
1985	181.4	7.36
1986	201.1	4.49
1987	151.8	9.12
1988	136.6	10.85
1989	124.2	12.75
1990	165.3	14.87
1991	200.7	12.58

2. First, a minor point: 1,000 percent annual inflation means that the price level is multiplied by 11. (A 100 percent increase means that something doubles, a 200 percent increase, that something triples, etc.) We use the compound interest formula to solve this problem. (See Review of Technique 18.) Thus, $11 = (1 + r)^{12}$. Solving, we write $(1 + r) = 11^{1/12} = 1.221$, or r equals 22 percent per month. We can solve the second question by writing $191 = (1 + r)^{365}$, or $1 + r = 191^{1/365} = 1.014$. The daily inflation rate is 1.4 percent.

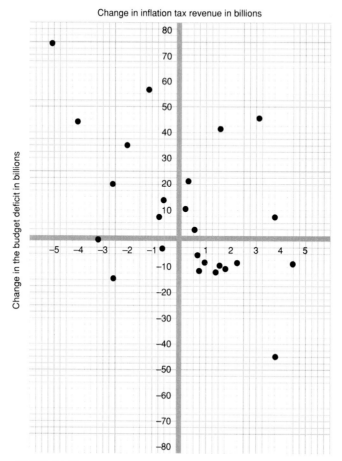

CHART 18-1*b*

3. To be precise, the nominal value will have grown to $100 \times (1 + 0.50)^{10} =$ $5,766.50 (Wow!). If we take today's price level as 1.0, the price level 10 years from now will have grown to $1.0 \times (1 + 0.48)^{10} = 50.42$ (oh, dear!). The real value of the investment will be $5,766.50/50.42 = $114.37. A quick and dirty way to find the same answer is to calculate the value of 10 years' compounding at the real interest rate, that is, $0.50 - 0.48 = 0.02$; $100 \times (1 + 0.02)^{10} =$ $121.90. You'll note that using the real interest rate introduces a small error in the final answer, but certainly puts you in the right ballpark.

TABLE 18-1*b*

Year	Change in the budget deficit from previous year, $ billions	Change in the inflation tax revenues from previous year, $ billions
1965	−3.9	
1966	2.7	0.74
1967	11.3	0.25
1968	−8.0	0.87
1969	−13.2	0.95
1970	21.8	0.38
1971	8.4	−0.76
1972	−4.4	−0.67
1973	−10.7	2.78
1974	5.0	4.64
1975	57.8	−1.34
1976	−16.5	−2.87
1977	−10.5	1.30
1978	−14.3	1.89
1979	−12.4	5.41
1980	44.4	3.91
1981	−1.3	−3.39
1982	76.7	−5.26
1983	44.6	−4.16
1984	−13.2	2.37
1985	14.5	−0.59
1986	19.7	−2.87
1987	−49.3	4.63
1988	−15.2	1.72
1989	−12.4	1.90
1990	41.1	2.12
1991	35.4	−2.29

CHAPTER 19

Graph It 19

Tables 19-1 and 19-2 appear below. In nominal terms, the end-of-year debt in year 5 was only 530.81 without inflation as opposed to 850.26 with inflation. But as you can see, the real comparison shows little real difference, only 530.81 versus 527.94.

TABLE 19-1

Year	1	2	3	4	5
Spending deficit	$100.00	$100.00	$100.00	$100.00	$100.00
Beginning debt	100.00	202.00	306.04	412.16	520.40
Interest	2.00	4.04	6.12	8.24	10.41
Price level, end of year	1.00	1.00	1.00	1.00	1.00
Real debt, end of year	102.00	206.04	312.16	420.40	530.81

TABLE 19-2

Year	1	2	3	4	5
Spending deficit	$100.00	$110.00	$121.00	$133.10	$146.41
Beginning debt	100.00	222.00	369.64	547.10	759.16
Interest	12.00	26.64	44.36	65.65	91.10
Price level, end of year	1.10	1.21	1.33	1.46	1.61
Real debt, end of year	101.82	205.49	311.04	418.52	527.94

Fill-In Questions

1. deficit
2. national debt
3. monetizing the debt
4. debt financing
5. money financing
6. primary deficit, inflation-corrected deficit
7. Gramm-Rudman-Hollings Act
8. the burden of the debt

True-False Questions

1. True.
2. True.
3. True.
4. False. In the United States, most of the deficit is financed by bond sales.
5. False. The Fed prints high-powered money.
6. True.
7. False. The Fed only buys up debt of the Federal government.

Multiple-Choice Questions

1. d   2. a   3. d   4. b   5. d   6. b   7. b   8. d   9. a

Worked-Out Problems

1. Use the formula $\Delta b = q[(r - y)b - x]$. We want to find the value of x that makes Δb equal to zero; that is, we want to find $x = (r - y)b$. The problem specifies $r = 0.02$ and $y = 0.027$. The Data Appendix in the text gives the 1988 ratio of debt to GDP as 52.9 percent, so $b = 0.53$. Thus, the highest sustainable level of x is -0.0037. In other words, the deficit can be 0.37 percent of GDP without causing the national debt to grow faster than GDP.

2. This is just a compound interest problem. At the end of 10 years, an amount P has grown to $P(1 + r)^{10} = 1.02^{10} = 1.22$. The debt will have grown to $244 billion.

3. a. $Y = 80 + 0.9YD + 600 = 680 + 0.9Y$
       which implies that $Y = 6,800$ and $C = 6,200$.

    b. $Y = 80 + 0.9YD + 600 + 50$
       $Y = 730 + 0.9(Y - 50) = 685 + 0.9Y$
       which implies that $Y = 6,850$ and $C = 6,200$. In all future years,
       $Y = 6,800$ and $C = 6,200$.

    c. $Y = 80 + 0.9YD + 600 + 50$
          $= 730 + 0.9Y$
       which implies that $Y = 7,300$ and $C = 6,650$.

       After the one-year road construction program is finished, the government has a debt liability of 50. At a 10 percent rate of interest, the government must make annual payments of 5, and so must raise taxes by 5 in all future years. Therefore, in all future years,

$$Y = 80 + 0.9YD + 600 = 680 + 0.9(Y - 5)$$
$$= 675.5 + 0.9Y$$

which implies that $Y = 6,755$ and $C = 6,155$. (Of course, the problem setup ignores the supply side completely.)

d. If the government finances the road construction project by debt, then consumption rises by 450 in the current year and falls by 45 thereafter. Notice that the present value of 45 is $45/0.10 = 450$.

The form of the consumption function is not consistent with Ricardian equivalence, since consumers look at current disposable income but not at future tax liabilities. Thus, consumers "overspend" during the first year and "underspend" later.

CHAPTER 20

Graph It 20

The regression of imports on GDP looks pretty reasonable. The coefficient a is 0.13. So a $1 billion increase in GDP increases imports by about $130 million. The regression of imports on the value of the dollar gives b equal to -3.4. Oops! The relation should be positive, not negative. This proves you can't always look at one factor at a time in a complex relation. The last regression gives $a = 0.16$ and $b = 0.91$, and so a billion-dollar increase in GDP increases imports by roughly $160 million and a 1 percent increase in the value of the dollar increases imports by about $910 million.

Fill-In Questions

1. sterilization
2. policy dilemma
3. policy synchronization
4. domestic credit
5. purchasing power parity
6. J curve
7. real exchange rate
8. spillover, interdependence
9. expenditure-switching policy

True-False Questions

1. False. Under flexible exchange rates, the terms of trade have fluctuated a great deal.
2. False. If the dollar is worth more, German goods are cheaper in the United States.
3. True.
4. True.
5. True.
6. True.
7. False. This requires flexible prices as well.
8. True.
9. True.

Multiple-Choice Questions

1. c   2. b   3. d   4. b   5. a   6. a   7. a   8. c

Worked-Out Problems

1. An investor could invest a dollar in the United States and end up with $1.12. Alternatively, she could buy 2 marks and end up with DM2.2. For the DM2.2 to equal $1.12, the exchange rate at the end of the year must equal 51 cents.

2. Yes. Take $1 and buy 2.5 marks. Exchange the 2.5 marks for 1.25 pounds. Exchanging the 1.25 pounds at the quoted dollar/pound exchange rate yields $1.875, for a pure, riskless profit of $0.875. This process will be repeated until the mark depreciates in terms of the pound from 2 marks to ($1.5 per pound/$0.4 per mark) = 3.75 marks per pound.

GLOSSARY

Accelerator model of investment   Theory that investment is proportional to the rate of change in output.

Accessions   People getting jobs.

Accommodation   Use of policy to offset a shock. For example, increase in money supply to prevent increase in interest rate when *IS* curve shifts out. See also *accommodation of supply shocks.*

Accommodation of supply shocks   Use of aggregate demand policy to maintain GDP when faced with a temporary drop in aggregate supply.

Action lag   Period between the time a policy is chosen and the time it is put into effect.

Activist policy   Policy that responds to current state of the economy.

Activists   Economists who believe the government should use stabilization policy.

Adaptive expectations   Expectations theory that expectations change gradually over time. Contrast *rational expectations.*

Adjustment of deficits   Alternative to financing deficits with central bank reserves. Policy measures can be used to reduce the deficit.

Adverse supply shocks   Upward movement of the aggregate supply curve; the OPEC oil price increase is the classic example.

Aggregate demand   Sum of all the purchases of final goods throughout the economy.

Aggregate demand curve   Amount of GDP demanded in the economy at a given price level.

Aggregate supply   Total production of all final goods in the economy.

Aggregate supply curve   Amount of GDP supplied by firms at a given price level.

Anticipated inflation   Inflation everybody can predict exactly in advance.

Asset budget constraint   The necessary condition that a household's investments in different assets must add up to total wealth.

Automatic stabilizer   Factors in the structure of the economy that reduce the impact of changes in the autonomous spending on the equilibrium level of GDP.

Balance of payments   Net flow of dollars into the country from abroad.

Balanced budget amendment   Proposed constitutional amendment requiring an annually balanced federal budget.

Balanced budget multiplier   Increase in GDP, given equal increases in government purchases and in taxes.

Barro-Ricardo equivalence   Theory that current tax changes do not affect interest rates because people anticipate that the changes must be reversed in the future. Named for Robert Barro and David Ricardo.

Base drift   Change over time in initial level of money stock used for money growth calculations. See *fan versus band.*

Beggar-thy-neighbor policy   Attempt to increase domestic GDP at the expense of GDP in foreign countries.

Bond   Promise by a borrower to repay a loan at a certain date and to pay interest in the interim.

Bracket creep   Process by which inflation pushes people into higher tax brackets.

Budget deficit   See *government budget deficit.*

Budget surplus   Excess of government revenue over government expenditure. (Opposite of *budget deficit.*)

Buffer-stock saving   Excess consumer savings used to maintain consumption when income is lower than normal.

Burden of the debt   Share of each individual in the national debt; note also that the "burden" should be corrected for the share of each individual in ownership of the debt.

Business cycle   Pattern of expansions and contractions of the economy around trend growth.

Business fixed investment   Annual increase in machinery, equipment, and structures used in production.

Capital account   Net flow of dollars into the country due to investment by foreigners in real and financial assets.

Capital mobility   Ability of financial assets to flow between countries.

Catching-up hypothesis   The hypothesis that poorer countries will eventually attain a level of economic well-being comparable to that of the world's wealthier economies.

Central bank independence   Policy that allows a central bank (such as the Fed) to make decisions independently from the national government, thus retaining its ability to control the stock of high-powered money.

Classical adjustment process   Process by which the economy automatically moves toward internal and external balance.

Classical aggregate supply curve   Vertical aggregate supply curve.

Classical case   Vertical *LM* curve; due to lack of interest sensitivity of money demand.

Classical labor market   Type of labor market where fully flexible wages ensure that the real wage is independent of the nominal price level. Unemployment is always at the natural rate.

Clean floating   Pure flexible exchange rate system in which central banks do not intervene. Contrast *dirty floating.*

Cobb-Douglas production function   Production function with characteristics of constant returns to scale, constant elasticity of output, and unit elasticity of substitution between input factors.

COLA   Cost-of-living adjustment clause that indexes wages to the inflation rate.

Cold turkey policy   Policy strategy of moving immediately to desired target.

Competitiveness   Price of foreign goods relative to domestic goods, $eP*/P$.

Composition of output   Relative amounts of consumption, investment, and government purchases that make up GDP.

Consumer durables   Consumer goods that yield services over a period of time, for example, washing machines.

Consumer price index (CPI)   Price index that measures the cost of goods bought by a typical urban family.

Consumption   Purchases of goods and services by households.

Consumption function   Equation relating consumption to spending.

Convergence   Tendency of economic growth rates of different countries to approach similar steady-state levels.

Coordination of policies   Policies agreed upon by countries. Because of international spillover effects, domestic economies can be best controlled by cooperation among countries.

Coordination problem (with reference to flexible prices)   Situation in which no single firm will adjust prices or wages until other firms have done so, resulting in price "stickiness."

Cost of cyclical unemployment   Principally, the loss of output associated with high unemployment.

Council of Economic Advisers (CEA)   The three-person body comprising the President's official economic policy advisers.

Crawling peg exchange rate policy   The exchange rate is depreciated at a rate roughly equal to the inflation differential between a country and its trading partners.

Credibility   The degree to which the public believes the government will implement announced policies.

Credit rationing   Limitation of the amount of money individuals are able to borrow, even if they are willing to pay the prevailing interest rate.

Crowding out   Displacement of some component of private aggregate demand by government spending.

Currency appreciation   Increase in the value of the dollar vis-à-vis other currencies.

Currency-deposit ratio   One of the primary determinants of the money multiplier.

Currency depreciation   Decrease in the value of the dollar vis-à-vis other currencies.

Currency reform   Change in unit of currency, for example, redefinition of Israeli pound as shekel.

Current account   Net flow of dollars into the country due to sales of goods and services and net transfers from abroad.

Cyclical deficit   Portion of the budget deficit due to deviation of GDP from potential. Contrast *structural deficit.*

Cyclical unemployment   Unemployment in excess of structural unemployment; it occurs when output falls below the full-employment level.

Debt-financed deficits   Budget deficits financed through sales of bonds to the public.

Debt-income ratio   The ratio of the national debt to GDP. The debt-income ratio cannot grow without limit.

Debt management   Policy of dividing financing of the national debt among bonds of various maturities and printing of high-powered money.

Debt problem   The inability to pay a debt. A nation has a debt problem when its real interest payments on the national debt, or the portion owed to foreigners, become so large that the nation is unable to meet the payment.

Decision lag   Period between the time a disturbance is discovered and the time a policy is chosen.

Depreciation   Wearing out of the capital stock.

Desired capital stock   Level of capital stock that maximizes profits.

Devaluation of the exchange rate   Intentional depreciation of the dollar (or other currency) under a fixed exchange rate system.

Development economics   Study of the economic problems of poor countries.

Dirty floating   Flexible exchange rate system in which central banks intervene in exchange markets to moderate short-run fluctuations in exchange rates.

Discount rate   Interest rate charged by the Fed on loans to banks.

Discounted cash flow analysis   The method of determining the present value of cash to be received in the future, based on applying a discount to future earnings in order to account for the interest differential between a dollar today and a dollar in the future.

Discretionary spending   Portion of the federal budget under immediate annual congressional control. Contrast *entitlement spending.*

Disintermediation   Withdrawal of deposits from financial intermediaries when market interest rates rise above regulated ceiling rates on time deposits.

Disposable personal income   Income available for the household to spend.

Dissaving   Negative saving, that is, expenditure out of wealth.

Duration of spells of unemployment   Length of unemployment; some individuals are unemployed for a very brief period, some for a long time.

Dynamic consistency   Carrying out an action, even when doing so is painful, because you promised to do so earlier and you want people to believe you next time.

Dynamic multiplier   Response over time of aggregate demand to increase in autonomous spending.

Econometric models   Single- or multiple-equation model used to make quantitative economic predictions.

Econometric policy evaluation critique   Criticism that existing econometric models are inappropriate for studying policy changes because the policy changes themselves change the responses of economic agents.

Economic development   The course of a country's economic well-being over a long period, especially the movement to a higher standard of living.

Economic disturbances   Shifts in aggregate demand or supply, or money demand or supply, that cause output, interest rates, or prices to diverge from the target path.

Efficiency wage   Theory attributing wage rigidity to losses in productivity that would occur if wages were cut.

Endogenous growth theory   Theory which asserts that the growth rate of output in the steady state is determined by endogenous and economic factors.

Endogenous variable   Factor that is determined within a particular economic theory or model.

Entitlement spending   Portion of the budget fixed as a result of prior program commitments, such as Social Security, unemployment insurance, and student loans. Contrast *discretionary spending*.

Equilibrium output   Level of output when aggregate demand equals the supply of goods.

Excess reserves   Reserves held by banks over and above the level required by the Federal Reserve.

Excess sensitivity of consumption   Evidence that consumption has a larger response to current income than is consistent with the life-cycle/permanent-income theory.

Exchange rate   Price of foreign currency in terms of the U.S. dollar.

Exchange rate expectations   Anticipated level of future exchange rates.

Exchange rate overshooting   Movement of the exchange rate past its target. Adjustment of exchange rates to long-run equilibrium is frequently accompanied by an interim move of the exchange rate past its final position.

Exogenous variable   Factor that is determined outside a particular economic theory or model.

Expansion   See *recovery*.

Expectations-augmented aggregate supply curve   Aggregate supply curve that includes inflationary expectations as a major determinant of the price level.

Expectations-augmented Phillips curve   Phillips curve that includes inflationary expectations as a major determinant of the inflation rate.

Expectations effect   Long-run increase in nominal interest rate following increased growth rate of the money supply due to increased inflationary expectations.

Expected depreciation   Anticiapted drop in the exchange rate. (Under perfect capital mobility, the nominal interest differential equals the expected depreciation rate.)

Expenditure reducing (or increasing) policies   Policies aimed at offsetting the effects of expenditure switching policy on aggregate demand.

Expenditure switching policies   Polices aimed at increasing purchases of domestic goods and decreasing imports.

Extended Phillips curve   Expectations-augmented Phillips curve with added term for the rate of change of unemployment.

Factor cost   Cost of goods net of indirect taxes. See *market prices*.

Factor shares   Portion of national income paid to each productive input (labor, capital, etc.).

Fan versus band   If the Fed follows the band operating procedure, last year's error is corrected in this year's money growth. If the Fed follows the fan operating procedure, each year starts from a fresh base. See *base drift*.

FDIC (Federal Deposit Insurance Corporation)   Government agency that insures deposits of most commercial banks and mutual savings banks to a maximum of $100,000.

Final goods   Production excluding intermediate factors of production.

Final sales to domestic producers GDP less net exports and inventory change.

Financing of deficits Use of reserves by a central bank to pay for temporary imbalances in the balance of payments.

Fine tuning Continuous attempts to stabilize the economy in the face of small disturbances.

Fiscal policy Government policy with respect to government purchases, transfer payments, and the tax structure.

Fiscal policy multiplier Increase in aggregate demand for a $1 increase in government purchases (or other changes in autonomous demand).

Fisher equation A relation in which the nominal interest rate equals the real interest rate plus the expected inflation rate.

Fixed exchange rates Exchange rates determined by governments and central banks rather than the free market.

Flexible exchange rates Exchange rates determined by supply and demand.

Floating exchange rates Synonym for *flexible exchange rates*.

Frequency of unemployment The average number of times, per period, that workers become unemployed.

Frictionless neoclassical model Model of a world with flexible prices and perfect competition.

Frictional unemployment Unemployment associated with the movement of workers in and out of jobs in "normal" times.

Full crowding out Total displacement of private spending by increasing government spending. See *classical aggregate supply curve* and *classical case*.

Full-employment (high-unemployment) surplus What the budget surplus would be (hypothetically) with existing fiscal policy if the economy were at full employment.

GDP deflator Measure of the price level obtained by dividing nominal GDP by real GDP.

GDP, nominal Measure of all goods and services produced within the country in one year, measured in dollars.

GDP, real Measure of all goods and services produced within the country in one year, measured in units of constant value.

Goodhart's law The theory that predicts that a stable relationship between nominal income and the quantity of *M2* cannot be sustained indefinitely.

Government budget deficit Excess of government expenditure over government revenue.

Government expenditure Total government spending; includes both government purchases and transfers.

Government purchases Government spending on goods and services. Contrast *government expenditure*.

Gradual adjustment hypothesis Theory that the change in the capital stock responds to the gap between desired capital stock and current capital stock.

Gradualism Policy strategy of moving toward a desired target slowly.

Gramm-Rudman-Hollings Act Federal law providing for automatic cuts in spending if the President and Congress do not agree on a balanced budget.

Gross domestic product   See *GDP, real.*

Gross national product (GNP)   Measure of the value of all final goods and services produced by domestically owned factors of production.

Growth   Increase in size of the economy.

Growth accounting   The theory of measurement of the sources of economic growth.

Growth of total factor productivity   See *technical progress.*

Guideposts   Advisory rulings for wage and price increases.

Heterodox programs   Combination of money, fiscal, exchange rate, and income policy designed to stabilize the economy.

High-powered money   Currency plus reserve deposits at the Federal Reserve.

Human capital   Education and training of individuals to increase productivity.

Hyperinflation   Very rapid price increase, usually defined as over 100 percent per month.

Imperfect information   Forecasts based on imperfect information will be less than fully accurate, though not necessarily biased.

Import substitution   The development strategy that protects domestic producers from foreign competition in an attempt to speed the pace of industrialization.

Imported inflation   Inflation due to increase in domestic prices of imported goods following currency depreciation.

Income effect   Increase in interest rate that follows initial drop in the rate (due to *liquidity effect*) after increase in money supply. Not to be confused with income effect of microeconomics as an "income and substitution effect."

Income velocity of money   Ratio of income to the money stock.

Incomes policies   Attempts to reduce inflation by wage or price controls.

Indexation   Automatic adjustment of prices and wages according to inflation rate.

Indexation of tax brackets   Automatic adjustment of tax brackets on the basis of the inflation rate. Prevents *bracket creep.*

Inflation   Percentage rate of increase in the general price level.

Inflation-corrected deficit   Measure of the budget deficit that corrects for effects of inflation; specifically, the correction reduces the measured budget deficit by the capital gain on nominal bonds.

Inflation tax   Revenue gained by the government because of inflation's devaluation of money holdings.

Infrastructure investment   Addition to a nation's physical plant—highways, schools, utilities, and the like—typically initiated by government.

Inside lag   Period between the time a disturbance occurs and the time action is taken.

Interdependence   Interconnection between national economies linked through international trade.

Intergenerational accounting   Evaluation of the costs and benefits of the entire fiscal system for various age groups in society.

Intermediate targets   Policy targets used for control rather than because of their inherent interest. For example, the money supply might be an intermediate target in the attempt to ultimately control inflation. Contrast *ultimate targets.*

Internal and external balance   *Internal balance* occurs when output is at potential GDP; *external balance,* when the trade balance is zero.

Intertemporal substitution of leisure The extent to which temporarily high real wages cause workers to work harder today and enjoy more leisure tomorrow.

Intervention Sales or purchases of foreign exchange by the central bank in order to stabilize exchange rates.

Inventory cycle Response of inventory investment to changes in sales that causes further changes in aggregate demand.

Inventory investment Increase in stock of goods on hands.

Inventory-theoretic approach Money demand models such as the Baumol-Tobin model.

Investment Purchase of new capital, principally by the business sector.

Investment subsidy Government payment of part of the cost of private investment.

IS-LM **curves** Goods market and money market equilibrium schedules.

J curve Curve that traces time path of response of imports to exchange rate changes.

Keynesian aggregate supply curve Horizontal aggregate supply curve.

Keynesians Members of a school of economic thought who argue for active government stabilization policy. Alternatively, those who argue for fiscal rather than monetary policy.

Labor productivity Average output per worker.

Laffer curve Relation between tax revenue and tax rates showing that tax revenue is maximized at a tax rate greater than zero and less than 100 percent.

Layoffs Term categorizing types of unemployment. A layoff occurs when the employer dismisses an employee but promises to recall the worker at a later date.

Life-cycle hypothesis Consumption theory emphasizing that consumers consume and save out of total life income and plan to provide for retirement.

Limits of growth Study of whether resource depletion will eventually eliminate economic growth.

Liquidity A measure of the ability to make funds available on short notice.

Liquidity constraints Limitations on ability to borrow in order to finance consumption plans.

Liquidity effect Initial drop in interest rate following increase in money supply due to movement in *LM* curve.

Liquidity trap Horizontal *LM* curve; due to extreme interest sensitivity of money demand.

Long-run aggregate supply curve Aggregate supply curve showing long-run tradeoff between GDP and the price level. Usually assumed to be vertical at potential GDP.

Long-run Phillips curve Long-run tradeoffs between inflation and unemployment (probably none).

Long-term labor market relations Observation that day-to-day changes in wages rarely clear labor markets. Employer-employee relations are generally based on understandings over months or years.

Lucas model Upward-sloping short-run aggregate supply curve based on the assumption that imperfect information prevents perfectly flexible wages.

Lucas supply curve Aggregate supply curve showing output to be positively related to the difference between the actual and expected price level (where the expected price level is formed with rational expectations).

M1 Currency plus checkable deposits.

M2 *M*1 plus small time and savings deposits, overnight repurchase agreements (RPs) and Eurodollars, and money market funds.

Macroeconomic models Simplified formal models used to study and predict the behavior of the nation's economy.

Managed floating See *dirty floating*.

Marginal product of capital Increment to output obtained by adding one unit of capital, with other factor inputs held constant.

Marginal product of labor (*MPL*) Increment to output obtained by adding one unit of labor, with other factor inputs held constant.

Marginal propensity to consume (*MPC*) Increase in consumption for each $1 increase in disposable income.

Marginal propensity to save (*MPS*) Increase in saving for each $1 increase in disposable income.

Market-clearing approach Theory that flexible prices clear all markets. See *frictionless neoclassical model*.

Market prices Cost of goods including indirect taxes. See *factor cost*.

Markup Increase of price over cost (often assumed to be constant, as an analytical convenience).

Measure of economic welfare (MEW) GDP measurement adjusted for nonmarket outputs, economic "bads," and growth in leisure.

Medium of exchange Asset used for making payments.

Monetarism See *monetarists*.

Monetarists Members of a school of economic thought which emphasizes the importance of the money supply.

Monetary accommodation Use of monetary policy to stabilize interest rates during active fiscal policy operations.

Monetary approach to the balance of payments Theory that emphasizes role of the money stock in determining the balance of payments.

Monetary base See *high-powered money*.

Monetary-fiscal policy mix Combination of fiscal and monetary policy chosen in recognition of differing effects of each policy on interest rates and investment.

Monetary policy Use of money supply and interest rate changes to influence aggregate demand.

Monetary policy multiplier Increase in aggregate demand for $1 increase in the money supply.

Monetary rule A rule setting the growth of the money supply; frequently, a constant growth rate without regard to current economic conditions.

Monetizing budget deficits Purchase of government debt by the Federal Reserve, thus indirectly funding the deficit by printing money.

Money (money stock) Assets that can be used for making immediate payment.

Money-financing Deficits financed by printing high-powered money.

Money illusion Incorrect belief that the numbers used to express prices have significance.

Money multiplier   Ratio of money stock to the monetary base.

Money stock and interest rate targets   The Fed can directly target either the money stock or the interest rate, but not both.

Money supply function   Function determined by the supply of high-powered money and the money multiplier.

Multiplier   Increase in endogenous variable for each $1 increase in exogenous variable. Particularly, increase in GDP for each $1 increase in government purchases.

Multiplier uncertainty   Uncertainty about effects of policy changes due to uncertainty about value of fiscal policy multiplier, monetary policy multiplier, etc.

Mundell-Fleming model   Model first proposed by Robert Mundell and Marcus Fleming that explores economy with flexible exchange rates and perfect capital mobility.

Myopia   Shortsightedness by households regarding future income streams.

National (public) debt   Accumulation of all past deficits; total outstanding government bonds.

National income   Total payments to factors of production. Net national product minus indirect taxes.

Natural rate of unemployment   The unemployment rate that is permanently sustainable given the institutions of the economy.

Neoclassical growth theory   Theory which asserts that the growth rate of output is determined by exogenous technological growth.

Net domestic product (NDP)   GDP minus allowance for depreciation of capital.

Net exports   Exports minus imports.

Net national saving   Total flow of savings from various sectors of the economy minus depreciation.

Neutrality of money   Proposition that equiproportional changes in the money stock and prices leave the economy unaffected.

New classical macroeconomists   Economists who believe that the private economy is inherently efficient and that the government ought not to attempt to stabilize output and unemployment.

New Deal   Slogan for Franklin D. Roosevelt's economic policy reforms.

New Economics   Economic policy of the Kennedy-Johnson years, emphasizing the use of Keynesian theory to maintain full employment.

New Keynesians   Set of eclectic economists who base their models on rational behavior and conclude that the economy is not inherently efficient and that, at times, the government ought to stabilize output and unemployment. Contrast *new classical macroeconomists.*

Newly industrializing economies (NIEs)   Economies such as South Korea, Taiwan, Hong Kong, and Singapore, which are characterized by high GDP growth rates.

Nominal interest rate   Stated rate of return without adjustment for inflation. See *real interest rate.*

Noninterest deficit   See *primary deficit.*

Okun's law   Empirical "law" relating GDP growth to changes in unemployment; named for its discoverer, the late Arthur Okun.

Open market operation Federal Reserve purchase or sale of Treasury bills in exchange for money.

Openness Extent to which the economy is involved with foreign trade as measured by the ratio of imports to GDP.

Output gap Difference between potential GDP and actual GDP.

Outside lag Time required for a policy change to take effect.

Outward-oriented strategy The development strategy that holds that competition from foreign producers improves the efficiency of domestic producers.

Overshooting Movement of an economic variable past its long-run value.

Peak High points of business cycle.

Permanent income Estimated lifetime income plus wealth.

Personal income Income received by households.

Phillips curve Relation between inflation and unemployment; in a sense, a dynamic version of the aggregate supply curve.

Planned aggregate demand Total planned spending on consumption, investment, and government purchases.

Policy coordination The combination of expenditure-switching policies and expenditure-increasing policies to achieve internal and external balance.

Policy dilemma Conflicts between achieving two inconsistent targets, for example, between *internal and external balance.*

Policy mix Combination of fiscal and monetary policy to achieve both *internal and external balance.*

Policy rule Activist but nondiscretionary policy guide.

Political business cycle Theory that politicians deliberately manipulate the economy to produce an economic boom at election time.

Portfolio decisions Decisions on how to divide wealth among different assets.

Potential output Output that can be produced when all factors are fully employed.

Precautionary demand Demand for money held against uncertain expenditure needs.

Present discounted value (*PDV*) Value today of a stream of payments to be made in the future.

Price controls Government-imposed restrictions against raising (and occasionally reducing) prices.

Primary deficit The budget deficit except for interest payments.

Producer price index (PPI) Price index based on a market basket of goods used in production. The PPI replaced the wholesale price index (WPI).

Production function Technological relation showing how much output can be produced for a given combination of inputs.

Profit sharing System in which part of workers' compensation is a share of profits rather than an hourly wage.

Propagation mechanism Mechanism by which current economic shocks cause fluctuations into the future, for example, *intertemporal substitution of leisure.*

Public debt See *national debt.*

Purchasing power parity (PPP) Theory of exchange rate determination arguing that the exchange rate adjusts to maintain equal purchasing power of foreign and domestic currency.

q theory   Investment theory emphasizing that investment will be high when assets are valuable relative to their reproduction cost. The ratio of asset value to cost if called *q*.

Quantity equation   Price times quantity equals money times velocity.

Quantity theory of money   Theory of money demand emphasizing the relation of nominal income to nominal money. Sometimes used to mean a vertical *LM* curve.

Quits   A quit occurs when the worker decides to leave.

Rational expectations   Theory of expectations formation in which expectations are based on all available information about the underlying economic variable. Frequently associated with new classical macroeconomics.

Rational expectations equilibrium approach   See *rational expectations*.

Reaganomics   Slogan describing the Reagan administration's economic program.

Real balance   Real value of the money stock (number of dollars divided by the price level).

Real business cycles   Theory that recessions and booms are due primarily to shocks in real activity, such as supply shocks, rather than to changes in monetary factors.

Real exchange rate   Purchasing power of foreign currency relative to the U.S. dollar.

Real interest rate   Return on an investment measured in dollars of constant value.

Real materials prices   Price of raw material relative to price of output.

Real wage rigidity   Situation in which formal or informal indexation of wages to the cost of living prevents economic adjustment through changes in real wages.

Recession   Period of economic weakness, with GDP below potential.

Recognition lag   Period between the time a disturbance occurs and the time policy makers discover the disturbance.

Recovery   Upward swing in business cycle.

Redistribution of wealth   Desired effect of mugging. Undesired side effect of unanticipated inflation.

Relative-income hypothesis   Consumption theory arguing that consumption is related to previous peak income as well as current income.

Rental cost of capital   Cost of using a dollar's worth of capital for a given unit of time, usually a year.

Repercussion effect   Feedback of domestic economic changes through foreign economies and back into the domestic economy.

Replacement ratio   The ratio of after-tax income while unemployed to after-tax income while employed.

Reserve-deposit ratio   One of the primary determinants of the money multiplier.

Residential investment   Investment in housing.

Revaluation of the exchange rate   Intentional appreciation of the dollar (or other currency) under fixed exchange rate system.

Rules versus discretion   Argument over whether policy should be on "automatic pilot" or whether (hard-to-predict) human judgment should be used.

Sacrifice ratio   During a period of anti-inflation policy, the ratio of cumulative GDP lost to reduction in the inflation rate.

Seigniorage   Revenue derived from the government's ability to print money.

Separations   People leaving jobs.

Short-run aggregate supply curve   Aggregate supply curve showing short-run trade-off between GDP and the price level. Usually assumed to be quite flat.

Short-run Phillips curve   Short-run tradeoff between inflation and unemployment, holding anticipated inflation constant.

Sluggish wage adjustment   Observation that wages adjust slowly rather than instantly, thus preventing labor markets from clearing in a competitive fashion.

Small menu costs   Theory suggesting that the very small costs of changing prices and wages may lead to large amounts of price and wage rigidity.

Sources of growth   Increases in factor inputs and improved technology.

Square-root formula   Demand-for-money schedule developed in Baumol-Tobin approach.

Stabilization policies   Use of fiscal and monetary policies to smooth fluctuations in output.

Stagflation   Simultaneous inflation and recession.

Standard of deferred payment   Asset normally used for making payments due at a later date.

Steady state   State in which real (per capita) economic variables are constant.

Sterilization   Open market purchase or sale by the Fed in order to offset effects of foreign exchange market intervention on the monetary base.

Sterilized and nonsterilized intervention   See *sterilization* and *intervention*.

Store of value   Asset that maintains its value over time.

Structural deficit   Deficit that would exist with current fiscal policy if the economy were at full employment. Formerly called "high-employment" or "full-employment" deficit. Contrast *cyclical deficit*.

Structural unemployment   See *frictional unemployment*.

Supply shock   An economic disturbance whose first impact is a shift in the aggregate supply curve.

Supply-side economics   School of economics that emphasizes changes in potential GDP rather than aggregate demand.

Synchronization   Coordinated exchange rate policies between trading countries.

Targeted programs   Employment programs aimed at special subsegments of the work force, such as youths or workers who have lost jobs to foreign competition.

Targets and instruments of policy   The *target* is the variable of policy instrument. The *instrument* is the variable to be manipulated in order to change the target variable.

Tax indexation   Under *tax indexation*, tax brackets move up with inflation. This eliminates *bracket creep*.

Tax surcharge   Temporary increase in tax rate.

Technical progress   Ability to produce more output with a given level of inputs; growth in total factor productivity.

Terms of trade   Ratio of import prices to export prices, a measure of competitiveness.

TIP (tax incentive policy)   Use of tax subsidies and penalties to persuade companies to reduce wage or price increase.

TISA   See *total incomes system of accounts*.

Total incomes system of accounts (TISA)   System of national income accounting that corrects traditional GDP measures, particularly with respect to measuring "non-market" goods.

Trade balance   Net flow of dollars into the country due to sales of goods abroad.

Transactions demand   Demand for money held to minimize costs associated with repeated "trips to the bank."

Transfers   Payments to a household other than as compensation for services, for example, Social Security.

Transmission mechanism   Process by which monetary policy affects aggregate demand.

Trend output   See *potential output.*

Trough   Low point of business cycle.

Twin deficits   The budget deficit and the trade deficit.

Ultimate targets   Policy targets of inherent interest. For example, the inflation rate might be an ultimate target. Contrast *intermediate targets.*

Unanticipated money   Changes to the money stock that were not anticipated by individuals or businesses.

Underground economy   Transactions executed in cash with the intention of confusing economic statistics.

Unemployment pool   Group of individuals in transition between jobs.

Unemployment rate   The fraction of the people in the labor force unable to find work.

Unintended inventory accumulation   Increase in stocks of goods when firms are unable to sell output as expected.

Unit of account   Asset in which prices are denoted.

Unit labor cost   Cost of enough labor to produce one unit of output.

User cost of capital   See *rental cost of capital.*

Value added   Increase in value of output at a given stage of production. Equivalently, value of output minus cost of inputs.

Wage and price controls   Regulation of wages and prices by law rather than by supply and demand.

Wage push   Demand for wage increases above inflation rate built into short-run Phillips curve.

Wealth budget constraint   The sum of a household's investment in different assets must equal its total wealth.

Zero inflation target   Plan to hold nominal prices constant.

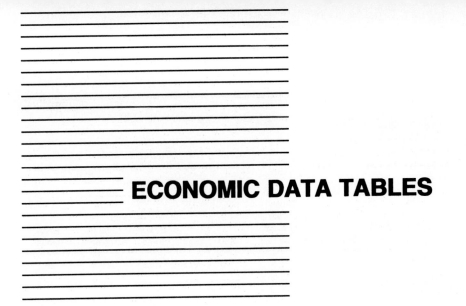

ECONOMIC DATA TABLES

TABLE A

GROSS DOMESTIC PRODUCT, 1959–1991 (Billions of dollars)

| | | PERSONAL CONSUMPTION EXPENDITURES | | | | | FIXED INVESTMENT | | | | |
| | | | | | | | | NONRESIDENTIAL | | | |
Year	Gross domestic product	Total	Durable goods	Non-durable goods	Services	Gross private domestic investment	Total	Total	Struc-tures	Producers' durable equipment	Resi-dential
1959	494.2	318.1	42.8	148.5	126.8	78.8	74.6	46.5	18.1	28.3	28.1
1960	513.4	332.4	43.5	153.1	135.9	78.7	75.5	49.2	19.6	29.7	26.3
1961	531.8	343.5	41.9	157.4	144.1	77.9	75.0	48.6	19.7	28.9	26.4
1962	571.6	364.4	47.0	163.8	153.6	87.9	81.8	52.8	20.8	32.1	29.0
1963	603.1	384.2	51.8	169.4	163.1	93.4	87.7	55.6	21.2	34.4	32.1
1964	648.0	412.5	56.8	179.7	175.9	101.7	96.7	62.4	23.7	38.7	34.3
1965	702.7	444.6	63.5	191.9	189.2	118.0	108.3	74.1	28.3	45.8	34.2
1966	769.8	481.6	68.5	208.5	204.6	130.4	116.7	84.4	31.3	53.0	32.3
1967	814.3	509.3	70.6	216.9	221.7	128.0	117.6	85.2	31.5	53.7	32.4
1968	889.3	559.1	81.0	235.0	243.1	139.9	130.8	92.1	33.6	58.5	38.7
1969	959.5	603.7	86.2	252.2	265.3	155.2	145.5	102.9	37.7	65.2	42.6
1970	1,010.7	646.5	85.3	270.4	290.8	150.3	148.1	106.7	40.3	66.4	41.4
1971	1,097.2	700.3	97.2	283.3	319.8	175.5	167.5	111.7	42.7	69.1	55.8
1972	1,207.0	767.8	110.7	305.2	351.9	205.6	195.7	126.1	47.2	78.9	69.7
1973	1,349.6	848.1	124.1	339.6	384.5	243.1	225.4	150.0	55.0	95.1	75.3
1974	1,458.6	927.7	123.0	380.8	423.9	245.8	231.5	165.6	61.2	104.3	66.0
1975	1,585.9	1,024.9	134.3	416.0	474.5	226.0	231.7	169.0	61.4	107.6	62.7
1976	1,768.4	1,143.1	160.0	451.8	531.2	286.4	269.6	187.2	65.9	121.2	82.5
1977	1,974.1	1,271.5	182.6	490.4	598.4	358.3	333.5	223.2	74.6	148.7	110.3
1978	2,232.7	1,421.2	202.3	541.5	677.4	434.0	406.1	274.5	93.9	180.6	131.6
1979	2,488.6	1,583.7	214.2	613.3	756.2	480.2	467.5	326.4	118.4	208.1	141.0
1980	2,708.0	1,748.1	212.5	682.9	852.7	467.6	477.1	353.8	137.5	216.4	123.3
1981	3,030.6	1,926.2	228.5	744.2	953.5	558.0	532.5	410.0	169.1	240.9	122.5
1982	3,149.6	2,059.2	236.5	772.3	1,050.4	503.4	519.3	413.7	178.8	234.9	105.7
1983	3,405.0	2,257.5	275.0	817.8	1,164.7	546.7	552.2	400.2	153.1	247.1	152.0
1984	3,777.2	2,460.3	317.9	873.0	1,269.4	718.9	647.8	468.9	175.6	293.3	178.9
1985	4,038.7	2,667.4	352.9	919.4	1,395.1	714.5	689.9	504.0	193.4	310.6	185.9
1986	4,268.6	2,850.6	389.6	952.2	1,508.8	717.6	709.0	492.4	174.0	318.4	216.6
1987	4,539.9	3,052.2	403.7	1,011.1	1,637.4	749.3	723.0	497.8	171.3	326.5	225.2
1988	4,900.4	3,296.1	437.1	1,073.8	1,785.2	793.6	777.4	545.4	182.0	363.4	232.0
1989	5,244.0	3,517.9	459.8	1,146.9	1,911.2	837.6	801.6	570.7	193.1	377.6	230.9
1990	5,513.8	3,742.6	465.9	1,217.7	2,059.0	802.6	802.7	587.0	198.7	388.3	215.7
1991	5,671.8	3,886.8	445.2	1,251.0	2,190.5	725.3	745.6	550.4	174.5	376.0	195.1

SOURCE: *Economic Report of the President*

	NET EXPORTS OF GOODS AND SERVICES			GOVERNMENT PURCHASES OF GOODS AND SERVICES						
						FEDERAL				
Change in business inventories	Net exports	Exports	Imports	Total	Total	National defense	Non-defense	State and local	Addendum: Gross national product	Percent change in GDP from preceding period
4.2	−1.7	20.6	22.3	99.0	57.1	46.4	10.8	41.8	497.0	
3.2	2.4	25.3	22.8	99.8	55.3	45.3	10.0	44.5	516.6	3.9
2.9	3.4	26.0	22.7	107.0	58.6	47.9	10.6	48.4	535.4	3.6
6.1	2.4	27.4	25.0	116.8	65.4	52.1	13.3	51.4	575.8	7.5
5.7	3.3	29.4	26.1	122.3	66.4	51.5	14.9	55.8	607.7	5.5
5.0	5.5	33.6	28.1	128.3	67.5	50.4	17.0	60.9	653.0	7.4
9.7	3.9	35.4	31.5	136.3	69.5	51.0	18.5	66.8	708.1	8.4
13.8	1.9	38.9	37.1	155.9	81.3	62.0	19.3	74.6	774.9	9.5
10.5	1.4	41.4	39.9	175.6	92.8	73.4	19.4	82.7	819.8	5.8
9.1	−1.3	45.3	46.6	191.5	99.2	79.1	20.0	92.3	895.5	9.2
9.7	−1.2	49.3	50.5	201.8	100.5	78.9	21.6	101.3	965.6	7.9
2.3	1.2	57.0	55.8	212.7	100.1	76.8	23.3	112.6	1,017.1	5.3
8.0	−3.0	59.3	62.3	224.3	100.0	74.1	25.9	124.3	1,104.9	8.6
9.9	−8.0	66.2	74.2	241.5	106.9	77.4	29.4	134.7	1,215.7	10.0
17.7	0.6	91.8	91.2	257.7	108.5	77.5	31.1	149.2	1,362.3	11.8
14.3	−3.1	124.3	127.5	288.3	117.6	82.6	35.0	170.7	1,474.3	8.1
−5.7	13.6	136.3	122.7	321.4	129.4	89.6	39.8	192.0	1,599.1	8.7
16.7	−2.3	148.9	151.1	341.3	135.8	93.4	42.4	205.5	1,785.5	11.5
24.7	−23.7	158.8	182.4	368.0	147.9	100.9	47.0	220.1	1,994.6	11.6
27.9	−26.1	186.1	212.3	403.6	162.2	108.9	53.3	241.4	2,254.5	13.1
12.8	−23.8	228.9	252.7	448.5	179.3	121.9	57.5	269.2	2,520.8	11.5
−9.5	−14.7	279.2	293.9	507.1	209.1	142.7	66.4	298.0	2742.1	8.8
25.4	−14.7	303.0	317.7	561.1	240.8	167.5	73.3	320.3	3,063.8	11.9
−15.9	−20.6	282.6	303.2	607.6	266.6	193.8	72.7	341.1	3,179.8	3.9
−5.5	−51.4	276.7	328.1	652.3	292.0	214.4	77.5	360.3	3,434.4	8.1
71.1	−102.7	302.4	405.1	700.8	310.9	233.1	77.8	389.9	3,801.5	10.9
24.6	−115.6	302.1	417.6	772.3	344.3	258.6	85.7	428.1	4,053.6	6.9
8.6	−132.5	319.2	451.7	833.0	367.8	276.7	91.1	465.3	4,277.7	5.7
26.3	−143.1	364.0	507.1	881.5	384.9	292.1	92.9	496.6	4,544.5	6.4
16.2	−108.0	444.2	552.2	918.7	387.0	295.6	91.4	531.7	4,908.2	7.9
36.0	−82.9	504.9	587.8	971.4	401.4	300.0	101.5	570.0	5,248.2	7.0
0.0	−74.4	550.4	624.8	1,042.9	424.9	313.4	111.5	618.0	5,524.5	5.1
−20.2	−27.1	593.3	620.4	1,086.9	445.1	323.4	121.7	641.8		2.9

TABLE B
GROSS NATIONAL PRODUCT IN 1987 DOLLARS, 1959–1991 (Billions of 1987 dollars, except as noted)

| | | PERSONAL CONSUMPTION EXPENDITURES | | | | | FIXED INVESTMENT | | | | |
| | | | | | | | | NONRESIDENTIAL | | | |
Year	Gross domestic product	Total	Durable goods	Non-durable goods	Services	Gross private domestic investment	Total	Total	Struc-tures	Producers' durable equipment	Resi-dential
1959	1,931.3	1,178.9	114.4	518.5	546.0	296.4	282.8	165.2	74.4	90.8	117.6
1960	1,973.2	1,210.8	115.4	526.9	568.5	290.8	282.7	173.3	80.8	92.5	109.4
1961	2,025.6	1,238.4	109.4	537.7	591.3	289.4	282.2	172.1	82.3	89.8	110.1
1962	2,129.8	1,293.3	120.2	553.0	620.0	321.2	305.6	185.0	86.1	98.9	120.6
1963	2,218.0	1341.9	130.3	563.6	648.0	343.3	327.3	192.3	86.9	105.4	135.0
1964	2,343.3	1,417.2	140.7	588.2	688.3	371.8	356.2	214.0	95.9	118.1	142.1
1965	2,473.5	1497.0	156.2	616.7	724.1	413.0	387.9	250.6	111.5	139.1	137.3
1966	2,622.3	1,573.8	166.0	647.6	760.2	438.0	401.3	276.7	119.1	157.6	124.5
1967	2,690.3	1,622.4	167.2	659.0	796.2	418.6	391.0	270.8	116.0	154.8	120.2
1968	2,801.0	1,707.5	184.5	686.0	837.0	440.1	416.5	280.1	117.4	162.7	136.4
1969	2,877.1	1,771.2	190.8	703.2	877.2	461.3	436.5	296.4	123.5	172.9	140.1
1970	2,875.8	1,813.5	183.7	717.2	912.5	429.7	423.8	292.0	123.3	168.7	131.8
1971	2,965.1	1,873.7	201.4	725.6	946.7	481.5	460.7	292.6	121.2	171.4	168.1
1972	3,107.1	1,978.4	225.2	755.8	997.4	532.2	509.6	311.6	124.8	186.8	198.0
1973	3,268.6	2,066.7	246.6	777.9	1,042.2	591.7	554.0	357.4	134.9	222.4	196.6
1974	3,248.1	2,053.8	227.2	759.8	1,066.8	543.0	512.0	356.5	132.3	224.2	155.6
1975	3,221.7	2,097.5	226.8	767.1	1,103.6	437.6	451.5	316.8	118.0	198.8	134.7
1976	3,380.8	2,207.3	256.4	801.3	1,149.5	520.6	495.1	328.7	120.5	208.2	166.4
1977	3,533.2	2,296.6	280.0	819.8	1,196.8	600.4	566.2	364.3	126.1	238.2	201.9
1978	3,703.5	2,391.8	292.9	844.8	1,254.1	664.6	627.4	412.9	144.1	268.8	214.5
1979	3,796.8	2,448.4	289.0	862.8	1,296.5	669.7	656.1	448.8	163.3	285.5	207.4
1980	3,776.3	2,447.1	262.7	860.5	1,323.9	594.4	602.7	437.8	170.2	267.6	164.8
1981	3,843.1	2,476.9	264.6	867.9	1,344.4	631.1	606.5	455.0	182.9	272.0	151.6
1982	3,760.3	2,503.7	262.5	872.2	1,368.9	540.5	558.0	433.9	181.3	252.6	124.1
1983	3,906.6	2,619.4	297.7	900.3	1,421.4	599.5	595.1	420.8	160.3	260.5	174.2
1984	4,148.5	2,746.1	338.5	934.6	1,473.0	757.5	689.6	490.2	182.8	307.4	199.3
1985	4,279.8	2,865.8	370.1	958.7	1,537.0	745.9	723.8	521.8	197.4	324.4	202.0
1986	4,404.5	2,969.1	402.0	991.0	1,576.1	735.1	726.5	500.3	176.6	323.7	226.2
1987	4,540.0	3,052.2	403.7	1,011.1	1,637.4	749.3	723.0	497.8	171.3	326.5	225.2
1988	4,719.6	3,162.4	428.7	1,035.1	1,698.5	773.4	753.4	530.8	174.0	356.8	222.7
1989	4,636.3	3,223.1	441.3	1,049.3	1,732.9	789.2	756.6	542.4	177.4	365.0	214.2
1990	4,884.9	3,262.6	438.9	1,050.8	1,773.0	744.5	744.2	548.8	177.9	370.8	195.5
1991	4,848.4	3,256.7	412.5	1,042.3	1,801.9	672.6	687.7	512.7	153.9	358.8	175.1

SOURCE: Department of Commerce, Bureau of Economic Analysis

	NET EXPORTS OF GOODS AND SERVICES			GOVERNMENT PURCHASES OF GOODS AND SERVICES						
						FEDERAL				
Change in business inventories	Net exports	Exports	Imports	Total	Total	National defense	Non-defense	State and local	Addendum: Gross national product	Percent change in GDP from preceding period
13.6	−21.8	73.8	95.6	477.8	268.2			209.6	1,942.1	
8.1	−7.6	88.4	96.1	479.2	261.3			217.9	1,985.1	2.2
7.2	−5.5	89.9	95.3	503.3	271.9			231.4	2,039.0	2.7
15.6	−10.5	95.0	105.5	525.9	289.0			236.9	2,145.0	5.1
16.0	−5.8	101.8	107.7	538.7	288.1			250.6	2,234.2	4.1
15.7	2.5	115.4	112.9	551.7	284.5			267.3	2,360.8	5.6
25.1	−6.4	118.1	124.5	569.9	285.1			284.8	2,491.9	5.6
36.7	−18.0	125.7	143.7	628.5	325.4			303.1	2,639.4	6.0
27.6	−23.7	130.0	153.7	673.0	356.1			317.0	2,707.8	2.6
23.6	−37.5	140.2	177.7	691.0	357.2			333.7	2,819.8	4.1
24.8	−41.5	147.8	189.2	686.1	344.2			341.9	2,895.0	2.7
5.9	−35.2	161.3	196.4	667.8	316.9			350.9	2,893.5	0.0
20.8	−45.9	161.9	207.8	655.8	294.2			361.6	2,985.2	3.1
22.5	−56.5	173.7	230.2	653.0	284.4	209.6	74.8	368.6	3,128.8	4.8
37.7	−34.1	210.3	244.4	644.2	265.3	191.3	74.1	378.9	3,298.6	5.2
30.9	−4.1	234.4	238.4	655.4	262.6	185.8	76.8	392.9	3,282.4	0.6
−13.9	23.1	232.9	209.8	663.5	262.7	184.9	77.8	400.8	3,247.6	−0.8
25.5	−6.4	243.4	249.7	659.2	258.2	179.9	78.3	401.1	3,412.2	4.9
34.3	−27.8	246.9	274.7	664.1	263.0	181.6	81.4	401.0	3,568.9	4.5
37.2	−29.9	270.2	300.1	677.0	268.6	182.1	86.5	408.4	3,739.0	4.8
13.6	−10.6	293.5	304.1	689.3	271.7	185.1	86.6	417.6	3,845.3	2.5
−8.3	30.7	320.5	289.9	704.2	284.8	194.2	90.6	419.4	3,823.4	−0.5
24.6	22.0	326.1	304.1	713.2	295.8	206.4	89.4	417.4	3,884.4	1.8
−17.5	−7.4	296.7	304.1	723.6	306.0	221.4	84.7	417.6	3,796.1	−2.2
4.4	−56.1	285.9	342.1	743.8	320.8	234.2	86.6	423.0	3,939.6	3.9
67.9	−122.0	305.7	427.7	766.9	331.0	245.8	85.1	436.0	4,174.5	6.2
22.1	−145.3	309.2	454.6	813.4	355.2	265.6	89.5	458.2	4,295.0	3.2
8.5	−155.1	329.6	484.7	855.4	373.0	280.6	92.4	482.4	4,413.5	2.9
26.3	−143.0	364.0	507.1	881.5	384.9	292.1	92.9	496.6	4,544.6	3.1
19.9	−104.0	421.6	525.7	886.8	377.3	287.0	90.2	509.6	4,726.3	3.9
32.6	−75.7	469.2	544.9	900.4	375.0	280.7	94.4	525.3	4,840.7	2.5
0.2	−51.3	505.7	557.0	929.1	380.9	281.3	99.5	548.2	4894.6	1.0
−15.1	−17.6	539.6	557.2	936.7	384.8	281.4	103.4	551.9		−0.7

TABLE C

CIVILIAN UNEMPLOYMENT RATE BY DEMOGRAPHIC CHARACTERISTICS, 1948–1991

Percent*

Year	All civilian workers	WHITE							AFRICAN AMERICAN						
		Total	MALES			FEMALES			Total	MALES			FEMALES		
			Total	16–19 years	20 years and over	Total	16–19 years	20 years and over		Total	16–19 years	20 years and over	Total	16–19 years	20 years and over
1948	3.8	3.5	3.4			3.8									
1949	5.9	5.6	5.6			5.7									
1950	5.3	4.9	4.7			5.3									
1951	3.3	3.1	2.6			4.2									
1952	3.0	2.8	2.5			3.3									
1953	2.9	2.7	2.5			3.1									
1954	5.5	5.0	4.8	13.4	4.4	5.5	10.4	5.1							
1955	4.4	3.9	3.7	11.3	3.3	4.3	9.1	3.9							
1956	4.1	3.6	3.4	10.5	3.0	4.2	9.7	3.7							
1957	4.3	3.8	3.6	11.5	3.2	4.3	9.5	3.8							
1958	6.8	6.1	6.1	15.7	5.5	6.2	12.7	5.6							
1959	5.5	4.8	4.6	14.0	4.1	5.3	12.0	4.7							
1960	5.5	5.0	4.8	14.0	4.2	5.3	12.7	4.6							
1961	6.7	6.0	5.7	15.7	5.1	6.5	14.8	5.7							
1962	5.5	4.9	4.6	13.7	4.0	5.5	12.8	4.7							
1963	5.7	5.0	4.7	15.9	3.9	5.8	15.1	4.8							
1964	5.2	4.6	4.1	14.7	3.4	5.5	14.9	4.6							
1965	4.5	4.1	3.6	12.9	2.9	5.0	14.0	4.0							
1966	3.8	3.4	2.8	10.5	2.2	4.3	12.1	3.3							
1967	3.8	3.4	2.7	10.7	2.1	4.6	11.5	3.8							
1968	3.6	3.2	2.6	10.1	2.0	4.3	12.1	3.4							
1969	3.5	3.1	2.5	10.0	1.9	4.2	11.5	3.4							
1970	4.9	4.5	4.0	13.7	3.2	5.4	13.4	4.4							
1971	5.9	5.4	4.9	15.1	4.0	6.3	15.1	5.3							
1972	5.6	5.1	4.5	14.2	3.6	5.9	14.2	4.9	10.4	9.3	31.7	7.0	11.8	40.5	9.0
1973	4.9	4.3	3.8	12.3	3.0	5.3	13.0	4.3	9.4	8.0	27.8	6.0	11.1	36.1	8.6
1974	5.6	5.0	4.4	13.5	3.5	6.1	14.5	5.1	10.5	9.8	33.1	7.4	11.3	37.4	8.8
1975	8.5	7.8	7.2	18.3	6.2	8.6	17.4	7.5	14.8	14.8	38.1	12.5	14.8	41.0	12.2
1976	7.7	7.0	6.4	17.3	5.4	7.9	16.4	6.8	14.0	13.7	37.5	11.4	14.3	41.6	11.7
1977	7.1	6.2	5.5	15.0	4.7	7.3	15.9	6.2	14.0	13.3	39.2	10.7	14.9	43.4	12.3
1978	6.1	5.2	4.6	13.5	3.7	6.2	14.4	5.2	12.8	11.8	36.7	9.3	13.8	40.8	11.2
1979	5.8	5.1	4.5	13.9	3.6	5.9	14.0	5.0	12.3	11.4	34.2	9.3	13.3	39.1	10.9

TABLE C (Continued)

		WHITE							AFRICAN AMERICAN						
			MALES			FEMALES				MALES			FEMALES		
Year	All civilian workers	Total	Total	16–19 years	20 years and over	Total	16–19 years	20 years and over	Total	Total	16–19 years	20 years and over	Total	16–19 years	20 years and over
1980	7.1	6.3	6.1	16.2	5.3	6.5	14.8	5.6	14.3	14.5	37.5	12.4	14.0	39.8	11.9
1981	7.6	6.7	6.5	17.9	5.6	6.9	16.6	5.9	15.6	15.7	40.7	13.5	15.6	42.2	13.4
1982	9.7	8.6	8.8	21.7	7.8	8.3	19.0	7.3	18.9	20.1	48.9	17.8	17.6	47.1	15.4
1983	9.6	8.4	8.8	20.2	7.9	7.9	18.3	6.9	19.5	20.3	48.8	18.1	18.6	48.2	16.5
1984	7.5	6.5	6.4	16.8	5.7	6.5	15.2	5.8	15.9	16.4	42.7	14.3	15.4	42.6	13.5
1985	7.2	6.2	6.1	16.5	5.4	6.4	14.8	5.7	15.1	15.3	41.0	13.2	14.9	39.2	13.1
1986	7.0	6.0	6.0	16.3	5.3	6.1	14.9	5.4	14.5	14.8	39.3	12.9	14.2	39.2	12.4
1987	6.2	5.3	5.4	15.5	4.8	5.2	13.4	4.6	13.0	12.7	34.4	11.1	13.2	34.9	11.6
1988	5.5	4.7	4.7	13.9	4.1	4.7	12.3	4.1	11.7	11.7	32.7	10.1	11.7	32.0	10.4
1989	5.3	4.5	4.5	13.7	3.9	4.5	11.5	4.0	11.4	11.5	31.9	10.0	11.4	33.0	9.8
1990	5.5	4.7	4.8	14.2	4.3	4.6	12.6	4.1	11.3	11.8	32.1	10.4	10.8	30.0	9.6
1991	6.7	6.0	6.4	17.5	5.7	5.5	15.2	4.9	12.4	12.9	36.5	11.5	11.9	36.1	10.5

*Unemployment as percentage of civilian labor force in group specified.

SOURCE: Department of Labor, Bureau of Labor Statistics

TABLE D

GOVERNMENT RECEIPTS AND EXPENDITURES (NATIONAL INCOME AND PRODUCT ACCOUNTS), 1959–1991

Billions of dollars; quarterly data seasonally adjusted annual rates

Calendar year	TOTAL GOVERNMENT			FEDERAL GOVERNMENT			STATE AND LOCAL GOVERNMENT		
	Receipts	Expenditures	Surplus or deficit (−)	Receipts	Expenditures	Surplus or deficit (−)	Receipts	Expenditures	Surplus or deficit (−)
1959	128.8	131.9	−3.1	90.6	93.2	−2.6	45.0	45.5	−0.5
1960	138.8	135.2	3.6	97.0	93.4	3.5	48.3	48.3	0.0
1961	144.1	147.1	−3.0	99.0	101.7	−2.6	52.4	52.7	−0.4
1962	155.8	158.7	−2.9	107.2	110.6	−3.4	56.6	56.1	0.5
1963	167.5	165.9	1.6	115.5	114.4	1.1	61.1	60.6	0.4
1964	172.9	174.5	−1.6	116.2	118.8	−2.6	67.1	66.1	1.0
1965	187.0	185.8	1.2	125.8	124.6	1.3	72.3	72.3	0.0
1966	210.7	211.6	−1.0	143.5	144.9	−1.4	81.5	81.1	0.5
1967	226.4	240.2	−13.7	152.6	165.2	−12.7	89.8	90.9	−1.1
1968	260.9	265.5	−4.6	176.8	181.5	−4.7	102.7	102.6	0.1
1969	294.0	284.0	10.0	199.6	191.0	8.5	114.8	113.3	1.5
1970	299.8	311.2	−11.5	195.2	208.5	−13.3	129.0	127.2	1.8
1971	318.9	338.1	−19.2	202.6	224.3	−21.7	145.3	142.8	2.5
1972	364.2	368.1	−3.9	232.0	249.3	−17.3	169.7	156.3	13.4
1973	408.5	401.6	6.9	263.7	270.3	−6.6	185.3	171.9	13.4
1974	450.7	455.2	−4.5	294.0	305.6	−11.6	200.6	193.5	7.1
1975	465.8	530.6	−64.8	294.8	364.2	−69.4	225.6	221.0	4.6
1976	532.6	570.9	−38.3	339.9	392.7	−52.9	253.9	239.3	14.6
1977	598.4	615.2	−16.8	384.0	426.4	−42.4	281.9	256.3	25.6
1978	673.2	670.3	2.9	441.2	469.3	−28.1	309.3	278.2	31.1
1979	754.7	745.3	9.4	504.7	520.3	−15.7	330.6	305.4	25.1
1980	825.7	861.0	−35.3	553.0	613.1	−60.1	361.4	336.6	24.8
1981	941.9	972.3	−30.3	639.0	697.8	−58.8	390.8	362.3	28.5
1982	960.5	1,069.1	−108.6	635.4	770.9	−135.5	409.0	382.1	26.9
1983	1,016.4	1,156.2	−139.8	660.0	840.0	−180.1	443.4	403.2	40.3
1984	1,123.6	1,232.4	−108.8	725.8	892.7	−166.9	492.2	434.1	58.1
1985	1,217.0	1,342.2	−125.3	788.6	969.9	−181.4	528.7	472.6	56.1
1986	1,290.8	1,437.5	−146.8	827.2	1,028.2	−201.0	571.2	517.0	54.3
1987	1,405.2	1,516.9	−111.7	913.8	1,065.6	−151.8	594.3	554.2	40.1
1988	1,492.4	1,590.7	−98.3	972.3	1,109.0	−136.6	631.3	593.0	38.4
1989	1,614.0	1,697.1	−83.0	1,055.2	1,179.4	−124.2	677.0	635.9	41.1
1990	1,697.1	1,836.7	−139.5	1,104.8	1,270.1	−165.3	724.5	698.8	25.7
1991	1,737.5	1,908.6	−171.2	1,119.1	1,319.8	−200.7	770.6	741.1	29.6

NOTE: Federal grants-in-aid to state and local governments are reflected in federal expenditures and state and local receipts. Total government receipts and expenditures have been adjusted to eliminate this duplication.

SOURCE: Department of Commerce, Bureau of Economic Analysis

TABLE E

MONEY STOCK MEASURES* AND LIQUID ASSETS, 1959–1991

(Averages of daily figures for December; billions of dollars)

Period	M1	M2	M3	L	Debt,[†] monthly average	PERCENT CHANGE FROM YEAR EARLIER[††] M1	M2	M3	Debt
1959	140.0	297.8	299.8	388.7	888.7				5.8
1960	140.7	312.4	315.3	403.7	923.9	0.5	4.9	5.2	4.0
1961	145.2	335.5	341.1	430.8	966.5	3.2	7.4	8.2	4.6
1962	147.9	362.7	371.5	466.1	1,018.8	1.9	8.1	8.9	5.4
1963	153.4	393.3	406.1	503.8	1,073.6	3.7	8.4	9.3	5.4
1964	160.4	424.8	442.5	540.4	1,136.6	4.6	8.0	9.0	5.9
1965	167.9	459.4	482.3	584.5	1,204.7	4.7	8.1	9.0	6.0
1966	172.1	480.0	505.1	614.8	1,272.1	2.5	4.5	4.7	5.6
1967	183.3	524.4	557.1	666.6	1,347.5	6.5	9.3	10.3	5.9
1968	197.5	566.4	606.3	729.0	1,439.9	7.7	8.0	8.8	6.9
1969	204.0	589.6	615.1	763.6	1,530.4	3.3	4.1	1.5	6.3
1970	214.5	628.1	677.4	816.3	1,620.6	5.1	6.5	10.1	5.9
1971	228.4	712.7	776.2	903.0	1,752.0	6.5	13.5	14.6	8.1
1972	249.3	805.2	886.0	1,023.0	1,906.9	9.2	13.0	14.1	8.8
1973	262.9	861.0	985.0	1,142.6	2,093.5	5.5	6.9	11.2	9.8
1974	274.4	908.6	1,070.4	1,250.3	2,265.4	4.4	5.5	8.7	8.2
1975	287.6	1,023.3	1,172.3	1,367.0	2,446.3	4.8	12.6	9.5	8.0
1976	306.4	1,163.7	1,311.8	1,516.6	2,689.3	6.5	13.7	11.9	9.9
1977	331.3	1,286.7	1,472.7	1,705.3	3,010.9	8.1	10.6	12.3	12.0
1978	358.4	1,389.0	1,646.7	1,910.8	3,392.8	8.2	8.0	11.8	12.7
1979	382.8	1,497.1	1,803.3	2,116.3	3,772.1	6.8	7.8	9.5	11.2
1980	408.8	1,629.8	1,987.5	2,324.2	4,104.5	6.8	8.9	10.2	8.8
1981	436.4	1,793.3	2,234.1	2,596.7	4,489.2	6.8	10.0	12.4	9.4
1982	474.4	1,952.9	2,441.7	2,851.4	4,886.1	8.7	8.9	9.3	8.8
1983	521.2	2,186.3	2,693.3	3,154.6	5,422.7	9.9	12.0	10.3	11.0
1984	552.2	2,374.7	2,986.2	3,527.5	6,176.5	5.9	8.6	10.9	13.9
1985	619.9	2,569.7	3,201.6	3,828.9	7,033.1	12.3	8.2	7.2	13.9
1986	724.3	2,811.6	3,492.6	4,133.2	7,921.5	16.8	9.4	9.1	12.6
1987	749.7	2,910.1	3,677.4	4,337.0	8,668.5	3.5	3.5	5.3	9.4
1988	786.4	3,069.9	3,919.1	4,676.0	9,437.5	4.9	5.5	6.6	8.9
1989	793.6	3,223.1	4,055.2	4,889.9	10,152.6	0.9	5.0	3.5	7.6

TABLE E (Continued)

Period	M1	M2	M3	L	Debt,[†] monthly average	PERCENT CHANGE FROM YEAR EARLIER[††]			
						M1	M2	M3	Debt
1990	825.4	3,327.8	4,111.2	4,966.6	10,792.4	4.0	3.2	1.4	6.3
1991	896.7	3,425.4	4,172.0			8.6	2.9	1.5	

*M1 = sum of currency, demand deposits, travelers checks, and other checkable deposits (OCDs). M2 = M1 plus overnight RPs (repurchase agreements) and Eurodollars, money market mutual fund (MMMF) balances (general purpose and broker-dealer), money market deposit accounts (MMDAs), and savings and small time deposits. M3 = M2 plus large time deposits, term RPs, term Eurodollars, and institution-only MMMF balances. L = M3 plus other liquid assets.

[†]Consists of outstanding credit market debt of the U.S., state, and local governments, and of private nonfinancial sector. Data are from flow-of-funds accounts.

[††]Annual changes are from December to December.

NOTE: The nontransactions portion of M2 is seasonally adjusted as a whole to reduce distortions caused by substantial portfolio shifts arising from regulatory and financial changes in recent years, especially shifts to MMDAs in 1983. A similar procedure is used to seasonally adjust the remaining nontransactions balances in M3.

SOURCE: Board of Governors of the Federal Reserve System

TABLE F
CONSUMER PRICE INDEXES, 1950–1991

1982–84 = 100

Year	All items	Year	All items	Year	All items
1950	24.1	1965	31.5	1980	82.4
1951	26.0	1966	32.4	1981	90.9
1952	26.5	1967	33.4	1982	96.5
1953	26.7	1968	34.8	1983	99.6
1954	26.9	1969	36.7	1984	103.9
1955	26.8	1970	38.8	1985	107.6
1956	27.2	1971	40.5	1986	109.6
1957	28.1	1972	41.8	1987	113.6
1958	28.9	1973	44.4	1988	118.3
1959	29.1	1974	49.3	1989	124.0
1960	29.6	1975	53.8	1990	130.7
1961	29.9	1976	56.9	1991	136.2
1962	30.2	1977	60.6		
1963	30.6	1978	65.2		
1964	31.0	1979	72.6		

NOTE: Data beginning 1978 are for all urban consumers; earlier data are for urban wage earners and clerical workers.

SOURCE: Department of Labor, Bureau of Labor Statistics

TABLE G
BOND YIELDS AND INTEREST RATES, 1929–1991
Percent per annum

Year	U.S. Treasury 3-mo. bills, new issues	Corporate bonds, Moody's, Aaa	New-home mortgage yields	Prime rate charged by banks	Discount rate, Federal Reserve Bank of N.Y.	Federal funds rate
1929		4.73		5.50–6.00	5.16	
1933	0.515	4.49		1.50–4.00	2.56	
1939	0.023	3.01		1.50	1.00	
1940	0.014	2.84		1.50	1.00	
1941	0.103	2.77		1.50	1.00	
1942	0.326	2.83		1.50	1.00	
1943	0.373	2.73		1.50	1.00	
1944	0.375	2.72		1.50	1.00	
1945	0.375	2.62		1.50	1.00	
1946	0.375	2.53		1.50	1.00	
1947	0.594	2.61		1.50–1.75	1.00	
1948	1.040	2.82		1.75–2.00	1.34	
1949	1.102	2.66		2.00	1.50	
1950	1.218	2.62		2.07	1.59	
1951	1.552	2.86		2.56	1.75	
1952	1.766	2.96		3.00	1.75	
1953	1.931	3.20		3.17	1.99	
1954	0.953	2.90		3.05	1.60	
1955	1.753	3.06		3.16	1.89	1.78
1956	2.658	3.36		3.77	2.77	2.73
1957	3.267	3.89		4.20	3.12	3.11
1958	1.839	3.79		3.83	2.15	1.57
1959	3.405	4.38		4.48	3.36	3.30
1960	2.928	4.41		4.82	3.53	3.22
1961	2.378	4.35		4.50	3.00	1.96
1962	2.778	4.33		4.50	3.00	2.68
1963	3.157	4.26	5.89	4.50	3.23	3.18
1964	3.549	4.40	5.83	4.50	3.55	3.50
1965	3.954	4.49	5.81	4.54	4.04	4.07
1966	4.881	5.13	6.25	5.63	4.50	5.11
1967	4.321	5.51	6.46	5.61	4.19	4.22
1968	5.339	6.18	6.97	6.30	5.16	5.66
1969	6.677	7.03	7.81	7.96	5.87	8.20

TABLE G (Continued)

Year	U.S. Treasury 3-mo. bills, new issues	Corporate bonds, Moody's, Aaa	New-home mortgage yields	Prime rate charged by banks	Discount rate, Federal Reserve Bank of N.Y.	Federal funds rate
1970	6.458	8.04	8.45	7.91	5.95	7.18
1971	4.348	7.39	7.74	5.72	4.88	4.66
1972	4.071	7.21	7.60	5.25	4.50	4.43
1973	7.041	7.44	7.96	8.03	6.44	8.73
1974	7.886	8.57	8.92	10.81	7.83	10.50
1975	5.838	8.83	9.00	7.86	6.25	5.82
1976	4.989	8.43	9.00	6.84	5.50	5.04
1977	5.265	8.02	9.02	6.83	5.46	5.54
1978	7.221	8.73	9.56	9.06	7.46	7.93
1979	10.041	9.63	10.78	12.67	10.28	11.19
1980	11.506	11.94	12.66	15.27	11.77	13.36
1981	14.029	14.17	14.70	18.87	13.42	16.38
1982	10.686	13.79	15.14	14.86	11.02	12.26
1983	8.63	12.04	12.57	10.79	8.50	9.09
1984	9.58	12.71	12.38	12.04	8.80	10.23
1985	7.48	11.37	11.55	9.93	7.69	8.10
1986	5.98	9.02	10.17	8.33	6.33	6.81
1987	5.82	9.38	9.31	8.21	5.66	6.66
1988	6.69	9.71	9.19	9.32	6.20	7.57
1989	8.12	9.26	10.13	10.87	6.93	9.21
1990	7.51	9.32	10.05	10.01	6.98	8.10
1991	5.42	8.77	9.32	8.46	5.45	5.69

TABLE H
EXCHANGE RATES, 1967–1991

Cents per unit per foreign currency, except as noted

Period	Belgian franc	Canadian dollar	French franc	German mark	Italian lira	Japanese yen
March 1973	39.408	0.9967	4.5156	2.8132	568.17	261.90
1967	49.689	1.0789	4.9206	3.9865	624.09	362.13
1968	49.936	1.0776	4.9529	3.9920	623.38	360.55
1969	50.142	1.0769	5.1999	3.9251	627.32	358.36
1970	49.656	1.0444	5.5288	3.6465	627.12	358.16
1971	48.598	1.0099	5.5100	3.4830	618.34	347.79
1972	44.020	.9907	5.0444	3.1886	583.70	303.13
1973	38.955	1.0002	4.4535	2.6715	582.41	271.31
1974	38.959	.9780	4.8107	2.5868	650.81	291.84
1975	36.800	1.0175	4.2877	2.4614	653.10	296.78
1976	38.609	.9863	4.7825	2.5185	833.58	296.45
1977	35.849	1.0633	4.9161	2.3236	882.78	268.62
1978	31.495	1.1405	4.5091	2.0097	849.13	210.39
1979	29.342	1.1713	4.2567	1.8343	831.11	219.02
1980	29.238	1.1693	4.2251	1.8175	856.21	226.63
1981	37.195	1.1990	5.4397	2.2632	1138.58	220.63
1982	45.781	1.2344	6.5794	2.4281	1354.00	249.06
1983	51.123	1.2325	7.6204	2.5539	1519.32	237.55
1984	57.752	1.2952	8.7356	2.8455	1756.11	237.46
1985	59.337	1.3659	8.9800	2.9420	1908.88	238.47
1986	44.664	1.3896	6.9257	2.1705	1491.16	168.35
1987	37.358	1.3259	6.0122	1.7981	1297.03	144.60
1988	36.785	1.2306	5.9595	1.7570	1302.39	128.17
1989	39.409	1.1842	6.3802	1.8808	1372.28	138.07
1990	33.424	1.1668	5.4467	1.6166	1198.27	145.00
1991	34.195	1.1460	5.6468	1.6610	1241.28	134.59

TABLE H (Continued)

Period	Netherlands guilder	Swedish krona	Swiss franc	United Kingdom pound	MULTILATERAL TRADE-WEIGHTED VALUE OF U.S. DOLLAR, March 1973 = 100	
					Nominal	Real
March 1973	2.8714	4.4294	3.2171	247.24	100.0	100.0
1967	3.6024	5.1621	4.3283	275.04	120.0	
1968	3.6198	5.1683	4.3163	239.35	122.1	
1969	3.6240	5.1701	4.3131	239.01	122.4	
1970	3.6166	5.1862	4.3106	239.59	121.1	
1971	3.4953	5.1051	4.1171	244.42	117.8	
1972	3.2098	4.7571	3.8186	250.34	109.1	
1973	2.7946	4.3619	3.1688	245.25	99.1	98.9
1974	2.6879	4.4387	2.9805	234.03	101.4	99.4
1975	2.5293	4.1531	2.5839	222.17	98.5	94.1
1976	2.6449	4.3580	2.5002	180.48	105.7	97.6
1977	2.4548	4.4802	2.4065	174.49	103.4	93.3
1978	2.1643	4.5207	1.7907	191.84	92.4	84.4
1979	2.0073	4.2893	1.6644	212.24	88.1	83.2
1980	1.9875	4.2310	1.6772	232.46	87.4	84.9
1981	2.4999	5.0660	1.9675	202.43	103.4	100.9
1982	2.6719	6.2839	2.0327	174.80	116.6	111.8
1983	2.8544	7.6718	2.1007	151.59	125.3	117.3
1984	3.2085	8.2708	2.3500	133.68	138.2	117.3
1985	3.3185	8.6032	2.4552	129.74	143.0	132.4
1986	2.4485	7.1273	1.7979	146.77	112.2	103.6
1987	2.0264	6.3469	1.4918	163.98	96.9	90.9
1988	1.9778	6.1370	1.4643	178.13	92.7	88.2
1989	2.1219	6.4559	1.6369	163.82	98.6	94.4
1990	1.8215	5.9231	1.3901	178.41	89.1	86.0
1991	1.8720	6.0521	1.4356	176.74	89.8	86.5

SOURCE: Board of Governors of the Federal Reserve System